America in an Interdependent World

Contributions by

Louis Morton / Michael Mazur / Kjell-Arne Ringbakk /
Donella Meadows / Nelson Kasfir / Howard Erdman /
Kalman Silvert / Laurence Radway / Donald McNemar

America in an Interdependent World
Problems of United States Foreign Policy

Edited by David A. Baldwin

Foreword by Gene M. Lyons

Published for Dartmouth College
by the University Press of New England
Hanover, New Hampshire, 1976

THE UNIVERSITY PRESS OF NEW ENGLAND

Sponsoring Institutions

Brandeis University
Clark University
Dartmouth College
University of New Hampshire
University of Rhode Island
University of Vermont

To the memory of Louis Morton
Teacher, Scholar, Colleague, Friend

Acknowledgments

Although the editor and contributors must bear responsibility for all errors and omissions in this volume, we must also acknowledge the many sources of help in creating and improving it.

The Dartmouth College Public Affairs Center, under the direction of Gene Lyons, provided the initial impetus toward launching the project and the efficient logistical support necessary to carry it to completion. The book grew out of the efforts of a study group preparing a report for the Department of State under research contract No. 1722-420140, part of a series sponsored by the Office of External Research in the Bureau of Intelligence and Research. Although William Trainor and his colleagues in the Office of External Research furnished valuable substantive suggestions at various stages of the project, the views contained in this volume should not be interpreted as representing the official opinion or policy of the Department of State.

Marion Chambers, a Dartmouth student, served as rapporteur during the early meetings of the group and contributed more than she realizes. Alan Horton of the American Universities Field Staff was a member of the study group and contributed a paper; unfortunately, other commitments deprived him of the time to revise the paper for inclusion in this volume. Both his wise comments and his useful paper, however, have contributed to the thinking contained in these essays.

Special thanks go to Christine Schile of the Public Affairs Center, who coordinated logistical support for the authors, reminded them of deadlines, and worked as energetically as anyone in the project. She was ably assisted by a number of typists, including Sharon H. Christie, Virginia Darrah, and Rhonda Martin.

The patience, encouragement, and advice of David Horne, editor of the University Press of New England, should also be acknowledged.

While this book was in press, we were saddened to learn of the death of one of the authors. It is with the greatest respect that we dedicate this volume to his memory.

D. A. B.

Hanover, New Hampshire
March 1976

Contents

Foreword

Gene M. Lyons

These essays on American foreign policy emerged out of a faculty study group organized at Dartmouth College under the auspices of the Public Affairs Center—one of several study groups created by the Center over the past decade and a half as part of its commitment to encourage and provide opportunities for faculty research and writing in the basic issues of public policy. There is, however, a special link between this book and another series of essays the Center sponsored and published in 1965 under the title, *America: Purpose and Power* (Chicago, 1965).

America: Purpose and Power was also the product of a faculty study group. Its purpose was to examine a range of public issues—urbanization, civil rights, and technological change, as well as international problems—and to do so in the perspective of America's historical development. One of the questions that we asked was whether, and how, major domestic issues in American life are affected by foreign policies—that is, whether any issue, however internal, can be meaningfully confronted without taking into account an international, as opposed to an exclusively national, context.

In the introduction to the earlier book, I tried to summarize what seemed to me to be the general conclusions we reached, first with regard to American history and then to the contemporary situation:

American historical development, no less than the present situation, is the product of the dynamic interplay of international and internal forces. Sometimes one set of forces has been more powerful, sometimes the other. Yet never was the

United States so detached from the rest of the world that its development could be carried on in isolation from what was happening elsewhere. If isolation was a policy of American governments, it never was a reality of American life. . . . The world is highly interdependent, however one may argue about the different degrees of dependent relationships. . . . We are . . . destined to exist in a divided but nevertheless interacting and increasingly interdependent world. The point of our history is that we have lived in interdependence throughout our development, no matter how much we have tried to glorify our freedom from foreign involvement. The point of our contemporary situation is the qualitative shift in our power relations with the rest of the world.[1]

The present book begins with the assumption of interdependence. It no longer needs to be argued. The problems each of the authors deals with are the consequences of interdependence for the United States and for American interests, each in a different field of foreign policy. Indeed, the study group was originally set up in response to an inquiry from the Department of State to identify major foreign-policy issues that the United States will face over the next five years in an increasingly interdependent world. Interdependence is now the overarching framework within which American foreign policy is being conducted, though the implications of interdependence still need to be defined and elaborated. These tasks are major themes of the present book.

Five years is not, of course, a long time. It is a safe time perspective, however, if we have a sense of the deeper strains that are moving under the surface. Only with that sense is it possible to find substantial meaning in unique events, or even in patterns of events. It is the "qualitative shift in our power relations with the rest of the world" that provides the long-range perspective against which short or mid-range responses must be tested. Until the end of the nineteenth century, the United States was dependent upon the rest of the world. With the turn of the twentieth century, the country began to build toward a position of greater independence, and from the early stages of the Second World War it has been the dominant power

---

1. Gene M. Lyons (ed.), *America: Purpose and Power* (Chicago, Quadrangle, 1965), pp. 11–13.

in world politics. The change through which we are now moving involves more than a loss of this dominance. Throughout its history the United States—dependent or independent—existed in a world in which power was centered in the West, first in Europe and then, for a shorter period, in the United States itself, and in which the prevailing ideologies favored liberal political systems and economic structures. These features are changing, and the qualitative shift, not over the next five years but, more likely, the next fifty, will be more drastic than any that has occurred since the country began; it is, in fact, a shift, for the first time in several centuries, from an exclusively western to a multicentered world.

The long-range question is whether a reasonable balance can be achieved between the centers of power which will emerge and those in the West which will attempt to sustain their influence and whether multilateral instruments of cooperation can be developed which will involve all the future major powers, however different their socio-economic systems. In the interim there will be great instabilities in world politics. The uncertainties of the situation already confronting American policy-makers have been described by Secretary of State Henry Kissinger:

> The world of the 1970's is less predictable, more fluid, than the world of 10 years ago. America's strength is less dominant, our margins for error narrower, our choices more complex and ambiguous. New centers of power and influence have emerged and over a hundred new nations have come into being, since the Second World War. What we once considered a monolithic Communist bloc has been fractured by profound divisions. Our alliances have taken on a new balance and are adjusting to new conditions. Developing countries are pressing their claims with fresh urgency and unity. Economic interdependence has become a fact of life. While the cold war structure of international relations has come apart, a new stable international order has yet to be formed.[2]

None of the essays in this book offers prescriptions for "a new stable international order." Within the midterm time span of their

---

2. Speech before the St. Louis World Affairs Council, reprinted in *The Secretary of State*, Bureau of Public Affairs, Department of State, May 12, 1975.

analyses, the authors deal with problems of transition without necessarily anticipating the structure of future international relations. For that matter, the time frame of the essays varies. That on nuclear proliferation strains against the day-by-day events that shape the future of this issue-area. The essays on food and population and on international organization assume a longer-range perspective. Yet, taken as a whole, all of them emphasize the interactions of major issues of American foreign policy and underscore the conceptual problem of recognizing the transformation of the international system through which we are passing.

Each of the essays can be read in its own right as a substantial discussion of a complex problem that United States foreign-policy makers face. But this approach would offer only partial insight into the deeper understanding that, together, they can provide of the broad changes we are witnessing in world affairs. Guided by the editor's introductory essay, the reader can begin to sense the perplexities of what one might call the globalization of world politics. In another, though not dissimilar, context Kissinger, before entering government, wrote: "In the years ahead, the profound challenge to American policy will be philosophical." At that time (1968) he was referring to a conceptual problem that we already face—"to develop some concept of order in a world which is bipolar militarily but multipolar politically."[3] The conceptual problem of the future would seem even more difficult: to develop a concept of order in a world of varying military, political, economic, social, and cultural pluralism, with multiple centers of power, influencing different issue-areas with different degrees of intensity and consistency. The challenge is, indeed, "philosophical."

This book is being published a little more than ten years after *America: Purpose and Power.* As I write this Foreword, I keep wondering what we might have to say ten years from now, in 1985. What will the world be like? How far will we have moved to that "multi-centered" world I have projected? Are the new centers becoming consolidated? What are the new centers? China? Probably. Brazil? Some emerging African regional group centered on Nigeria? Possibly. Will Europe be more closely united? How will the

---

3. Henry A. Kissinger, *American Foreign Policy* (New York, Norton, 1969), p. 79.

Soviet Union have survived its transitions of authority? And the United States? What will be America's purpose and what will be the state of America's power?

Perhaps we should pledge to meet again in ten years' time. We could check, against time and events, how accurately each writer diagnosed critical phenomena and, to the extent that prediction was attempted, how close to reality he came. But perhaps most important would be to judge whether this book of essays helped Americans cope with the transformations that have occurred in world politics and provided a perspective that stimulated a creative response to the changing role of the United States. Now, today, there is little cause for encouragement. Many Americans are frustrated by world affairs, having become accustomed to the dominance of the United States and feeling bewildered by the limits of what is still significant American power. This frustration is understandable, but it is the result of a short view of history and a narrow, material idea of power as much as it is of the perplexity of immediate events and changes. These essays can help us all deal with the "philosophical" problem we face, the uncertainties of a world in transformation, with intelligence and with the reasoning that makes it possible to cope with change.

Notes on Contributors

David A. Baldwin. John Sloan Dickey Third Century Professor in the
Social Sciences; Dartmouth College, Ph.D., Princeton, 1965.
Publications include *Economic Development and American
Foreign Policy* (1966); and *Foreign Aid and American Foreign
Policy: A Documentary Analysis* (1966).

Howard L. Erdman. Professor of Government, Dartmouth College;
Ph.D., Harvard, 1964; Fulbright Awards for research in India,
1961–63 and 1971–72; Visiting Research Scholar, Institute of
Commonwealth Studies, London, fall 1969 and fall 1971.
Publications include *The Swatantra Party and Indian Conserva-
tism* (1967); *Political Attitudes of Indian Industry* (1971); and
Politics and Economic Development in India (1973).

Gene M. Lyons. Professor of Government, Dartmouth College; Ph.D.,
Columbia, 1958; Director, Department of Social Sciences,
UNESCO, 1970–72; Senior Staff, Division of Behavioral Sciences, National Research Council, 1966–68. Publications
include *Education and Military Leadership* (co-author, 1959);
Military Policy and Economic Aid (1961); *Schools for Strategy*
(co-author, 1965); and *The Uneasy Partnership: Social Science
and the Federal Government in the Twentieth Century* (1969).

Michael P. Mazur. Assistant Professor of Economics, Dartmouth
College; Ph.D., Massachusetts Institute of Technology, 1972;
Consultant, Rand Corporation, 1968–69. Publications include
"Economic Development of Jordan," in Cooper and Alexander,
*Economic Development and Population Growth in the Middle
East* (1972).

Donald W. McNemar. Assistant Professor of Government, Dartmouth College; Ph.D., Princeton, 1971; Visiting Fellow, Center of International Studies, Princeton, 1973–74. Publications include "The Post-Independence War in the Congo," in *Proceedings of the American Society of International Law* (1967); "The Future Role of International Institutions," in Black and Falk, *The Future of the International Legal Order* (1972); and *The United Nations and World Order* (co-author, 1975—forthcoming).

Donella H. Meadows. Assistant Professor of Environmental Studies, Dartmouth College; Ph.D., Harvard, 1968; Research Fellow, Argonne National Laboratory, 1961–63; Co-director of the Club of Rome's Project on the Predicament of Mankind, 1968–72. Co-author of *The Limits to Growth* (1972); *Toward Global Equilibrium* (1973); and *Dynamics of Growth in a Finite World* (1974).

Louis Morton. The late Daniel Webster Professor of History, Dartmouth College; Ph.D., Duke, 1938; Chief, Pacific Branch, Office of Military History, Department of the Army, 1946–59; Rockefeller Public Service Award, 1959; editor, multivolumed series on Wars and Military Institutions of the United States. Publications include *The Fall of the Philippines* (1953); *War in the Pacific: Strategy and Command* (1963); *Schools for Strategy* (co-author, 1965); and *The Historian and the Diplomat* (co-author, 1967).

Kjell-Arne Ringbakk. Associate Professor of International Management, Tuck School of Business Administration, Dartmouth College; Ph.D., Wisconsin, 1968; faculty member, Centre d'Etudes Industrielles, Geneva, Switzerland, 1969–73; consultant to Stanford Research Institute, 1967–68. Publications include *Organized Planning in 40 Major U.S. Corporations*, SRI Report (co-author, 1968); "Multinational Corporate Planning—the Current State of the Art," in *Newsletter of European Society of Corporate and Strategic Planners* (1972); and "Monitoring the Multinational Corporate Environment," in *Planning Review* (1974).

Nelson M. Kasfir. Assistant Professor of Government, Dartmouth College; Ph.D., Harvard, 1973. Publications include "Prismatic Theory and African Administration," *World Politics* (1969); *Getting*

People Out of Politics: Ethnicity and Participation in African Politics—with a Case Study of Uganda (1975); "Organization Theory and Uganda Cooperative Unions," in C. Widstrand, *Co-operatives and Rural Development in East Africa* (1970); "Cultural Subnationalism in Uganda," in V. A. Olorunsola, *Cultural Nationalism in Africa* (1972); and "Theories of Administrative Behavior in Africa," in *The African Review* (Dar es Salaam, 1972). Taught Political Science in Uganda for four years.

Laurence I. Radway. Professor of Government, Dartmouth College; Ph.D., Harvard, 1950. Publications include *Soldiers and Scholars: Military Education and National Policy* (1957); *Foreign Policy and National Defense* (1969); "Militarism," in *International Encyclopedia of Social Science.*

Kalman H. Silvert. Professor of Government, New York University, 1967–present; The Ford Foundation, 1967–present; Ph.D., University of Pennsylvania, 1948. Publications include *The Conflict Society: Reaction and Revolution in Latin America* (1961); and *Chile, Yesterday and Today* (1965).

America in an Interdependent World

I.
Foreign Policy Problems, 1975–1980: Framework for Analysis

David A. Baldwin

American foreign policy is currently going through a major transition, a process likely to continue for the rest of this decade. This transition involves far more than identifying and responding to specific problems during the next five years. It involves developing the ability to perceive such problems in the context of an international system that is undergoing fundamental changes. Old perceptions of America as the world's policeman, as the world's breadbasket, as the world's conscience, as the leader of a cohesive anticommunist alliance, and as an invulnerable fortress are being reconsidered in terms of changes in the international system. These changes include the diffusion of power in the world as the bipolar system gives way to a multipolar one, the emergence of new "actors" such as the giant multinational corporations, and rapid multiplication of the number of vital issues demanding the attention of United States foreign-policy makers. This situation is often characterized as increasing international interdependence. No matter what label one applies, however, it is clear that some fundamental rethinking about America's world role is in order.

In this volume, nine scholars from four disciplines describe and analyze selected American foreign-policy problems from the perspective of their disciplines and in the context of current trends in the international system. Although each problem-study is designed to stand independently, an effort has also been made to relate each essay to a common conceptual framework. The problems include nuclear proliferation, international monetary stability, development in the Third World, the multinational corporation, the population-food problem, domestic constraints on foreign policy, and the United

Nations. In addition, there are two articles with geographic foci (South Asia and Latin America) which cut across the other areas.

It is obvious that such a list does not constitute a comprehensive examination of America's foreign-policy problems. The problems chosen, however, are all likely to command serious attention from United States foreign-policy makers during the next five years. In addition, these problems illustrate the kind of rethinking about American foreign policy that is necessitated by current trends in the international system.

CONCEPTUAL PROBLEMS AND THE INTERNATIONAL SYSTEM: WHY BOTHER?

Conceptual problems are not often thought of as being of immediate practical relevance to policy-making. In relatively stable periods of history, most of the time is spent in gathering additional facts to refine one's understanding of concrete problems. In an age of revolutionary changes, however, it is necessary to give more attention to perspectives and general intellectual orientations. The recent oil shortage, for example, could be viewed from numerous perspectives. Was it a problem of underproduction by the exporting nations or overconsumption by the importing nations? Was it a limited tactical move in the Arab-Israeli dispute, the culmination of a long-term trend toward using up nonrenewable resources at an ever increasing rate, a manifestation of the North-South split, a victory for communism, an indication of a fundamental long-term shift in the "world balance of power," or a straightforward attempt to exploit a monopoly position? The appropriate United States policy response would vary with one's perception of the problem.

The facts of the oil shortage were relatively easy to grasp: the difficulty was to choose a context in which to view those facts. In a revolutionary age, imagining the future may well be the policy-maker's most challenging task. Academics can help by explicit identification of alternative intellectual perspectives and by sharpening the focus of each alternative. In the studies that follow, the primary purpose, therefore, is not to provide new facts but rather to provide different perspectives on problems in order to help foreign-policy makers to imagine the future with clarity, precision, relevance, and humanity of purpose.

TRENDS IN THE INTERNATIONAL SYSTEM: THE BASIC ANALYTICAL FRAMEWORK

Multipolarity

The observation that the bipolar world of the immediate postwar period has given (is giving?) way to a multipolar world has become a cliché. Like all clichés it can be an important source of misunderstanding if everyone assumes that others share their definition of it. It calls to mind the time-honored but increasingly questionable tendency to divide the society of nations into so-called Great Powers, who must be consulted on virtually every issue, and small powers, who need to be consulted on virtually no issue.

Much depends, of course, on how one defines power. In most discussions of national power, there is a persistent temptation to define it in military terms. Thus a statement about increased multipolarity often refers to the spread of nuclear weapons. This is, of course, an example of increased multipolarity, but it is neither the sole nor the most important example. Indeed, Morton's study of nuclear proliferation suggests that acquisition of nuclear weapons may even *weaken* a nation's international political position.

Perhaps the most misleading aspect of the multipolarity concept is the implication that a single pattern of polarity prevails for all issue areas. In today's world it would be more accurate to speak of multiple patterns of polarity, since many nations are powerful with respect to some issues and weak with respect to others. Although the Soviet Union and the United States still dominate the nuclear arena, they do not dominate the United Nations as they used to. Saudi Arabia and Iran are extremely important in discussions of energy or international finance; but they play virtually no role in nuclear disarmament talks. Very few nations—perhaps only the United States—are so potentially influential that they must be consulted on practically every major issue.

The trend toward a wider distribution of power seems to hold for most issue areas. The studies that follow contain many examples of such a trend. In Latin America it has been obvious for at least twelve years that United States relations with Cuba must take account of Soviet intentions and capabilities. Brazil, Chile, Cuba, Mexico, Argentina, and Venezuela are emerging not only as regional actors but as global actors with respect to some issues. In its relations with India the United States must now consider the capabilities and intentions of at least four nuclear nations—itself, India, China, and the Soviet Union. In the Middle East the Arabs have demonstrated a startling increase in their military capability to hurt Israel and their economic capability to disrupt the United States and Western Europe. In international finance the United States can no longer exercise the influence it once had on exchange rates. In development financing for the Third World the United States will never again be as alone as it was during the decade 1950-60. No matter what the issue area, the trend seems to be toward an increasing number of "poles": nations that are too important to be ignored.

The policy implications of increased diffusion of power are not self-evident. Clearly this development means an increase in the complexity of the problems facing policy-makers. Increased effort to develop a complex policy to fit new and more complex situations is one plausible response, but it is possible also to adopt a simple response—to develop a single policy for a whole set of similar problems.[1] Nor is it all clear whether American interests are threatened or helped by wider dispersion of power. Without compelling evidence it would be unwise for United States foreign-policy makers to view this trend as ominous.

The waning of bipolarism is not equivalent to the end of the tension between the United States and communist nations often labeled the "cold war." There is no denying, however, the splintering of the once cohesive communist bloc, especially the split between China and the Soviet Union. There is also no denying that other issues have intruded into the foreign-policy realm. Relations with communist nations do not have the salience relative to other issues

---

1. For a provocative if not convincing argument along this line, see Max Singer and Aaron Wildavsky, "A Third World Averaging Strategy," *U.S. Foreign Policy: Perspectives and Proposals for the 1970's,* ed. Paul Seabury and Aaron Wildavsky (New York, McGraw-Hill, 1969), pp. 13-35.

that they once had, and they are unlikely to regain this salience in the next five years. Will détente with the Soviet Union continue to grow stronger? Will arms control negotiations make progress? Will relations with China continue to improve? Almost every problem area of American foreign policy will be affected by the answers to such questions. Whether it is the Arab-Israeli dispute, the oil shortage, nuclear proliferation, or development in the third world, the answers to such questions are relevant. During the next five years one of the most important tasks American policy-makers face is estimating the impact of new United States relations with Russia and China on old and emerging problems in many issue areas.

Multiple Levels

The international system is pluralistic rather than monolithic. Issues, actors, and power vary from one level to another. United States relations with Canada, for example, can be considered at the bilateral level, the hemispheric level, the North Atlantic level, or the global level. One of the most important questions a policy-maker faces is deciding which problems to consider at which level at which time.

The global approach has recently come under fire as the key to understanding the "lesson" of Vietnam. Why did the United States get drawn into Vietnam? Because events there were analyzed on the wrong level. Instead of viewing this situation from the perspective of a global battle against communism, policy-makers should have viewed it in bilateral or regional terms. This type of reasoning typically leads to a rejection of "misguided universalism" in favor of a policy of withdrawal and noninvolvement or a policy of doctrinaire regionalism.[2]

"Doctrinaire regionalism" argues for carving the whole world into regions and treating each region separately. William Bundy, for example, argues that the "regions of the world have reasserted a life of their own; their resistance to outside domination and influence is much greater; most are, in the true sense, nonaligned; and the number of nations entitled to rank as major powers is much larger, with

---

2. See William P. Bundy, "International Security Today," *Foreign Affairs*, 53 (October 1974), 24–44.

some of them aspiring to dominant roles within their regions." In this "new situation," he concludes, "it makes sense on the face of things for American policy to handle each regional arena as separately as possible . . ."[3]

Without defending "misguided universalism," one might ask whether noninvolvement and doctrinaire regionalism are the only alternative policies worth considering. What about "enlightened universalism"? Is it so ridiculous to suggest the possibility of American foreign-policy makers replacing "misguided universalism" with a global approach enlightened by learning from past mistakes and by knowledge of probable trends in the international system? What about "pragmatic regionalism"? It does not insist on a regional approach everywhere; rather it advocates regional approaches in some areas but not in others. There is no particular virtue in consistency regarding this matter. American foreign-policy makers may well decide to emphasize regionalism in dealing with Latin America; but they may also decide that a regionalist approach to Asia (West, South, Southeast, East, and Northeast) makes very little sense. Both the Erdman and the Silvert papers are examples of pragmatic regionalism. Silvert suggests that a regionalist approach to Latin America makes sense because of the unique "special relationship" these nations have had and continue to have with the United States. He views this special relationship as based not only on the romantic tradition of pan-Americanism but also on a number of political, socioeconomic, and ideological similarities between that region and the United States. Likewise, Erdman argues for a regional (South Asian) approach to United States relations with India on the basis of the particular geopolitical situation in that area at this time.

The approach in this volume highlights the need to *combine* enlightened and properly humble globalism with pragmatic regionalism. Bundy concludes that America should pursue "many policies rather than a single over-arching one, accepting complexity as a fact of life, and adapting the American role not to any single vision of the world but to the realities of power and political attitudes in its diverse parts."[4] In contrast, the papers presented here suggest the need to *combine* a single vision of the world with regional approaches that

---

3. Ibid., pp. 26–27.
4. Ibid., p. 44.

take account of the realities of power and political attitudes in diverse regions. Regardless of the success of this particular study in providing such a global vision, United States foreign-policy makers should not abandon the search for an overarching concept of world order to guide various regional or bilateral policies. Trends toward increased global interdependence must not be ignored or forgotten in overzealous attempts to retreat from the "misguided universalism" that allegedly got us into Vietnam. Treating the world as if it were nothing but separate regions would be just as unwise as a global approach that ignored the unique aspects of different nations and groups of nations.[5]

Multiple Units

The actors in the international arena used to be confined to nation states—about 60 at the end of World War II. Now there are about 140 nation states, over 200 international organizations, and at least 50 (by anyone's criteria) giant multinational corporations interacting on the international stage. Although hopes or fears of the imminent demise of the nation state as the dominant actor in world politics are unjustified, no important problem of American foreign policy can be understood without reference to non-national actors.

Silvert notes that "the core of international studies is not how one government affects another, or one army another, but rather how one total social order affects others. Relations among formal states are the day-to-day symptoms of the underlying question of how societies play on each other internally and, in so doing, how the latent, longer-term effects of such interactions work themselves out." One expects discussions of development, such as those by Silvert, Erdman, Kasfir, and Mazur, to refer to the multinational corporation. It is more surprising, however, to find that the multinational corporation is also deeply involved in such problems as nuclear proliferation.

---

5. One weakness in any regional approach is, of course, the lack of consensus on what constitutes a region. Latin America and sub-Saharan Africa are relatively easy; Europe is more difficult; and Asia is almost impossible. The trouble is that more than one plausible scheme for dividing the world into regions can be imagined. Whereas Erdman considers India in the context of South Asia, Bundy (ibid.) treats the Balkans, South Asia, and the Middle East as a single region.

Indeed, one would be hard pressed to find a single mid-term United States foreign policy problem that did not involve multinational corporations in some significant way.

Multi-issue World Politics

The United States national interest is getting harder to calculate. This is not to say that it was ever easy; it is only that the national interest is easier to determine in some situations than in others. It is easiest when two conditions prevail—(1) when clearcut criteria for subordinating one national goal to another exist and (2) when resources are so abundant that all or most goals can be pursued simultaneously. During World War II the United States faced a scarce resource situation, but there was widespread agreement that winning the war should be the basic criterion for allocating such resources. From 1945 to 1965 the United States national interest could be (not to say should have been) calculated in terms of what was perceived to be a worldwide struggle against communism. Whatever helps us hurts them and vice versa was the basic rule of thumb by which many policy-makers seemed to operate. In addition to the prevalence of anticommunism as a guide to establishing priorities among goals, the foreign-policy maker's job was simplified by a relative abundance of political and economic resources. Domestic political stability, a comfortable lead in the arms race, a reservoir of international good will created during World War II, and a lack of a colonialist past constituted major political resources that strengthened the United States ability to accomplish its foreign-policy objectives. Steady economic growth, food surpluses, an abundance of energy resources, low awareness of environmental problems, and international monetary stability (at least from the United States point of view) were major economic resources behind United States foreign policy.

In this situation policy-makers could pursue such basic goals of United States foreign policy as survival, preserving the American way of life, and promoting economic welfare without having to subordinate one to the other to any great extent.[6] The primary threat to

---

6. There are various ways to formulate the basic or core values underlying American foreign policy. For purposes of this study the differences among them do not seem very important. The particular scheme employed here is based on William D. Coplin, Patrick J. McGowan, and Michael K. O'Leary, *American Foreign Policy* (North Scituate, Mass., Duxbury Press, 1974), pp. 67–96.

United States survival came from the same source as the threat to the American way of life. Deterring thermonuclear war and containing communism did not require policy-makers to subordinate one to the other except insofar as the goals themselves were incompatible, as in the case of the Cuban missile crisis. Preserving the American way of life was also viewed as compatible with promoting economic welfare at home and abroad. Both the reconstruction of Europe and the promotion of development in the Third World were viewed as measures that simultaneously inhibited communism, promulgated and protected the American way of life, and enhanced economic well being.

Today's foreign-policy makers face a more difficult situation. Avoiding thermonuclear war may require the United States to modify the American way of life in order to build bridges to the communist powers. Economic welfare both at home and abroad may require Americans to modify their wasteful consumption habits and their environment-destroying production habits. The abundant political and economic resources available from 1945 to 1965 are severely depleted. The Vietnam war and the Watergate scandal have weakened domestic political support; the Russians have achieved parity in the arms race; the world image of the United States has been badly tarnished; the economy has stopped growing; food surpluses have disappeared; energy shortages are imminent; international monetary relations are in a highly volatile state; and environmental deterioration is becoming apparent even to the man in the street.

American foreign-policy makers face a multiplicity of vital issues with inadequate resources to deal with all of them and no clearcut criteria by which to establish priorities among them. Such a situation is likely to lead to a style of foreign-policy making in which short-term considerations predominate and overall integration of policy-making is weak. Dealing with the problems of increased global interdependence will be difficult under such circumstances.

International Interdependence

The prime contender as a replacement for anticommunism as a conceptual guide for American foreign-policy makers is "interdependence." Unfortunately, neither academics nor policy-makers have clarified this concept sufficiently to make it of much use as a basis for policy formulation.[7] Only one thing is certain: the concept is much more complex than is commonly supposed by many who use it.

In one sense, professional diplomats should be comfortable with the concept. Part of their traditional job has always been to convince those at home that they were underestimating the importance of foreign affairs. To the extent that interdependence is used merely to underscore the point that other nations matter, it is a useful and familiar idea for diplomats but hardly a basis for policy. Yet when it is used to imply something more precise, difficulties arise.

One way to clarify the concept of interdependence is to say what it is not. First, interdependence is *not* necessarily symmetrical. To affirm that nations are mutually dependent is not to say that they are equally dependent on one another. Canada and the United States are mutually but not equally dependent on each other. Latin America and the United States are also asymmetrically interdependent. An interdependent world is compatible with a world in which some nations are more dependent than others.

Second, interdependence is not unidimensional. The degree, the direction, and the rate of change varies with the issue. For example, interdependence is probably increasing much faster with regard to managing a nation's economy than it is with regard to maintaining internal order. Interdependence also varies from one level of the international system to another. Thus regional interdependence may be decreasing at the same time that global interdependence is increasing or vice versa. Given the multidimensional nature of interdependence, it would probably be preferable to speak of multiple interdependencies rather than interdependence.

---

7. There is, however, a body of academic literature that constitutes a very respectable beginning at clarifying our understanding of the concept of interdependence. See the following: Oran Young, "Interdependencies in World Politics," *International Journal,* 24 (Autumn 1969), 726–750; Richard Rosecrance and Arthur Stein, "Interdependence: Myth or Reality?" *World Politics,* 26 (October 1973), 1–27; Richard N. Cooper, "Economic Interdependence and Foreign Policy in the Seventies," *World Politics,* 24 (January 1972), 159–181; and Robert O. Keohane and Joseph S. Nye, "International Interdependence and Integration," *The Handbook of Political Science,* ed. Fred Greenstein and Nelson Polsby (Reading, Mass., Addison-Wesley, in press).

Third, interdependence does not necessarily lead either to conflict or to stability. In the eighteenth and nineteenth centuries geographic isolation was probably the most important obstacle to interdependence. The technological revolution in transportation and communication, however, has reduced the significance of distance and has increased opportunities for both conflict and cooperation among nations. Rising levels of international trade may be an example of system-stabilizing interdependence just as proliferation of nuclear weapons may be an example of system destabilizing interdependence. One cannot say a priori whether United States foreign-policy makers should regard increased interdependence as desirable or undesirable.

Granted the multidimensional nature of interdependence, is it meaningful to speak of an overall global trend toward increased interdependence among nations? The answer is a qualified yes, as long as one keeps in mind the caveats mentioned above. Such a statement should be understood to mean something like the following: *Most (many?) nations are encountering an increasing number of issue-areas in which their ability to achieve their policy goals is significantly affected by events and policies in other nations.*

Policy-makers are confronted with what might be called the "paradox of interdependence." This paradox grows out of the fact that interdependence means an increased ability for all (or most) nations to influence other nations, but it also means a decrease in usable influence because of the increased costs of exercising each influence. Whereas growing interdependence necessitates a global outlook, global definition of problems, and global concern, it also reduces the usable global power of the United States. In such a situation the problem is not so much finding ways to exert "leverage" on other nations as it is ensuring that the wrong lever is not pulled inadvertently. In an interdependent world American foreign-policy makers may have to worry less about how to influence intentionally other nations and more about how to monitor United States influence in order to avoid unintentionally influencing them.

MAKING FOREIGN POLICY

It is difficult to separate policy processes from policy problems.

Although the primary focus in this volume is on substantive policy problems, the potential organizational implications of our increasingly complex world should be noted.

Domestic and Foreign Policy

The increased interdependence of nations has further blurred the distinction between foreign and domestic policy problems. The old bipartisan admonition to "stop politics at the water's edge" never did work very well; but it would be virtually impossible to obey today, since domestic and international politics have become so closely intertwined. Radway's paper discusses a number of difficulties American foreign policy makers are likely to encounter as a result of this intertwining.

In addition to increased domestic sensitivity to external events, Americans face the problem of revising their image of themselves. They have not in the past spent much time worrying about the national image. In general they have taken pride in the role they perceived the nation as playing in world affairs; and foreign opinion of them, while not unqualifiedly admiring, at least reflected toleration, respect, and even friendliness. Attempts to characterize America as a threat to world peace, as an international bully, or as a gluttonous consumer of precious resources were rarely taken seriously by most people either at home or abroad. Since 1960, however, such perceptions have received serious attention from growing numbers of people both at home and in other countries.

To what extent should this concern United States foreign-policy makers? On the one hand, the weakening of national self-confidence could make it harder to generate support for foreign policy. On the other hand, receptivity to proposals for a new world role for the United States may be enhanced because of doubts about the older image held by many Americans. In the aftermath of Watergate and Vietnam, the question of restoring national self-respect cannot be taken lightly.

The Policy-Making Time Frame

Although mid-term foreign policy problems are defined in terms of a five-year time horizon, the question of longer-term considerations cannot be excluded from the analysis of such problems. Most mid-term problems cannot be defined or solved without reference to such longer-term problems as population growth, environmental deterioration, depletion of nonrenewable resources, energy sources, and food supplies. Lord Keynes's dictum that we are all dead in the long run should not be used to justify excluding long-run considerations from the policy-planning process. (He did not, after all, identify an antecedent for "we.")

In general, inclusion of long-run considerations in discussing mid-term United States foreign-policy problems leads to a stronger sense of urgency. Should American policy-makers approach their job during the 1975–80 period in a business as usual way or on a crash-planning basis? No clear answer emerges from the papers in this volume. Such studies as those supported by the Club of Rome suggest, however, that this is an increasingly important question for policy-makers to consider.

Geography vs. Function

Should the foreign-policy making process be oriented primarily toward geography or toward issue-areas? This question is not new to American foreign-policy makers, but emerging trends suggest its continued and even increased importance. It is no accident that the twentieth century trends toward global economic, social, and political interdependence have been paralleled by the emergence of functionally based foreign-policy making units. Since the turn of the century, offices concerned with such matters as commercial policy, aviation, petroleum, telecommunications, and shipping have taken their places beside the traditional geographic offices in the Department of State. Indeed, the organizational history of American foreign policy during this century could be written largely in terms of the tension between geographic and functional orientations. Although it is not the purpose of this study to explore organizational questions, the probability of continued or increased tension between a functional approach, based on trends toward interdependence, and a geographic approach, based on the continued viability of the territorially based nation-state, cannot be ignored in discussing mid-term or long-term problems of United States foreign policy.

The question whether to emphasize geographic or functional

considerations cannot be separated from questions about how much interdependence is emerging, how fast, in which issue-areas, and in which parts of the world. There is a tension between a multipolar world and a multi-issue world. On the one hand, dispersal of power strengthens the appeal of regional approaches. On the other hand, the multiplication of issues that cut across geographic boundaries points toward a functional approach. Multipolarity, for example, may mean increased power for India as the dominant actor in South Asia; but multi-issue politics means that CIA activities outside the region (Chile?) may affect United States relations with India.

Long-run trends toward a global village suggest that the functionalist emphasis on issues rather than regions will eventually prevail. For the next five to ten years, however, continued reliance on geographic orientation may be desirable. The crucial factor in deciding which approach to emphasize is the extent to which issues are linked. To what extent can the population-growth issue be uncoupled from the nonrenewable resources issue? To what extent can the food issue be isolated from the energy issue? To what extent can the issue of human rights be separated from issues of trade policy? To what extent can the issue of terrorism be divorced from the Arab-Israeli dispute? To the extent that linkages among issues are weak, a geographic approach makes sense; to the extent that such linkages are strong, a functional approach makes sense.

Four types of linkages are relevant to this discussion. First, issues may be linked in terms of opportunity costs. More money spent on military hardware may mean that less is available for development. Second, issues may be linked by perceptions. A widespread belief that the price of oil is related to the Arab-Israeli dispute is a significant linkage regardless of the accuracy of such perceptions. Third, causal linkages among issues may exist even though they are not widely perceived. Thus the linkage between pollution and industrial growth is not new, despite the fact that widespread awareness of the linkage is relatively recent. A fourth type of linkage is deliberately created for bargaining purposes. Thus arms sales may become linked to oil supplies simply because the Arabs declare these issues to be linked. Similarly, the United States could create a linkage between food exports and oil imports by committing itself to withhold food exports from nations that charge too much for their oil. Any or all of these linkages may make it hard for policy-makers to isolate one problem from another.

The kind of tactics employed depend partially on the number and strength of such linkages. Those who believe that linkages are relatively weak are likely to emphasize geographic approaches, regionalism, multipolarity, incremental policy changes, and avoidance of bargaining across issue-areas. Those who believe that linkages are relatively strong are likely to favor functional approaches, globalism, comprehensive planning, and bargaining across issue-areas. Lags in perceiving emerging trends toward interdependence combined with traditional American pragmatism are likely to bias American foreign-policy-making processes against the latter approach.

The Role of Multilateralism

The United States is currently reevaluating the utility of international organizations as arenas in which to pursue American foreign-policy goals. The unseating of Nationalist China in the United Nations; increasing harassment of Israel in United Nations organs; Third World domination of United Nations debates, agendas, and votes; and increasing criticism of America's role in the world economy have all contributed to United States disillusionment with multilateral tools of foreign policy.

The United States ambassador to the United Nations denounced the "tyranny of the majority" before the General Assembly, while his successor called for the United States to go into "opposition" in the international arena.[8] Clearly, the United States can no longer hope to dominate international organizations as it once did.

Although reexamination of America's role in these groups is in order, care must be taken to avoid two pitfalls. First, we must be careful to determine the extent to which changes in the United States role in the United Nations merely reflect underlying changes in the nature of the international system. The United Nations should not be blamed for events beyond its control. And second, the United States must resist the childish desire to take its ball and bat and go home whenever it fails to get its way in an international organization.

---

8. Text of address by Ambassador John Scali before the United Nations General Assembly, *New York Times,* December 7, 1974; and Daniel P. Moynihan, "The United States in Opposition," *Commentary* (March 1975). See also Harlan Cleveland, "The U.S. vs. the U.N.?" *New York Times Magazine* (May 4, 1975).

Constructive criticism, even hard-hitting denunciations, are appropriate United States actions; it would not be in the United States interest to damage the United Nations or similar organizations in any fundamental way. Survival in an increasingly interdependent world may not require the use or existence of any particular international institution, but it will certainly necessitate the existence and use of some.

ISSUE AREA LINKAGES IN UNITED STATES FOREIGN POLICY

Identifying the nature and number of linkages among foreign-policy issues will be one of the most challenging tasks facing American foreign-policy makers in the next several years. No effort to summarize each of the following essays will be made, but the actual or potential linkages among the issues should be pointed out.

Louis Morton, in his study of nuclear proliferation (Chapter II), predicts that at least six more nations will acquire nuclear weapons by the end of the century, but he thinks that rapid proliferation during the next five years is unlikely. Slow proliferation of such weapons may be the best one can expect in today's world, but it is a rather disconcerting prospect.

Morton envisions two kinds of violent crises involving nuclear weapons. First, the introduction of such weapons into hot spots, such as South Asia or the Middle East, could set off a volatile chain reaction of further proliferation. If Israel were to acquire nuclear weapons, for example, the Arabs would not be far behind. Likewise, India's nuclear "device" has greatly increased the incentive for Pakistan to develop such a "device."

A second potential crisis as envisioned by Morton is nuclear blackmail by nongovernmental terrorist groups. Ever-increasing quantities of plutonium will require much stricter measures to safeguard such material from would-be terrorists. Nuclear devices are dangerous enough when controlled by governments, but they are more so when controlled by free-lance terrorists.

In addition to its relevance to the paper on South Asia, Morton's discussion suggests a number of linkages with other foreign-policy issue-areas. First, the energy problem is linked because nuclear energy is one of the most salient alternatives to fossil fuels and because peaceful uses of atomic energy create the potential for not-so-peaceful uses. Second, critical shortages of a critical resource, such as food or oil, make it easy to imagine situations in which countries with nuclear reactors are willing to trade them for such resources. Such shortages may thus exacerbate the nuclear proliferation problem. Third, the multinational corporation is linked to the issue because of the deep involvement of such corporations in the nuclear power industry. The difficulties of regulation and control by governments are thus compounded. A fourth problem linked to nuclear proliferation is the rich–poor, North–South, or developed–less developed problem. Nuclear reactors are not only a potential energy source for third-world nations, they are also a potential source of both domestic and international prestige. Unfortunately, all four of these linkages seem to enhance the probability of nuclear proliferation.

In South Asia, Howard Erdman (Chapter VIII) identifies Bangladesh and the India-Pakistan situation as likely catalysts of violence in the next five years. This becomes a problem for American foreign policy primarily in terms of its potential effects on regional stability and India's role as the dominant actor in South Asia. Doubts about Bangladesh's viability as a political and economic unit, for example, make a major crisis likely in the next few years. Such a crisis could lead to actual or threatened intervention by Russia, China, India and/or Pakistan. Thus could problems of poverty, ignorance, and disease be converted into confrontation among nuclear powers.

Although Erdman sees the Bangladesh problem as linked with the more general problems of development, population control, and food shortage, he sees little hope of progress on these fronts during the next five years in Bangladesh. The most significant linkages for United States policy makers are with extraregional problems, such as United States relations with Russia and China. In an interdependent world small problems in very weak countries can rapidly grow into big problems for very strong nations.

The problems of food scarcity, overpopulation, and resource depletion are so closely linked that they can be viewed as a single constellation. As a major food producer and exporter the United States can expect increased pressure to provide food for other nations. Dealing with such external pressures will not be nearly so easy as it was when grain surpluses were so big that the government defined the problem in terms of finding ways to get rid of such surpluses. As Laurence Radway points out (Chapter X), domestic pressures to "feed Americans first" are likely to increase simultaneously with foreign pressure to export food.

The food shortage, of course, is a function of the number of mouths to be fed. Whatever the differences among people, they all have one thing in common—the need to eat. Population growth, however, is usually perceived as a long-term rather than a mid-term problem. Donella Meadows suggests (Chapter VI) two arguments for viewing the problem in more immediate terms. First, preventing food shortages is easier and cheaper than trying to end them once they appear. And second, the dynamics of the population growth process magnify the effects of early successes (or failures) in population control.

The most visible example of resource depletion is, of course, the oil situation. On the one hand, some see this as the first step toward ever-increasing crises in resource shortage. Michael Mazur, on the other hand (Chapter V), raises doubts about cartels similar to OPEC being formed in other primary commodity markets. There is also another sense in which resource depletion may be a problem for United States foreign-policy makers. The knowledge that the United States consumes about a third of the resources used by the entire world in a year has strengthened resentment of American power, wealth, and status. Such a perception can have great political significance regardless of the validity of the view from a strictly economic standpoint.

The food-population-resources problem provides an excellent example of the importance of linkages among issues. At the World Population Conference in Bucharest, Rumania (August 1974), the United States took the position that excessive population growth was a problem for other nations but not for the United States and that American consumption levels had little or nothing to do with the population problem. At the World Food Conference in Rome three months later the American delegation showed increased awareness of linkages. The Americans seemed willing at least to consider the possibility that United States consumption habits might be part of the problem. The tendency to deny the existence of linkages among issues and to treat every problem in isolation is a sign of a pre-interdependence type of thinking. As interdependence increases,

United States foreign-policy makers will have to learn to think of excessive population growth and food shortage not just as "their" problems but as "ours."

The problem of third-world development is so closely intertwined with food-resources-population that many would question separating them. Development, however, is more than just food, population, and resources. It is a complex social process that concerns fundamental changes in a whole society. It is a psychological, social, and political phenomenon as well as an economic one. Third-world development presents the United States with some very difficult problems. The United States is both a symbol of development and a potential source of aid. Such a situation makes American insensitivity to third-world difficulties all the more frustrating to less-developed countries. Also, as Nelson Kasfir points out (Chapter VII), a school of thought has emerged that blames the United States as much for what it has done as for what it has not done. There is now a great deal of ambivalence and skepticism as to whether the United States ought to try to promote development in other countries, which means are likely to be effective, and whether the United States can afford to use such means. As Radway's paper notes, economic aid is one of the least popular foreign-policy expenditures in domestic political arenas.

The linkages between development and other world problems have been magnified and multiplied by deliberate acts of third-world diplomats, who are determined to demonstrate the intensity of their feelings about the problem by capitalizing on every opportunity to remind the rich nations of this point. Third-world countries are not proceeding toward multi-issue foreign policies nearly so fast as the rich nations. The overriding issue of development still serves as a touchstone for many. Any major foreign-policy problem the United States is likely to encounter in the next five years—nuclear armaments, oil shortages, inflation, population growth, environmental deterioration, the Arab-Israeli dispute, or whatever—will have to be analyzed in terms of implications for third-world development. The leaders of the less developed countries will make sure that questions about such implications are raised.

The two schools of thought on development which Kasfir discusses provide an excellent illustration of the duality of the role of multinational corporations. On the one hand, such organizations serve as channels for spreading technology and for internationalizing production. On the other hand, they often generate friction in developing countries and are frequently viewed as the symbols and/or agents of economic imperialism. Although multinational corporations are not governmental agencies, their activities are important determinants of the way foreigners perceive the United States.

Much of the current conventional wisdom about multinational corporations should be viewed, however, with caution. Kjell-Arne Ringbakk suggests (Chapter IV) that the "multinational era" dates from about 1958 and that the next five years may not see just more of the same tendencies toward more and bigger MNC's. He argues that MNC's evolve through a life cycle in which the mature stages may be characterized by "fragmentation, stagnation, retraction, and diminution of headquarters control." Such possibilities suggest that close scrutiny of MNC's during the next five years is in order, but they also suggest the need to be wary of making premature judgments about the role of the MNC during the next five years.

Michael Mazur views the MNC (Chapter V) as having much different significance for more developed nations than for less developed ones. For developed nations competition to attract MNC investments and frictions regarding national antitrust regulations are seen as salient mid-term problems. For less developed nations bargaining about the terms of entry and operation are likely to be of primary importance.

International monetary relations are often considered the polar opposite of international political and military relations. Whereas threats, violence, and intense emotions often characterize politico-military depictions of international relations, international finance tends to be viewed in terms of technical, rational, nonpolitical agreements. This view of the world of international finance never was very accurate; it is less so today. Questions about exchange-rate stability and short-term capital flows are not only important issues in their own right, they are also linked to a number of other issues.

The oil shortage, third-world development, and the multinational corporation are among the more important issues to which international monetary problems are linked. The oil price revolution has suddenly increased Arab control of huge and rapidly growing amounts of foreign exchange. Balance-of-payments crises and the possibilities for recycling these funds are problems stemming from the recent rise in oil prices. Multinational corporations are linked to international monetary questions. As Mazur notes, "the spread of the multinationals has been one of the prime forces increasing the mobility of short-term capital." The question of how changes in the international monetary system would affect the operations of MNC's is likely to be an important consideration for United States foreign-policy makers during the coming five years. Any attempt to revamp international monetary arrangements will also trigger demands for special treatment of less developed countries. From the standpoint of the third world, the symbolism of such measures matters as much as the substance; and third-world leaders will undoubtedly try to link long-term development issues with the issue of international monetary reform.

AMERICA AND THE WORLD: DIRECTION, ORIENTATION, AND STYLE IN FOREIGN POLICY

Each of the essays prepared for this volume focuses on a particular problem area of American foreign policy, but there are also questions that cut across several papers or that relate to the overall pattern found in the essays. Such questions are not so much about tactics or game plans as they are about deciding which game to play. What sort of general orientation should America have toward the rest of the world? If the phrase "long-range goals" implies an unjustified and misleading degree of concreteness, then what vague general sense of direction should infuse the American foreign-policy making process? To such questions we now turn. Although no answers are provided, the identification of the right questions is an important first step in rethinking America's world role.

The single most important question facing United States foreign-policy makers is how to respond to the emerging interdependent world. This question is really a bundle of smaller ones and can be answered piecemeal. Still, the overall orientation to such questions matters. The alternative "dominant strategies" available to the United States include insulation, promotion, retardation, and adaptation.

Insulating itself from the international system would not be an unprecedented policy orientation for America. "No entangling alliances" could simply be updated and expanded to read "No entangling relationships of any kind." Americans could learn to live without, or develop substitutes for, imported goods and services. Developing self-sufficiency in energy resources is one example of a policy designed to insulate the United States from the actual or potential effects of interdependence.

Although the United States is one of the few nations that can even contemplate a policy of insulation, there are a number of drawbacks associated with such an approach. First, some problems simply do not permit the United States to insulate itself. Short of a gigantic canopy erected over the entire nation, it is difficult to imagine the country remaining aloof from global environmental problems, such as destruction of the earth's atmosphere, pollution of the oceans, weather modification, melting the polar ice cap, etc. Similar difficulties arise with respect to national security. In a dangerous world with many dissatisfied nations, terrorists, and mounting stocks of nuclear devices, the United States cannot unilaterally ensure its own national security. A second disadvantage of insulation is the tremendous economic and social costs of such a policy. Taken to an extreme it would entail eliminating (or minimizing) all communication, travel, and commerce with the rest of the world. A third drawback of such an approach would be impairment of the American self-image. It is one thing to rationalize failure to help others with their problems in terms of one's inability; it is another to proclaim one's unwillingness to help. Unless Americans are willing to contemplate withdrawal from the human race, no very extensive uncoupling from the international system seems feasible. Selective insulation on such issues as energy may indeed be appropriate, but an overall dominant strategy of cutting loose from the rest of the world would not.

A second strategy available to United States policy-makers is *active promotion* of interdependence on either a global or a regional basis. Supporting the formation of new international institutions, encouraging higher levels of international trade, and promoting global communication via satellites are examples of policies that would strengthen trends toward interdependence.

Two major difficulties are encountered with such an approach. First, since interdependence can have destabilizing effects on the international system, it would be important to avoid promoting some kinds of interdependence. And second, attempts by the United

States to promote interdependence are likely to be interpreted by the rest of the world as designed to preserve and enhance United States hegemony.

On balance, this strategy is unlikely to be adopted primarily because adjusting perceptions to existing interdependence trends is difficult enough without deliberate attempts to magnify such trends. Still, the possibility that interdependence, including United States dependence, might serve United States interests should at least be considered. The proposition that American dependence on other nations for energy resources is undesirable has assumed the status of a self-evident truth. If, however, such dependence serves to increase American awareness of the need to cooperate with other nations, it might well be that the long-run interests of the nation would be served better by dependence than by interdependence. The Secretary of State can give any number of speeches on interdependence, but none will drive the point home to the American people as effectively as doubling the gasoline prices. This is not to say that increased American dependence is always desirable; it is only to suggest that policy-makers should seriously consider the desirability of increased American dependence to some extent and in some areas.

The counterpart to a strategy of promoting interdependence is a strategy of trying to *retard* it. This is similar to a policy of insulation, except that the United States would be promoting the insulation of all nations rather than just itself. Encouraging autarkic trends in other nations, inhibiting foreign investment, and discouraging international communication would be examples of such policies. Self-sufficiency for everyone, not just for the United States, would be the earmark of this approach. Whether the United States has the ability to affect the overall trends toward interdependence, however, is open to serious question. If a strategy of insulating the country would be difficult, a strategy of insulating others would be more so. If promoting interdependence would stimulate suspicions about American motives, attempts to retard interdependence would do the same.

Attempts to manipulate worldwide trends toward interdependence and attempts to insulate America from the effects of such trends are worth consideration by United States foreign-policy makers even though immense difficulties are associated with each strategy. A fourth approach deserving consideration is *adapting*

American society to the emerging interdependent world.[9] Whereas promoting or retarding strategies are attempts to manipulate global trends, the adaptive approach accepts such trends as givens. Whereas insulation tries to preserve and protect America from the effects of such trends, the adaptive approach tries to change America to bring it into harmony with worldwide trends.

Thus far the history of American foreign relations could be divided into two stages: an early stage, during which the dominant strategy was to ignore the rest of the world, and a later stage, during which the dominant strategy was to reform the rest of the world. The adaptive approach suggests a third stage, in which the United States learns to accept and live with the rest of the world. The transition to such a third stage has been characterized as moving from an "engineering perspective" to an "ecological perspective" on foreign policy.[10] Whereas the engineering perspective emphasizes solving individual problems, the ecological perspective emphasizes the linkages among problems and the need to adapt to certain environmental conditions. In the opinion of some, "the engineering perspective that pervades the foreign and domestic policies and statecraft of most governments today is possibly the most formidable obstacle to effective concerted attack on the long and lengthening list of international problems that arise from the inescapable interdependence of all nations upon this increasingly crowded planet."[11] Not every paper in this study would go so far, but many of them emphasize the need to give serious consideration to an overall dominant strategy which emphasizes adaptation.

The adaptive approach would not be an easy one to choose. In addition to such traditional activities as diplomatic negotiation and foreign aid disbursement, the adaptive approach calls upon foreign-policy makers to begin thinking in terms of getting Americans to

---

9. A foreign policy characterized by an adaptive orientation is discussed by James N. Rosenau, "Adaptive Polities in an Interdependent World," *Orbis*, 16 (Spring 1972), 153–173; Harold and Margaret Sprout, *Multiple Vulnerabilities*, Princeton University Center of International Studies, Research Monograph 40 (April 1974); and Harold and Margaret Sprout, *Toward a Politics of the Planet Earth* (New York, Van Nostrand, 1971).

10. Sprout and Sprout, pp. 17–18.

11. Ibid.

change personal values and life styles and to alter the allocation of resources radically. Such measures as the allocation of 10 percent of the gross national product for nonmilitary international affairs, gasoline rationing, or prohibitions on meat production are likely to generate intense domestic opposition. In addition, such an approach constitutes a reduced emphasis on the optimistic pragmatism that has been one of the important sources of strength in American foreign policy.

The essays that follow do not point unequivocally to a single response to interdependence. They do, however, identify several midterm problems and underscore the need to consider policy responses in terms of broader trends in the international system. The choices made by United States policy-makers during the next five years will have important effects on the world for the rest of this century. If these essays facilitate the making of wise and humane choices, they will have served their purpose.

EDITOR'S NOTE

No issue more graphically illustrates the hopes and fears associated with increasing interdependence than that of nuclear proliferation. On the one hand nuclear energy has a great potential for increasing human welfare; but on the other hand it also generates fears of nuclear war.

Professor Morton examines the problem of nuclear proliferation and surveys some of the policy options available to the United States. He concludes that the United States should try to retard the spread of nuclear weapons while simultaneously exploring ways to limit the further accumulation of such weapons by those who have already "gone nuclear."

AUTHOR'S NOTE

This paper was written more than a year ago. The discussion and analysis of the problems of nuclear proliferation was based therefore on developments of the spring and early summer of 1974. They are as valid today (August 1975) as they were then. Events of the past year have not altered the nature of the problems of nuclear proliferation or the dangers inherent in nuclear technology. Rather, they have confirmed the analysis and conclusions of the paper, for at the time it was written, it was already evident that India's explosion of a nuclear device in May of that year and the oil embargo of 1973 and the energy crisis that followed had released forces that greatly increased the danger of proliferation. The only developments of the past year not anticipated in the present study are the dimensions of the increased sales of nuclear power plants, including West Germany's four-billion-dollar agreement with Brazil; additional strong evidence of the risks inherent in industrial nuclear technology; and President Ford's proposal in June 1975 to turn over to private industry the manufacture of enriched uranium in order to increase the supply and improve the United States position in the growing international competition for nuclear sales.

Much has been written on the subject of nuclear proliferation and the technology of nuclear energy. A good deal of this literature is in the form of journal articles, government documents, and the reports of a variety of scientific governmental and international organizations. Though I have utilized this material, I have not documented the paper, since it was based very largely on newspaper stories, government reports, and discussions with colleagues. For the convenience of the reader, however, a select bibliography of convenient and accessible sources (exclusive of journal articles) is included at the end of the essay.

II.

Who Next?
The Spread of Nuclear Weapons

Louis Morton

> The more nations that have the power to trigger off a nuclear war, the greater the chance that some nation might use this power in haste or blind folly.
>
> *Christian Herter*

> The unleashed power of the atom has changed everything save our modes of thinking, and thus we drift to unparalleled catastrophe.
>
> *Albert Einstein*

The problem of proliferation, a shorthand term for the spread of nuclear weapons to other nations, is not new. It came into existence with the test at Alamogordo and the bombing of Hiroshima and Nagasaki in 1945 and with the passage the following year of the McMahon Act. This Act, the first dealing with nuclear matters, prohibited the sharing of American atomic weapons or technology with any other nation, including the British, who had helped develop the bomb. In the Acheson-Lilienthal proposals presented to the United Nations in 1946 as the Baruch Plan, men had for one brief moment a vision of a world without nuclear arms. But the Soviet Union found the proposals unacceptable and pressed forward with a nuclear program of its own. In 1949 it exploded an atomic bomb, thus breaking the American monopoly and setting off the spread of nuclear weapons. A few years later the United Kingdom joined the first two by testing its own nuclear device. By the end of the decade, whether as a result or because of their independence from the two superpowers, France and China embarked on a nuclear program. The former joined the nuclear club in 1960, the latter in 1964.

The tests by France and China, coming so close together, raised the specter of the rapid spread of nuclear weapons to other nations and created an atmosphere that encouraged negotiations on the limitation of nuclear armaments between the United States and the Soviet Union, even while each was engaged in a nuclear race with the other. In 1963 the two nations signed the "Hot Line" Agreement (renewed in 1971) establishing direct and immediate communications between Washington and Moscow, and, the same year, a Limited Test Ban Treaty barring nuclear tests in the atmosphere, in outer space, and under water. Agreement on a comprehensive test ban proved impossible then and still is, but the principle of test limitations, already in effect for the Antarctic region (signed in 1959) was extended to outer space in 1967, to Latin America in 1968, and to the ocean floor in 1971. At the Moscow summit in June of 1974, the two nations extended this principle by limiting the yield as well as the location of the nuclear explosion by an agreement prohibiting underground tests in excess of 150 kilotons. Most important of the agreements were the Non-Proliferation Treaty (NPT) and SALT I. Other nations, it is true, signed many of these agreements, but it was the signatures of the United States and the Soviet Union which gave them force and significance.

Between 1946 and 1949 the world had stood at a crossroads, with a choice between a non-nuclear and a nuclear world. That golden opportunity slipped by. Between March 1970, when the NPT went into effect, and the spring of 1974, before India set off a nuclear explosion, the world had a second opportunity to choose. Would the number of nuclear nations remain at five or would it gradually increase as more and more nations acquired a nuclear technology? India's test seemed to settle that question.

THE PROBLEM

The Indian explosion on May 18, 1974, opened up the prospects of a new round of proliferation and a renewal of the arms race between the United States and the Soviet Union. This event, combined with the effects of the oil embargo and the spread of nuclear technology with its terrifying potential for increasing the stockpiles of deadly plutonium, made the dangers of proliferation a very real possibility. In this section I propose to describe the events that raised anew the specter of proliferation during the summer of 1974 and place them in context. The second section discusses the political and technological aspects of proliferation in general terms; and in the final section the various policy options are summarized.

India

On May 18 India exploded a nuclear device in a shallow (one-hundred-foot-deep) underground test in the northern desert of Rajasthan, thus joining the exclusive five-member nuclear club. The yield of the plutonium explosive was in the range of 10 to 15 kilotons, somewhat less than that of the Hiroshima bomb. The device, the Indian government explained to a skeptical world, was not a bomb and had no military significance whatsoever; its purpose was entirely peaceful, to explore the possibilities of utilizing nuclear power for earth-moving and mining. "We do not intend to be a nuclear weapons power and we will use atomic energy for peaceful purposes only," said Dr. Homi Sethna, head of the Indian Atomic Energy Commission. "We are interested, essentially, in gas and oil exploration."

India's protestations notwithstanding, it was believed that any explosion of a nuclear device, whatever its purpose, had to be regarded as a nonpeaceful use of nuclear power and potentially a military weapon. As one informed critic observed, "no fundamental difference exists between the innards of a weapon and a 'peaceful' explosive."

The fissionable material for the explosion in the Rajasthan desert had presumably come directly or indirectly from the reactors furnished by Canada almost twenty years earlier. Although no safeguards had been established at the time to ensure that the reactors would be used only for peaceful ends, the Indian Government had agreed in 1971 to inspection by the Vienna-based International Atomic Energy Administration (IAEA). This agreement was to apply only to the Canadian installation.

Despite these regulations, India had managed to evade detection and obtain enough plutonium to set off the explosion, an action that the Canadians considered a clear violation of the 1971 understanding. The United States had indirectly contributed to the Indian explosion

by providing heavy water for the Canadian reactor. It had also supplied India with two atomic power plants, with the proviso that they
be subject to international controls by the IAEA to limit their use to
peaceful purposes—a requirement to which the Indians agreed in
1963 but later insisted did not apply to "peaceful" explosions.
Despite the United States and Canadian restrictions, rumors that the
Indians were stockpiling plutonium persisted, one study estimating in
July 1972 that India had a plutonium stockpile of 95 kilograms,
more than enough for a significant number of bombs. The plutonium
presumably had come from the Canadian research reactor.

India was not one of the signatories to the Non-Proliferation
Treaty (NPT). In that treaty the non-nuclear powers had pledged
themselves not to develop nuclear weapons, and the nuclear powers
had agreed not to help other nations acquire such weapons. As of
May 1974, over 80 nations had signed and ratified the treaty; 62 had
either not signed or not ratified. Of these about 25 could be considered critical. Those that had signed but not ratified included such
countries as Japan, West Germany, Italy, and Belgium—all capable of
manufacturing nuclear weapons should they choose to do so. The
non-signers included—in addition to India—Israel, South Africa,
Argentina, Brazil, and Pakistan.

India's move into the nuclear club was not altogether unex-
pected. Among nations that had been considered likely candidates
for such a move, she stood high. She had steadfastly refused to sign
the NPT, was extremely sensitive to the presence of a nuclear China
on her border and of a recently defeated Pakistan close by, had a
well developed nuclear technology, and perhaps aspired to leadership
in the Third World.

Prestige and domestic politics probably played as large a role in
India's decision as any other factor. The *Times of India* spoke of a
nation "thrilled" by the event which "scientists, politicians and the
common man hailed as a great landmark in India's nuclear research."
Significantly, the *Times* failed to mention the military, but an
accompanying cartoon pictured Mrs. Gandhi in tattered sari entering
a clubroom occupied by male members representing the five nuclear
powers, holding aloft a dove of peace with an olive branch.

Despite her protestations, the explosion of a nuclear device did
have significant potential military implications for India. The explosion did not give her a military nuclear capability, but the distance

between a device and a bomb is comparatively short. Nor was a delivery system beyond her capabilities, at least not the kind she might need to influence her neighbors. She did not need a system comparable to that of the United States or Russia to pose a military threat to Pakistan or even, minimally, to China. An arms race with China might well be financially ruinous, but it was no more necessary for India to match China's nuclear power than it was for the French *force de frappe* to match Soviet missile strength. The point was that India's nuclear capability would have to be taken into consideration by China in any future strategic calculations.

The Indian military was silent on India's need for nuclear weapons, but Dr. K. Subrahmanyam, director of the foremost Indian "think tank," said "I am in favor of a weapons program." He recognized the cost would be high, however, and he therefore favored deferring the decision for the present but allocating sufficient funds to prepare for it. "I suppose it would be possible for us now to build a few droppable plutonium bombs each year. . . . You've got to provide security for your government."

Egypt and Israel

On June 14, less than a month after the explosion at the underground test site in northern India, President Nixon on a tour of the Middle East startled the American people with the announcement that the United States had agreed to provide Egypt with a nuclear technology for peaceful purposes. This sale, announced jointly with President Sadat, was presented as part of a broad program of cooperation formalizing the new relationship between the two countries. Under this agreement, which had been worked out earlier with Secretary of State Kissinger, the United States would sell Egypt two nuclear reactors and fuel (i.e., fissile materials) under safeguards that presumably would ensure their peaceful use. A similar agreement, it was announced, would be concluded (as indeed it was only a few days later) with Israel. The nuclear reactors in question, the experts pointed out, were each capable of producing 150 kilograms of plutonium annually, which would yield after reprocessing about twice that amount of weapons-grade fissionable material.

At the time Nixon made his announcement, Egypt already had two Soviet reactors, but Sadat, apparently seeking the best of both worlds, wanted American reactors as well so that he would not be dependent upon Russia for fuel. Under the agreement announced by Nixon, the sale of enriched uranium was to begin immediately and after safeguard arrangements had been completed for inspection by the IAEA and direct controls by the United States, the U.S. Atomic Energy Commission and the Egyptian Ministry of Electricity were to work out the details of an accord. By the early 1980's it was expected that Egypt would have a nuclear power plant capable of generating enough electric power to "support its rapidly growing development needs."

Israel, too, already had nuclear facilities. In fact, the Israelis possessed both the technology and the scientific expertise for the manufacture of nuclear explosives. There were even rumors that they had already built one or more bombs, and estimates placed Israel's stockpile of plutonium at 40 kilograms. If the Israelis had a bomb, they had evidently not tested it yet. The plutonium for such weapons, if they did have a stockpile, presumably came from the 5-7 megawatt reactor at Dimona built with French assistance. This reactor, which the French had offered without safeguards, was capable of producing enough plutonium for one bomb of Nagasaki size each year. In recent years the United States had been selling fuel to Israel for its reactor, and American intelligence had long assumed that Israel had, at the least, a stockpile of fissionable material and the ability to construct nuclear weapons.

The announcement of the introduction of nuclear materials into the explosive Middle East coming so closely on the heels of the Indian explosion was greeted in the United States with alarm and consternation on Capitol Hill and throughout the country. Hearings by Senate and House committees in June and July made it evident that Nixon's offer to Egypt and Israel would not be routinely approved. "With all the problems in the Mideast today," asked Rep. Lee H. Hamilton (D., Ind.), "why is it so essential to make agreements for the export of nuclear technology? . . . We are creating problems. I am hard put to see why we don't do other things that don't have the risks this appears to."

Before Congress at this time was a proposal to amend the Atomic Energy Act of 1954 to give Congress a voice in the approval of international agreements for the peaceful cooperation in nuclear technology. During the debate, it became clear that the critical question was the adequacy of safeguards, both of the Atomic Energy Commission and of the International Atomic Energy Administration. As an example, proponents of the measure pointed to the unwillingness of responsible officials in the Atomic Energy Commission and the State Department to guarantee that the reactors the President had offered to the Mideast countries would be used only for peaceful uses. Other concerns expressed at the time included doubts about Egypt's need for new sources of power, or for a technology that required huge capital investments that neither Egypt nor Israel could afford, and the possibility of nuclear accidents or theft of plutonium by terrorists.

In an effort to calm these fears, Secretary Kissinger held a news conference to explain that the safeguards to be taken for "the storing and disposition of the end product of these reactors," i.e., the plutonium, would be "substantially foolproof." Just how this would be accomplished, Mr. Kissinger did not explain. The United States, Kissinger reminded the correspondents, had negotiated similar agreements with twenty-nine other countries. To the criticism that the introduction of nuclear technology into the sensitive Middle East could create a dangerous situation, Kissinger responded that "there is no reason to suppose that other countries, and not only those of Eastern Europe, would have been quite prepared to engage in nuclear discussions on peaceful energy with Egypt, or perhaps even other countries of the Middle East."

Kissinger's reassurance did not convince opponents of the sale, and when President Nixon resigned, Senator Henry Jackson, a member of the Joint Committee on Atomic Energy, called on the new president to reconsider the Nixon offer. There was no way, he said, to ensure that plutonium could not be diverted from the reactor. To date President Ford has taken no steps to remove what Jackson described as "a most unfortunate legacy" of the Nixon years. Nor has he given any indication that he intends to do so. But, neither, so far as we know, has he delivered the reactors promised by Nixon to Egypt or Israel.

Iran

The next development in the introduction of nuclear technology into the Mideast came at the end of June 1974 with the announcement that France had signed a ten-year, 4 billion dollar pact with Iran which included the sale of five 1,000 megawatt nuclear reactors valued at well over a billion dollars. The prime supplier of the nuclear plant was the Creusot-Loire Company, whose earnings, said the Finance Minister, would be "fabulous." The French government agreed also to train Iranian scientists and technicians and to assist in the establishment of an Iranian nuclear research center. No mention was made of safeguards against the use of the reactors for military purposes, but both parties agreed to respect their international obligations. Since France had signed the Euratom Treaty (which prohibited dissemination of weapons or weapons-making capacity), and Iran the nuclear Non-Proliferation Treaty (which calls for safeguards and inspection by the IAEA) it was generally assumed that safeguards would probably be established. This assumption, it must be observed, is not necessarily correct; Canada, it will be remembered, believed it had imposed similar obligations on India.

The announcement of Iran's decision to acquire a nuclear technology did not come as a complete surprise. A month earlier, almost immediately after the Indian test explosion, there was a report that Iranian officials had been discussing for several months the terms of nuclear assistance with a number of countries, including the United States, Russia, and Canada. The Shah, it was further reported, had repeatedly asserted his intention to bring his country into the nuclear age. In April of 1974 he had created an Atomic Energy Commission and early in May he had welcomed the former President of Argentina's Atomic Energy Commission on his arrival in Teheran to act as adviser on atomic affairs. About the same time, Prime Minister Gandhi had visited the Shah, at which time she may have informed him of India's decision to explode a nuclear device. And finally, on May 21, an American atomic delegation headed by Dixie Lee Ray, Chairman of the Atomic Energy Commission, arrived in Iran to discuss plans for development of a major nuclear energy complex. None of these reports hinted at the negotiations with the French, who ultimately were successful in concluding arrangements with Iran under which France would not only ease her balance of payments problem but be assured of an adequate supply of oil and the opportunity to develop Iranian natural gas to transport to Europe.

But American industry did not lose out altogether in the

Franco-Iranian agreement. Westinghouse had a 45 percent interest in Creusot-Loire and orders for sixteen nuclear units from the French— at that time the largest nuclear power order ever placed—in addition to six previous orders. The total value of the twenty-two units was placed at about 1.5 billion dollars. Some idea of the extent of Westinghouse's commitment to the nuclear power industry can be gained from the fact that in addition to the French order the company had twenty-three other overseas units and seventy-seven units in operation, under construction, or on order in the United States. Additional orders were expected from other European nations and Japan in the near future, and predictions for total industry sales for 1974 were placed at about 45 million kilowatts. "The energy crisis helped people to understand what was to be done"—said Westinghouse President John W. Simpson—"that there are no real alternatives to nuclear energy which is cheaper and less subject to inflationary pressures than any other system." He did not mention consumer opposition or the potential dangers of the system that opponents were concerned about.

The Moscow Summit

This series of events reached a disheartening climax early in July 1974 with the failure of the Nixon-Brezhnev meeting in Moscow. People all over the world had hoped that following SALT I in May 1972, the United States and the Soviet Union would arrive at an agreement providing long-term and effective limits on offensive strategic nuclear arms. The failure to do so and to make the 1972 interim agreement permanent now opened the way to a resumption of the nuclear arms race and the expenditure of additional billions on military hardware.

The interim agreement on offensive weapons in SALT I had given the Russians superiority in the number of land and sea-based missiles and in "throw-weight" (more powerful missiles) but left the United States with overall superiority in nuclear weapons. The United States had a clear superiority in long-range bombers that could carry 60 percent of its destructive force, and had begun in 1970 to MIRV its land and submarine missiles—i.e., to equip them with multiple independently targeted warheads. This agreement on offensive weapons was due to expire automatically in 1977, by which time the Americans, thanks to the MIRV, expected to have 2½ times more warheads than the Russians (10,120 to 3,950). In addition, the Americans had begun developing an improved nuclear submarine, the Trident, carrying MIRV-equipped missiles with a range of almost 5,000 miles, and were planning for a new long-range bomber, the B-1.

The Russians had not been idle either. Their missiles, already more powerful than the American Minuteman III, were made even more powerful and given the capability of carrying multiple warheads. Thus the so-called SS-18 with a throw-weight of 16,500 pounds would carry many more warheads than the Minuteman, which had a throw-weight of about a ton. The SS-17 and SS-19, though not as powerful, still had far greater throw-weight than the Minuteman. Given their superiority in the number of missiles (approximately 2,500 to 1,700), the Pentagon estimated, the Russians with their newly acquired MIRV capability and their greater throw-weight could conceivably achieve by 1977, when the interim agreement on offensive weapons would expire, a greater offensive capacity than the United States.

It was at this time that Secretary of Defense James Schlesinger and his Pentagon planners proposed that the United States develop missiles with a greatly improved accuracy so that they could knock out Soviet "hardened" missile sites as well as cities—a policy that was interpreted by its critics as giving the United States a first-strike capability and therefore essentially destabilizing. In addition, Secretary Schlesinger, supported by such powerful senators as Barry Goldwater, brought pressure on the negotiators at Geneva and on Secretary Kissinger to limit Soviet MIRV deployment.

But even Kissinger's famed powers of persuasion proved unequal to the task of selling this program to the Russians, who had their own Pentagon to satisfy. As a result, the agreement concluded in Moscow was limited to the ABM (reduced from two to one) and to underground testing, setting an upper limit of 150 kilotons to such tests, to go into effect in March 1976—a restriction that did not seriously limit any tests the two might wish to conduct. "One way of describing these negotiations at the summit," said Alexander Rich, professor of biophysics at MIT, "is [that] it's the military of both sides negotiating with the civilian components of both sides. The net result . . . was a clear-cut victory for the military of both sides and a clear-cut defeat of [civilians]."

However it is viewed, the Moscow meeting was a failure in that it reached no agreement on offensive weapons. All that the two parties could agree upon was that they would continue to seek to negotiate an interim agreement on offensive weapons to extend through 1985. "If we have not reached an agreement well before 1977," warned Secretary Kissinger, "then I believe you will see an explosion of technology and an explosion of numbers at the end of which we will be lucky if we have the present stability." Two months later, in mid-September, the two countries resumed negotiations in Geneva on strategic arms in an effort to halt the seemingly "inexorable arms race."

The failure of Nixon and Brezhnev to reach agreement on limitation of offensive weapons undercut the argument for the Non-Proliferation Treaty and had the effect of encouraging a trend toward proliferation. The link between arms limitation and the NPT lay in the expectation of the non-nuclear powers that the superpowers were committed to genuine nuclear disarmament. They were persuaded to accept the treaty on that understanding, and Article 6, one of the key provisions of the NPT and one that the non-nuclear powers had insisted upon, was the agreement by the nuclear powers to "pursue negotiations on effective measures relating to cessation of the nuclear arms race at an early date and to nuclear disarmament." Commenting on the failure to reach agreement at the Moscow summit meeting, Abram Chayes, Harvard law professor and former legal adviser to the Secretary of State, expressed concern over the effect on the NPT. "Now the non-nuclear powers have clearly been dissatisfied with the progress that has been made," he said. "When you add that to the Indian test, the question arises whether the non-nuclear powers now will feel that things have gone so far that there is nothing left for them in the treaty." The Test Ban Treaty, SALT I, and other agreements had held out the promise of progress in arms control and encouraged support of the NPT. The Moscow summit, in the view of many, put an end to such hopes for the time being.

DISCUSSION

There was a real concern in the United States that these events were a frightening portent of worse still to come, that they would give impetus to the further spread of nuclear weapons and soon other nations would decide to acquire a nuclear capability. It was possible to make an argument for proliferation of nuclear weapons on the ground that it would enhance the stability of the international order and lessen the prospects of a nuclear war. But most American officials and students of the subject believed with Christian Herter that the spread of nuclear weapons only increased the chances of a nuclear conflict. Meeting in mid-July, the executive committee of the prestigious "Pugwash" conference, an international group of distinguished scientists and other experts from over thirty countries, expressed its alarm over these developments, all of which in their view emphasized anew the threat of nuclear war. The group had become complacent over the years, but recent events had forced a "rude awakening," said the executive committee, and had restored "a sense of urgency and concern." "For individuals as for nations," it declared, "an ethic of arms control must replace the ethic of the arms race."

This sentiment was echoed by the editors of the *Bulletin of Atomic Scientists*, whose cover each issue pictured the "doomsday" clock. Since June 1972, after the signing of the SALT I Treaty, the hands of the clock had been set at 12 minutes to midnight. In August, the hands were moved three minutes closer to midnight, the fatal hour, in recognition of the setbacks suffered since May. In the view of the editors these setbacks as well as the continued development of new generations of nuclear weapons and delivery systems augured ill for the future. They noted also the failure of governments generally to deal with the problems created by the energy crisis and the rapid spread of nuclear power plants, the disposal of waste products, safeguards, security, the production of ever-increasing quantities of plutonium, and the threat of nuclear sabotage, blackmail, and terrorism.

Political and Strategic

Any discussion of the spread of nuclear weapons is necessarily concerned with uncertainties of all kinds—technological, political, financial, and military. Since the present study is focused on the short range, i.e. four to ten years, it is necessary to keep in mind that we are dealing with *trends* toward a nuclear capability rather than with the *actual* acquisition of a complete nuclear weapons system. In this time frame it is safe to say that the balance of nuclear power will not change materially. Such a change, as well as fundamental shifts in international relationships, ordinarily occurs over long periods of time even when conditions favor change.

Viewed from this perspective, the effect of the nuclear explosion in the Indian desert, aside from all other considerations, is significant largely as a symbol, an indication of what may come to pass in the future. It did not give India an operational nuclear capability; that will require perhaps five or ten years to achieve, assuming that the Indian government makes the decision to develop such a weapons system. Other countries less advanced technologically than India and less favored by geography, population, and resources would require an even longer period to achieve what India has already accomplished. Even for such advanced industrial non-nuclear states as West Germany, Sweden, and Japan, assuming all conditions were favorable, the manufacture of a nuclear warhead and a delivery system would take at least a few years. Thus the addition of a seventh or eighth or tenth member of the nuclear club will occur, if at all, gradually and over a period of time.

The overriding consideration in dealing with the spread of nuclear weapons is the avoidance of nuclear war and the maintenance of a secure and stable world order. To put the issue this way implies the answer to a prior question: whether proliferation increases or diminishes the likelihood of nuclear conflict or stability. This paper will not develop the arguments for and against the question; it assumes the truth of the proposition that an increase in the number of nuclear powers increases the risks of nuclear war. This is the official position of the United States government, and has been at the root of United States negotiations on nuclear matters since 1946. "I ask you," said President Kennedy, with perhaps pardonable exaggeration, "to stop and think for a moment what it would mean to have nuclear weapons in so many hands, in the hands of countries large and small, stable and unstable, responsible and unresponsible, scattered throughout the world."

If we accept the desirability of limiting nuclear weapons, how can we limit their spread? Proliferation depends on a variety of factors, and its potential effect is related to the rate of proliferation, the size, location, and political relationships of the nation or nations involved, and the reasons for the decision to go nuclear. At present, at least a dozen nations—some estimate as many as twenty-four—have or can acquire the capability to manufacture nuclear weapons, though in some cases the effort to do so would clearly require great sacrifice. But as more states acquire a nuclear power technology and with it a supply of plutonium, the possibility of additional states acquiring the capacity to produce nuclear bombs increases.

A nuclear arms capability need not consist of a complex system of warheads and a delivery system comparable to that of the superpowers; a few bombs and the planes to deliver them a comparatively short distance may be all that is necessary for the nation that faces the hard decision of whether to go nuclear. Nor need nuclear war consist of a major nuclear exchange between the superpowers culminating in millions of casualties and vast destruction, as is commonly assumed. Nuclear exchanges that are limited in yield, area affected, and extent of damage are conceivable under a variety of circumstances. In the case of the superpowers such exchanges are less likely (except for accident or miscalculation) because of the danger of escalation, but in the case of the smaller powers with only a few low-yield bombs, they are not only possible but probable.

Since the technological capability and the knowledge to produce a bomb are so widespread, why then, one may ask, do not more states do so? The answer to this question is to be found more in the political than the technological realm and is concerned with intentions rather than capabilities—a more complex and difficult problem. In this realm the most important consideration is security, which in turn is dependent on a number of other factors: alliance relationships, treaty obligations, geography, domestic politics, and the anticipated long-range consequences of any action taken. When all of these considerations—and others—are weighed, the advantages of a nuclear capability, which appear so numerous from a distance, may not be at all clear. In fact, it is not difficult to envisage any number of situations in which the acquisition of nuclear weapons by a middle-range or small power may be clearly disadvantageous and result in weakening its political position.

But security may not be the issue at all; a decision for nuclear weapons may be made for reasons of domestic politics, or to achieve less tangible but equally important goals such as the fulfillment of national pride, or to reach and maintain a higher status. India's decision to explode a nuclear device was made for reasons of prestige as much as anything else; certainly there were no political or military considerations so important and far-reaching as to warrant a decision certain to draw the criticism of world opinion and the opposition of the United States and the Soviet Union. Though her political and military position has undoubtedly been altered as a consequence, it is difficult to see how, except for status in the third world and prestige, India has profited from the test. It has not eased the food problem—famine still threatens—diminished the birth rate, increased production, or materially improved her military posture. And it may have added enormously to her problems.

It may be useful to consider the possibilities of proliferation in terms of the patterns that may be expected to take shape rather than in terms of individual choices. The first and least likely pattern is one in which a large number of states that have or can acquire the capability for building a nuclear bomb decide to do so. Some nations may even find available another option: purchasing nuclear weapons or a nuclear technology complete and ready-made.

This last option is available only to the few nations that have very large funds and can find a nuclear supplier, preferably one with an unfavorable balance of trade or anxious to enter the trade in nuclear technology. In a sense, this is what Iran is doing; other OPEC states, hard pressed to find an outlet for the vast funds they are now accumulating, might conceivably elect to follow Iran's example, though it is difficult to imagine to what use they could put nuclear power plants or bombs if they had them. Still, one ought not to rule out this possibility altogether. The expenditure of several billion dollars or more is not beyond their means, and it should not be forgotten that Iran and Saudi Arabia are, with Israel, the largest purchasers of military equipment from the United States.

In 1973 oil revenues to the Middle East states amounted to some $22 billion; the estimate for 1974 is more than $100 billion. With these funds, the OPEC states may acquire a role in nuclear politics in another way, by buying a large share of the nuclear power industry, which may seem to them an attractive field for investing part of their huge balances. The incentive for such a sale may appear attractive to industrialized nations with a nuclear technology if it opens up the possibility of special access to unlimited quantities of oil. In this way the oil rich states may, in a sense, become nuclear powers without actually acquiring a nuclear capability.

The possibility is remote that a large number of states, or even the half dozen or so that have the requisite industrial base, will follow the lead of India in acquiring a nuclear weapons capability in the immediate future. The state most directly concerned, Pakistan, is still a long way from such a capability, though the incentive to develop one is certainly strong. And the decision of these nations that may have the capability—Israel, West Germany, Sweden, Japan—is not likely to be affected by India's actions. Nor is there any evidence to date that it has. There are other circumstances, however, that might induce them to do so. In Western Europe the decision of West Germany, Sweden, or Switzerland to go nuclear appears largely to hinge on estimates of Soviet action and on the guarantee of United States nuclear protection, not on India, though these states might well decide to export their nuclear technology rather than manufacture bombs. The case of East Europe—East Germany, Poland, Czechoslovakia, and others—is somewhat comparable, with the additional factor that Soviet approval would probably be required.

In the Western Hemisphere, Canada, which has large deposits of uranium ore and a well-developed nuclear technology, has thus far refused to develop a nuclear weapons program. In the past, Canada has been one of the staunchest opponents of proliferation. It is difficult to imagine the circumstances that would alter this view, except perhaps some difference with the United States so serious as to threaten a basic national interest. But to the south of the United States, in Latin America, the situation is different. Argentina and Brazil, for reasons of prestige and the former with the assistance of India, appear to be not only interested in but actively seeking to develop nuclear technology, with the possibility of ultimately testing an explosive device.

Far across the Pacific, Australia appears to be far removed from conflict. But their sparsely settled subcontinent, the Australians feel, presents an attractive target, and for this reason the Australian government has indicated an interest in nuclear weapons. Like the South Africans, the Australians feel threatened by neighbors of a different race and should the situation warrant, might well opt for a nuclear capability. Or they might seek an arrangement with the United States or Britain for nuclear defense, and since both have an interest in Australia's security they might furnish the necessary guarantees. Neither could supply nuclear weapons even if they wanted to, since such action is prohibited under the terms of the Non-Proliferation Treaty.

South Africa is in a different situation than Australia and cannot count on American support: domestic opposition would be too strong, even if the State Department favored it. Though the threat in Africa is probably greater, there is little possibility that a major nuclear power would provide support. But South Africa has a plentiful supply of uranium ore and might elect to develop its own bomb. Its use, however, is doubtful except under the most extreme conditions, for to do so would probably bring intervention by the nuclear powers.

In light of the events of May and June of 1974 as well as recent developments in Latin America and Africa, it would not be entirely unreasonable to predict that one or more of the nations in either region may decide to join the nuclear club. Already India has agreed to cooperate with Argentina in a program to develop nuclear technology. Such a program would inevitably provide the Latin American country with an independent source of plutonium with which to build a "peaceful" nuclear device, as did India. India would hardly be in a position to protest. Furthermore, Argentina's move may provide the incentive for other Latin American nations, Brazil for one, to seek assistance in developing their own nuclear technology.

Japan is a special case. One of the most industrialized nations in the world, with a nuclear power plant of her own, Japan has the capability of manufacturing nuclear weapons should she choose to do so. But as the only nation ever to experience nuclear bombing, she has strong, built-in inhibitions against the development or use of such weapons. The conventional view is that for this reason alone the Japanese would not at any time in the near future elect this option. But Japan was slow in signing the NPT and has not yet ratified. Moreover, a new generation has grown up since Hiroshima, and the situation in Asia has changed markedly. Hostility toward the United States (with whom relations recently have deteriorated), or fear of China, her traditional enemy, might provide the incentive for developing a nuclear arms capability. Or Japan might adopt an alternative course: to assist India by providing technological assistance for an Indian rocket program as a counter to a hostile China. In any case, a decision would seem to be some distance off, a nuclear arms capability even further.

In summary, there is little likelihood in the short run of general proliferation by those nations that have the capability, and little evidence that India's test has set off a new round of proliferation. Pakistan does not have the capability, Japan the inclination, West Germany or Sweden the incentive, and Israel's decision will be made on the basis of her own security needs. In the long run, i.e. by the end of the century, however, a large number of states will have acquired the capability of manufacturing nuclear explosives very quickly should the situation demand it, and unless something is done, a half-dozen nations will have built the bomb.

That the nuclear club will continue indefinitely with only six members is most unlikely. The most probable pattern is of selective or limited proliferation. The reaction thus far to India's test explosion confirms such a pattern, though it may still be too soon to tell. The technology and fissionable material for building the bomb are spreading rapidly, aided by an industry that has a large financial stake in the expansion of nuclear power. Only political and strategic considerations impose restraints on the states that have the capability at present, and those who do not now possess it look forward to the day when they will. Whatever the consideration, possession of a nuclear technology increases a nation's options, and that in itself is a powerful incentive for acquiring a nuclear power plant.

Proliferation is a dynamic process in which the behavior of one nation affects the behavior of all others, or at least influences their decision. For example, India's decision clearly increases the likelihood of a Pakistan program, even at great national sacrifice; Japan's response to India's nuclear device, however, is more ambiguous. Her decision depends on a number of other considerations, including her perception of the threat and the extent of India's program. The last is a particularly important factor in estimating the possibilities of proliferation, for India may choose, or be persuaded, not to build nuclear weapons but to rest content with the prestige she has already won.

None of the responses in Asia are likely to bring nuclear intervention of the superpowers into the region. But if Israel were to acquire a nuclear capability, the Soviet Union would probably aid the Arabs to acquire their own. If both Israel and the Arabs acquire nuclear weapons, there would seem to be little advantage and great danger to both. Perhaps under the circumstances the Israeli stance of leaving the matter speculative is the best course.

The action of India, and perhaps possible action in the next few years by Canada or a non-Western state such as South Africa or Australia, probably will not by itself trigger a response by one of the European states or by Japan, but it does increase the odds in favor of such action, other things being equal. In part, the response depends on the nature of the capability (i.e., whether it consists merely of a device or of an entire weapons system), and the size and location of the country. Why would Sweden or Switzerland feel impelled to go nuclear because Australia has tested a bomb, even though Japan might? And why should Japan respond to a South African test?

Technological

In the United States, the scientific community and other experts were fully aware before the Indian explosion of the problem of proliferation and the relationship between a nuclear power technology and the spread of nuclear weapons. That event, the subsequent offer by Nixon to Egypt and Israel, and the French sale to Iran aroused the concern of the general public and the interest of the press. The spate of articles and news stories which followed highlighted the problem and alerted the public to the dangers that lay ahead. The provisions of the NPT and other agreements, which the public had largely ignored or forgotten, and the implications of the spread of nuclear power plants were described in full and sometimes frightening detail.

"Nuclear Club Could Add 24 Nations in 10 Years" headlined the *New York Times* on July 5, 1974. The gist of this excellent survey, based largely on interviews with United States arms control officials, was that unless "technical and political barriers" were strengthened, the spread of nuclear power plants to more and more countries would in time provide fissionable material, the technology, and enough trained manpower to enable an estimated twenty-four nations to manufacture nuclear weapons within the decade. Already, the *Times* pointed out, such weapons were within the reach of half a dozen or more nations and others, it concluded, could be expected to join this company within a few years.

Plants for the production of nuclear energy have spread rapidly in recent years, sparked by the oil embargo and the subsequent rise in the cost of energy. A nuclear power technology is neither easy nor inexpensive to acquire, and the less developed nations can only

secure it by purchase (or other means) from the more highly industrialized states. Such a technology is characterized by high capital
costs, a sophisticated infrastructure of supporting technical and
industrial products and services, highly trained personnel, and a
reliable source of supply for nuclear fuels. It is not surprising, therefore, that nuclear power was developed first in the United States and
Europe. As of 1972 there were 28 operable nuclear power stations in
the United States and 38 in Western Europe, including 14 in the
United Kingdom; 8 in France; and 5 in West Germany. Thanks in
large part to the energy crisis and President Eisenhower's "atoms for
peace" program, nuclear technology is now spreading to other less
industrialized states through the good offices of the United States
(and France) and of such heavily financed transnational corporations
as Westinghouse and General Electric. A summary of nuclear facilities
in non-weapons states indicated that in 1973 17 nations had 69
power reactor sites, in addition to 50 low-power research reactors.
The number of reactor sites, it was estimated, would increase to 200
in 1980, by which time 8 more nations would have joined the group.
Only 4 of the countries were expected to have plutonium fabrication
plants, but all would presumably produce the toxic substance. By
1982, according to another estimate, the world's nuclear power
stations are expected to produce about 100,000 kilograms of plutonium a year—enough for thousands of explosive devices.*

These statistics emphasize the fact that the spread of nuclear
weapons is only part of the problem. After all, India declared it had
not built a bomb and certainly has not yet developed a significant
military nuclear capability. The growth and rapid expansion of a
nuclear power technology by a powerful group of international corporations supported by their governments represents perhaps as real
a danger as the increase in the number of nuclear states.

A civilian nuclear energy program is intimately related to the
development of a military nuclear capability, since plutonium, the
end product of the production of nuclear power, is also one of the
two fissionable materials needed for the construction of a nuclear
bomb. (U-235, the other fissionable material for a bomb, is much
more difficult to obtain.) Under present plans the United States

---

*No more than 8 kilograms of plutonium are required to manufacture a
nuclear warhead with a yield of about 20 kilotons.

would have by the year 2000 over 2,000 nuclear power plants capable of producing 60 percent of its electricity—and with it 660,000 pounds of plutonium a year. World-wide projections for that date called for a large-enough number of nuclear plants to produce over two million pounds of plutonium each year—assuming the development of the "breeder" reactor.

Not only is the supply of fissionable material increasing rapidly and becoming more readily available, but the technology for building a nuclear warhead is well understood and widely known. The Atomic Energy Commission, it is reported, conducted a study to determine whether two new Physics Ph.D.'s could design a bomb using only the literature available to the public. The two men built so well that the device exploded with a force within 10 percent of the predicted yield.

The opportunities thus opened for nuclear blackmail by terrorists with access to ever larger stockpiles of plutonium—a highly toxic substance with a life span of thousands of years—is enough to worry the most sanguine citizen. A one-kiloton nuclear explosive—it need not be a bomb—detonated during the lunch hour in the Wall Street area would kill several hundred thousand people. Similar horrors could be multiplied by the score: a small bomb to blow up the Hoover Dam releasing the largest body of water in the United States; a fiftieth of a kiloton in the Rose Bowl during a game; a tenth of a kiloton next to a nuclear reactor to eliminate the core-cooling system and release more long-lived radioactivity than a 100 megaton bomb; a bomb inside one of the World Trade Center towers in lower New York City or along the Massachusetts Turnpike below the Prudential Center in Boston could bring down either structure; another exploded near the Capitol during the State of the Union message would kill virtually every important official in the government, including the Cabinet, the nine justices of the Supreme Court, the head of every important agency, and everyone in the line of Presidential succession.

Because of the relationship between a civilian nuclear power technology and a nuclear weapons program, as well as for other reasons, it may be possible to solve the problem of proliferation by curtailing the spread of nuclear energy technology and discontinuing the manufacture of reactors. Though Secretary of State Kissinger hinted at this possibility in his September 23, 1974, address to the United Nations, and though there is considerable support for such a policy among consumer groups, it is not likely to be adopted. The crisis in energy is real and the nuclear power industry is well established and exercises considerable influence on all levels of government and banking. It has made enormous investments in nuclear technology and power plants and would oppose any regulations that restrict its operations or diminish its profits. Any major change in the industry that would affect its investments seriously and adversely could be expected to call forth from the powerful industry all its instruments of influence and public relations in opposition. Until another source of energy is developed, the demand for nuclear power plants is certain to grow.

The problem of regulation and control is complicated by the international nature of the nuclear power industry and the multinational character of the corporations that control it. The Westinghouse-Creusot-Loire connection already mentioned illustrates this aspect of the spread of nuclear technology. The multinationals have an important stake in the nuclear industry and play a vital role in its expansion at home and overseas. Westinghouse is only one of several corporations that have entered into arrangements with European and other corporations to develop the nuclear industry. This development poses difficult problems of national and foreign policy involving the transfer of nuclear technology and fissionable materials, the influence of powerful economic interests in the regulation of nuclear power, and the safeguards established for the safety of the nuclear plants and the control of their fissionable by-product.

Another approach to the problem of proliferation is to adopt safeguards to ensure that the plutonium produced by reactors is fully accounted for and not used for other than peaceful (nonexplosive) purposes. How effective actually are the safeguards established to control the plutonium? There is no simple answer to this question. In addition to the controls exercised by the United States through the Atomic Energy Commission over its own plants and some overseas, there are two international organizations that monitor the use of nuclear fuels: the Vienna-based International Atomic Energy Administration (IAEA), established in 1957 largely as a result of President Eisenhower's Atoms for Peace proposal; and Euratom, which performs a similar function for its Western European members in addition to its program for fostering the development and use of nuclear power in the region.

None of these organizations, however rigid its inspection, is in a position to assure the safety of the nuclear plant or prevent all possible diversion of nuclear materials. As a matter of fact, as a recent study claimed, the regulations of the AEC not only raised questions about the safety of nuclear reactors but were also considered "entirely inadequate" to protect fissionable materials in private hands from theft by a determined group of terrorists, saboteurs, or ordinary criminals. Moreover, the accounting system utilized by the AEC and the IAEA to control possible diversion of plutonium, accurate and detailed as it may be, is no more perfect than a bank audit—in fact, less so. (And there are no guards to prevent theft, as in a bank.) Already, it is estimated, thousands of pounds of plutonium and enriched uranium are unaccounted for, presumably lost in the industrial process. According to some physicists, about 2 percent of the plutonium produced in reactors would inevitably be uncontrollable and unaccounted for no matter what safeguards were adopted. In short, there is no foolproof system.

Since it is a fundamental objective of United States foreign policy to prevent proliferation and to discourage non-nuclear states from making nuclear weapons, it is surprising that it does not require that a non-nuclear state receiving nuclear assistance from the United States sign the Non-Proliferation Treaty, which, among its other provisions, establishes safeguards against the diversion of fissionable materials. As the leading manufacturer and exporter of nuclear reactors and fuels, the United States presumably is in a position to lay down such conditions. The reasons why it does not do so should be reexamined in the light of the danger of proliferation.

There are other difficulties about safeguards. Some nations have raised objections about the cost of international inspection, especially a system designed to achieve more than a 90 percent effectiveness. Others have expressed fears about the danger of commercial espionage by inspectors and possible interference with the normal operation of nuclear power plants generating electricity for a large urban and industrial area during inspection. And even if some diversion of fissionable material is detected, there is no provision in the NPT for corrective and punitive action by the IAEA or any of the signers of the treaty. Of course, one of the nuclear powers could cut off the supply of fuels or foreign aid, but there might be important reasons for not doing so.

One would suppose that the development, storage, and transport of so important and dangerous a substance as plutonium would be subject to the strictest security and watched over with the greatest care. In point of fact the opposite is true, as the nuclear scientist Theodore Taylor pointed out to a Senate Committee. Nuclear fuel fabricated in North Carolina may go to reactors in California and then to Morris, Illinois, to be reprocessed. During the journey back and forth across the country plutonium may be hauled along the public highways by truck within easy reach of determined hijackers and subject to accidents of all kinds. Or it may be flown in the cargo hold of commercial aircraft, whose passengers and crew remain totally unaware of its presence. Or the plutonium may be shipped by rail to various points throughout the country, wherever a reactor is located, without special marking or handling. No guards watch over its safety, no convoys accompany it, no local authorities are aware of its presence throughout this entire time. It is entirely possible to lose an entire shipment of plutonium; in fact, this has happened at least once. Under the circumstances, wrote Paul Leventhal, special counsel to a Senate subcommittee that reviewed the organization of the AEC, the spread of nuclear power technology "is a form of insanity that may overtake the world before its awesome dimensions are realized."

CONCLUSION

The questions raised by the events of the summer of 1974 (and confirmed by events since) may be stated succinctly as follows:

—What measures can be adopted to dissuade India from developing a nuclear weapons capability and a delivery system?

—How can the United States discourage other nations from following India's lead?

—Should the United States seek to limit or control the spread of nuclear power technology, and, inferentially, to regulate the American nuclear industry?

—What measures can be taken to increase the effectiveness of the safeguards established by the United States Atomic Energy Commission and the International Atomic Energy Administration to prevent diversion of plutonium or theft by terrorist groups or criminals?

—How can the United States continue and increase its efforts to secure wider acceptance of the Non-Proliferation Treaty, including the signatures of those nuclear states that have not signed, and adherence to its provisions?

—Is the present policy of the United States with respect to nuclear testing and arms control agreements consistent with the aims of the NPT, and will this policy militate against acceptance of the treaty?

Although most of these questions have been considered above, it may be useful here to respond directly and briefly. With respect to the first, it should be noted that it may actually be too late to affect India's decision, which may already have been made. In a cable to Secretary Kissinger in mid-September 1974, the then United States ambassador to India, Daniel Moynihan, predicted categorically and without qualification that India would "proceed to develop nuclear weapons and a missile delivery system, preaching non-violence all the way." Since the Indian Government and a number of officials had repeatedly asserted that the explosion had been for peaceful purposes only, this prediction did nothing to increase Mr. Moynihan's popularity in New Delhi.

But even if Moynihan was wrong or the decision is not firm, there is little that the United States can do now to affect India's policy on nuclear weapons. The Canadian government had protested vigorously this violation of the 1971 agreement, without visible effect. Cutting off the supply of uranium ore while continuing other forms of aid proved equally ineffective. At first the United States did nothing, and even shipped a supply of uranium fuel, with a request for an explanation of India's action. None came, and in September 1974 the United States halted further deliveries of the enriched uranium, declaring that it would not resume deliveries until the Indian government "clarifies its policy on nuclear tests." So far as the United States government is concerned, there is no distinction between a "peaceful" and a "military" nuclear explosion, and it sought assurance from New Delhi that none of the plutonium produced in reactors supplied or fueled by the United States would be used for tests. This the Indians refused to give.

In the long run, withholding the uranium fuel may have some effect on India's policy, but there is a real possibility that it may worsen the relations, already strained, between the two countries.

Other measures, such as cutting off food or other forms of aid, or supporting Pakistan more strongly, would probably only make matters worse. In short there would seem to be little that the United States can do under the circumstances, and it is doubtful whether the action already taken will achieve its purpose—or even whether, in the interests of maintaining friendly relations between the two countries, it was a wise move.

What measures can the United States adopt to discourage further diffusion of nuclear weapons (or explosive devices)? Proliferation, unavoidably, may take on the nature of a chain reaction. India's test made her the sixth member of the club and the first to enter that exclusive circle in a decade. It is doubtful that another decade will pass before another country sets off a nuclear explosion, "peaceful" or otherwise. The decision of the seventh will probably be easier than that of the sixth, and the eighth easier still. The largest gap in the chain reaction, if there is one, was between the fifth and the sixth. But there is nothing inevitable about the process, and it may not take place at all.

If a seventh country is to join the club in the feared diffusion process, the most likely candidates in terms of political incentives are either Israel or Pakistan. Unlike Pakistan, Israel's decision will depend not on India but on the tangled political situation in the Middle East. But if Pakistan had the technological capability, it would probably move immediately to construct a bomb and a delivery system. "If India builds a bomb we will eat leaves, grass, and even go hungry," said Pakistan's prime minister, "but we have to get one of our own. We have no alternative." But Pakistan does not have a nuclear power plant, plutonium, the industrial base, or the trained manpower to build a bomb, and it will take her a long time to acquire them. There are other possibilities, however: (1) to obtain assurances of nuclear protection from the superpowers or from China; (2) to persuade one of them to base nuclear warheads in Pakistan as a deterrent; or (3) to obtain the warheads from one of the nuclear powers. Under the terms of the NPT, however, the United States and Russia are prohibited from providing any non-nuclear power with nuclear weapons. But France and China did not sign the treaty, and the latter has a strong interest in supporting Pakistan.

Israel and Japan presumably are in a position to build and

deliver one or more nuclear bombs fairly soon, but there are many disincentives in both cases. Israel is at present the more likely candidate, especially if she falls so far behind the Arab nations in conventional capability that she feels her survival is at stake. In this respect military aid to Israel may be critical in preventing proliferation. As long as Israel can stand off the Arabs and can count on United States support, she gains no advantage from nuclear bombs, especially if Egypt also acquires nuclear weapons. Israel did not sign the NPT, and there is much speculation about her possession of a bomb. Israeli leaders neither deny nor confirm these speculations. Indeed, it is to Israel's interest to encourage such speculation.

Japan is a special case, and there are very strong inhibitions of an emotional rather than political nature to nuclear weapons. But the possibility of one or the other, Japan or Israel, acquiring nuclear capability by 1980 is not altogether out of the question. Certainly it is a possibility that must be viewed as a realistic contingency.

For reasons of prestige Iran and Argentina may follow India's lead, or each other's lead, by constructing a nuclear device. With this prestige, of course, would come certain political and strategic advantages—for the former in the Persian Gulf and the latter in Latin America. But with the prestige and political advantages would also come liabilities—and the displeasure of the Soviet Union in the first instance and the United States in the second. Finally, it should be noted that the incentives of any one of these states to build a bomb may well depend on what the others do. There is not much prestige to membership in a nonexclusive club and not much advantage to possession of a weapon that cannot be used without the possibility of incurring severe penalties.

Should the United States try to limit the spread of a nuclear power technology, and, inferentially, to regulate more closely its nonprivate nuclear industry? Closely related to this question is that of the controls and safeguards established by IAEA. Are these safeguards adequate, and if not, what measure can be taken to make them more effective? Can they entirely eliminate the possibility of diversion of fissionable materials?

The first question is probably an idle one. It would be extremely difficult to halt or even slow the spread of nuclear power plants all over the globe. It is even doubtful, in view of the increased cost and declining stocks of fossil fuels, that it should be. If that is the case, we can expect that increasing quantities of plutonium will be available in all industrialized states and in many others. Secretary Kissinger recognized this fact in his address to the United Nations General Assembly on September 23. Reminding his listeners that the United States and others had furnished nuclear technology to nations for peaceful use and that the amount of plutonium generated in this way was increased rapidly, he warned that "this policy cannot continue if it leads to the proliferation of nuclear explosives."

Control and safeguards, both internal and external, over plutonium and plutonium production is of the utmost importance. Present safeguards, no matter how rigorously enforced, cannot provide 100 percent effectiveness in detecting diversions of fissionable material, and even when they do detect a suspected diversion, there is no established mechanism for dealing with it other than, as the United States did with India, to halt further nuclear assistance. Clearly, safeguards are not enough. They can only set off a warning; what is required is an enforcement system backed by preventive action and sanctions.

But even within the present system there are ways in which the possibility of diversions could be discouraged if not halted entirely. One of them would be to require as a condition of sale that all reprocessing be done by the United States, and that the non-nuclear power agree not to construct reprocessing or chemical separation facilities. It might be practical even to consider that these facilities be placed under international control (IAEA) and that the plutonium itself either be returned to the nation that furnished assistance in the first place or placed under the same international control. This may not be a foolproof system or provide for enforcement, but it does afford greater security than we now have.

The Non-Proliferation Treaty is an essential instrument in furthering the United States effort to prevent proliferation and should be supported and extended by all possible means. Any weakening of the treaty increases the possibilities of proliferation and works against United States interests in preventing nuclear war. Conversely, to the extent that the treaty is strengthened by increased membership and strict adherence to its provisions, to that extent is the possibility of nuclear war diminished. And of critical importance in strengthening the bonds of the treaty is the injunction in Article 6 to pursue means for limiting nuclear arms, including the prohibitions on testing.

It is true that states tend to act in what they consider their own interests, or, negatively, to avoid or oppose action they consider to be against their interests. Though it may appear that a prohibition against building a nuclear weapon is against a nation's interests, it is possible to offer inducements for a nation to accept such a prohibition. The Non-Proliferation Treaty contains such inducements, and it should be an important goal of American foreign policy to link nuclear aid and, where possible, other forms of assistance to signing the Treaty and adhering to its provisions.

Ratification of the NPT does not in itself guarantee that a signatory nation will never go nuclear. It is not unreasonable to suppose that in the event of a coup or a change of government by other means, a nation might very well decide for political reasons or for reasons of prestige to develop a nuclear capability. Finally, neither France nor China, both nuclear powers, have signed the treaty and continue to refuse to do so. Presumably both are free, except that France is limited by membership in Euratom, to supply nuclear technology and fuels to other countries without inspections or safeguards.

Although a state may with proper notice withdraw or even violate the NPT if it believes itself threatened, it is more likely to feel inhibited if it is a signatory to the treaty than if it is not. Moreover, reasons for withdrawal must appear compelling or at least convincing, and outright violation may bring unpleasant consequences. In either case the onus is on the nation withdrawing from the treaty. The NPT offers no guarantee, but it does make a decision to go nuclear more difficult and slows up the rate of proliferation. After all, said Secretary Rusk in response to a question from Senator Pastore during the Hearings on the NPT, "A treaty which has 100 signatures puts the world in a vastly better position than the world would be in if there were no treaty at all. . . . It also means that 100 nations or more will have accepted an obligation not to develop their own weapons even without the assistance of existing nuclear powers. So that, again, the total situation is greatly enhanced even though the treaty does not achieve perfection in terms of total adherence."

Even under favorable conditions, the NPT can be expected to restrain the non-nuclear states for only a limited period of time—hopefully the twenty-five years covered by the treaty. By that time either new solutions must be found or the existing system in which a few nations are permitted nuclear weapons must somehow be made acceptable to those who do not have them. Almost certainly, if pro-liferation is to be contained, the nuclear arms race must be brought under control, and the ban on testing, now limited, should be made complete.

One of the obligations of the nuclear powers under the NPT is to pursue negotiations looking toward nuclear disarmament. The results of the Moscow summit conference, which failed to produce an agreement on offensive weapons or a complete ban on testing, was hardly calculated to further the cause of nonproliferation—already damaged by India's test explosion. Non-nuclear states, especially those with a developed industrial base and a nuclear technology, cannot be expected to refrain indefinitely from acquiring nuclear weapons if the nuclear nations continue to develop, build, and test more weapons of increasingly advanced design. After all, prolifera-tion can be of two kinds—horizontal and vertical. The former has to do with their spread to other countries, the latter with the number and types of arms in the nuclear arsenal. It is scarcely realistic to expect to stop one while the other continues. In a real sense, there-fore, perhaps the essential condition for halting the spread of nuclear weapons, or limiting it to a restricted few, depends in the final analysis on the willingness of the United States and the Soviet Union to put a complete ban on nuclear tests and to halt the upward spiral of the race in offensive nuclear weapons as a preliminary to an agree-ment on measures to reverse the process.

Only a week after the SALT negotiations were resumed at Geneva and four months after the Indian test explosion, Secretary Kissinger on September 23, 1974, told the United Nations General Assembly that "political inhibitions" against proliferation "are in danger of crumbling" and that the expansion of nuclear technology was threatening to put nuclear weapons into the hands of an in-creasing number of nations. "We realize," he said, "that we cannot expect others to show restraint if we do not ourselves practice restraint." The task, he told the Assembly, "is to realize the peaceful benefits of nuclear technology without contributing to the growth of nuclear weapons or to the number of states possessing them." This, indeed, was the challenge for the United States and for the entire community of nations.

SELECT BIBLIOGRAPHY

Beaton, Leonard. *Must the Bomb Spread?* Baltimore, Penguin Books, 1966.
—— and John Maddox. *The Spread of Nuclear Weapons.* London, Chatto and Windus, 1962.

Buchan, Alastair, ed. *A World of Nuclear Powers?* Englewood Cliffs, Prentice-Hall, 1966.

Gelber, Harry. *Nuclear Weapons and Chinese Policy*, Adelphi Paper No. 99. London, International Institute for Stratetic Studies, 1973.

Inglis, David R. *Nuclear Energy: Its Physics and Its Social Challenge.* Reading, Mass., Addison-Wesley, 1973.

International Atomic Energy Agency (IAEA). *Peaceful Uses of Atomic Energy.* New York and Geneva, United Nations (1953, 1958, 1965, 1972). See also the IAEA *Market Surveys* and other publications.

Kramish, Arnold. *The Watched and the Unwatched: Inspection in the Non-Proliferation Treaty*, Adelphi Paper No. 36. London, International Institute for Strategic Studies, 1967.

Leachman, Robert D., and Philip Althoff, eds. *Preventing Nuclear Theft: Guidelines for Industry and Government.* New York, Praeger, 1972.

Maddox, John. *Prospects for Nuclear Proliferation*, Adelphi Paper No. 113. London, International Institute for Strategic Studies, 1975.

Marks, Anne W., ed. *NPT: Paradoxes and Problems.* Washington, D.C., Arms Control Association, 1975.

McAfee, John. *The Curve of Binding Energy.* New York, Farrar, Straus and Geroux, 1973.

McKnight, Allan. *Atomic Safeguards: A Study in International Verification.* New York, United Nations, 1971.

Novick, Sheldon. *The Careless Atom.* Boston, Houghton Mifflin, 1968.

Newhouse, John. *Cold Dawn: The Story of SALT.* New York, Holt, Rinehart and Winston, 1973.

Quester, George. *The Politics of Nuclear Proliferation.* Baltimore, The Johns Hopkins University Press, 1973.

Rosencranz, R. N. *Problems of Nuclear Proliferation: Technology and Politics.* Security Studies Paper No. 7, University of California Press, Los Angeles, 1966.

Redick, John R. *Military Potential of Latin American Nuclear Energy Programs.* Beverly Hills, Sage Publications, 1971.

Som Dutt, Maj. Gen. D. *India and the Bomb*, Adelphi Paper No. 30. International Institute for Strategic Studies, 1966.

Speth, J. Gustave, Arthur R. Tamplin, and Thomas B. Cochran. *The Plutonium Decision: A Report on the Risks of Plutonium Recycle.* Washington, D.C., Natural Resources Defense Council, 1974.

Stockholm International Peace Research Institute. *The Near Nuclear Countries and the NPT.* Stockholm, 1972.

—— *Nuclear Proliferation Problems.* Stockholm, 1974.

United States Arms Control and Disarmament Agency. *Documents on Disarmament.* Annual Publications, 1967 to date. Washington, D.C., Government Printing Office, 1968 et seq.

United States House of Representatives. *Commercial Nuclear Power in Europe: The Interaction of American Diplomacy with a New Technology.* Subcommittee on National Security Policy and Scientific Development of the Committee on Foreign Affairs. Washington, D.C., Government Printing Office, 1972.

United States Senate, *Hearings on the Non-Proliferation Treaty.* 90th Cong. 2nd Sess., Committee on Foreign Relations; Part I, July 1968; Part II, February 1969. Washington, D.C., Government Printing Office, 1968–69.

Williams, Shelton L. *The U.S., India and the Bomb.* Baltimore, The Johns Hopkins University Press, 1969.

Willrich, Mason, ed. *Civil Nuclear Power and International Security.* New York, Praeger Publishers, 1971.

—— *Global Politics of Nuclear Energy.* New York, Praeger Publishers, 1971.

—— *International Safeguards and Nuclear Industry.* Baltimore, The Johns Hopkins University Press, 1973.

—— *Non-Proliferation Treaty: Framework for Nuclear Arms Control.* Charlottesville, The Michie Company, 1969.

—— and Bennett Boskey, eds. *Nuclear Proliferation: Prospects for Control.* New York, The Dunellen Company, Inc., 1970.

—— and Theodore Taylor. *Nuclear Theft: Risks and Safeguards.* Cambridge, Mass., Ballinger Publishing Company, 1974.

Yager, Joseph A., and Eleanor B. Steinberg. *Energy and U.S. Foreign Policy.* Cambridge, Mass., Ballinger, 1974.

Young, Elizabeth. *The Control of Proliferation: The 1958 Treaty in Hindsight and Forecast,* Adelphi Paper No. 56. London, International Institute for Strategic Studies, 1967.

Zuckerman, Sir Solly, Alva Myrdal, and Lester B. Pearson. *The Control of Proliferation: Three Views,* Adelphi Paper No. 29. London, International Institute for Strategic Studies, 1966.

In addition, the reader will find excellent discussions of the subject in the New York *Times,* the Washington *Post,* and other newspapers, as well as in such journals as *Foreign Affairs, Foreign Policy, Orbis,* and *Scientific American.*

EDITOR'S NOTE

In the past, discussions of the international economy have often focused on the theme of a "return to normalcy," implying that the current economic order is in some way an aberration from the norm. Professor Mazur looks foward, however, rather than backward. He suggests that policy planning should focus on learning to live with floating exchange rates rather than on ways to resurrect the Bretton Woods system.

Three factors that have increased international economic interdependence since World War II are identified—increased mobility of short-term capital, the expansion of multinational corporations, and the increased relative importance of foreign trade for most countries. These factors increased international interdependence to the point that nations turned to floating exchange rates in order to regain some of their rapidly diminishing national autonomy.

A nation may mitigate the effects of increased interdependence, but it cannot escape them. Mazur notes that "the existence of international capital mobility under a system of floating-exchange rates increases the potential for conflict between countries over ostensibly domestic macroeconomic policy actions because such actions may stabilize one country at the expense of another."

The major policy implication arising from Mazur's analysis is the need for the United States to develop a policy toward the foreign capital controls which are likely to develop during the next few years.

III.
Interdependence, Flexible Exchange Rates, and Capital Controls: The International Monetary Order in Transition

Michael P. Mazur

Since the devaluation of the pound in November 1967, the international monetary system has been moving in the direction of greater flexibility of exchange rates. The greatest failing of the Bretton Woods monetary system of fixed, but occasionally adjusted, exchange rates was excessive exchange-rate rigidity. The rigid fixity of exchange rates was inconsistent with the desire of national governments for autonomy in macroeconomic policy. Since this desire for a considerable degree of national macroeconomic autonomy can be expected to continue well into the future, it seems certain that whatever form international monetary relations take in the future, exchange-rate flexibility will be greater than it was before 1967. Since early 1963, flexibility has been achieved by "managed" or "dirty" floating between the major currencies of the world. This system (or, more properly, absence of a system) now enjoys the force of inertia, particularly since it entails minimum formal international agreement, lacking even the commitment not to intervene required by truly floating rates. Therefore, in examining the future of international monetary relations, we should begin not by designing an ideal international monetary system, but by identifying the problems that may appear if the present system of managed floating is continued. If there are no such problems serious enough to warrant an international effort to adopt new arrangements, it does not much matter whether we can design a marginally better arrangement than the present one, for inertia is then likely to maintain the existence of the present international monetary order.

INTERDEPENDENCE AND THE BRETTON WOODS SYSTEM

The concept of economic interdependence, recently demonstrated most vividly by the impact of the oil embargo and price increase, has almost come to be a cliché.[1] Like the old joke about the man who disliked Shakespeare's plays because they contained so many clichés, people may underestimate the significance of economic interdependence because of the familiarity of the concept. Yet the recent history of the international financial system may be viewed as the interplay of structural changes, increasing economic interdependence, with institutional changes intended to cope with interdependence or to counteract it.

Increased economic interdependence has come in a variety of forms, but the one most significant for the international monetary system has been the vast increase in the mobility of short-term capital between the developed countries, a phenomenon associated especially with the rise of the Eurodollar market but not limited to it.[2] Among the factors contributing to greater international mobility of liquid capital are the increased convertibility of most major currencies since 1958 and the spread of the multinational corporation. The multinational corporation not only contributes to international short-term capital mobility by its ability and willingness to participate in different national money markets, but is in itself another of the most significant manifestations of increased economic interdependence, requiring accommodation in such areas of national economic policy as export and technology controls, corporate taxation, and antitrust policy.

A third way in which economic interdependence has increased since World War II is the rise in the magnitude of foreign trade in relation to aggregate economic activity, at least among the industrialized countries.[3] Primarily, this is due to reductions in transportation

---

1. See especially Richard N. Cooper, *The Economics of Interdependence: Economic Policy in the Atlantic Community* (New York, McGraw Hill, 1968).

2. For a concise analysis of the Eurodollar market and its implications for the Bretton Woods system see Geoffrey Bell, *The Euro-Dollar Market and the International Financial System* (New York, John Wiley & Sons, 1973).

3. Marina v. N. Whitman, "The Current and Future Role of the Dollar: How Much Symmetry?" *Brookings Papers on Economic Activity*, no. 3 (1974), p. 553. Although there seems to have been an increase in the relative importance

costs and to the reduction of tariffs and other barriers to trade among the industrialized countries. The postwar rise in the relative size of international trade has increased international economic interdependence directly,[4] but it has also contributed indirectly to an increase in the volume of internationally mobile short-term capital, since an increase in foreign trade impels an increase in trade financing.[5]

The aforementioned factors increasing economic interdependence may be termed "structural," in that the increase in interdependence is largely the result of changes in the economic environment or structure, and only to a much smaller degree and indirectly, the result of conscious policy decisions by governments. In contrast, "institutional" factors involve government actions directly intended to alter the degree of interdependence.[6] Although the distinction cannot be a precise one, it is useful to differentiate changes in interdependence to which governmental policy-makers may react from changes in interdependence consciously engineered by policy-makers (perhaps in response to changes in structural interdependence).

The adoption of a fixed-exchange-rate system at Bretton Woods in 1944 may be viewed as an increase in institutional interdependence. Fixed exchange rates increase interdependence in the short run

---

of foreign trade in the developed countries during the postwar period, the relative importance of foreign trade declined during the years between the two world wars. See Simon Kuznets, *Modern Economic Growth: Rate Structure and Spread* (New Haven, Yale University Press, 1966), pp. 310-321.

4. Cooper, *The Economics of Interdependence*, chap. 3. Cooper does not stress the increased relative size of foreign trade so much as the increased sensitivity of international trade movements to relatively small variations in incomes, costs, and prices.

5. Particularly when a change in an official parity is anticipated, changes in the timing of foreign trade credits may lead to large movements of capital in a short period through the phenomenon of changes in "leads and lags." For example, if devaluation of the pound were anticipated, payments for British imports would tend to be speeded up, while credit terms on Britain's exports would tend to be lengthened, the net effect being increased capital outflow from Britain.

6. The expressions "structural interdependence" and "institutional interdependence" are taken from Richard N. Cooper, "Economic Interdependence and Foreign Policy in the Seventies," *World Politics*, 24 (1972), 163. The definitions of these terms used here are, however, not the same as Cooper's.

because they transmit the business cycle from one country to another. Fixed rates increase interdependence in the long run because they require countries to maintain similar long-run rates of inflation. The fundamental reason for the breakdown of the Bretton Woods system in 1973 was that a high degree of exchange-rate rigidity was inconsistent with longer-term changes in the international competitiveness of countries and with national differences on macroeconomic policy directed toward inflation and unemployment. The degree of macroeconomic interdependence imposed by the Bretton Woods system was incompatible with national desires for independence in macroeconomic policy.

The great postwar increase in international mobility of liquid capital played an important role in the demise of the Bretton Woods system. Although not itself the fundamental source of the breakdown, increased short-term capital mobility conditioned the environment so that the inconsistency between fixed rates and differing national macroeconomic policy had greater and more sudden consequences. In a sense, increased mobility of liquid capital gave the international monetary system a hair trigger, greatly shortening the period during which national monetary policies could diverge. The steady increase in international capital mobility magnified the stresses on the Bretton Woods system in several interrelated ways: by decreasing the effectiveness of monetary policy, increasing the tendency of fixed rates to spread inflation, and increasing the magnitude of currency speculation. To take an important example and oversimplify it, contractionary monetary policy in Germany to combat inflation "imported" from the United States leads to increased capital inflows into Germany as foreign funds are attracted by the rise in interest rates induced by Germany's tight monetary policy. The resulting surplus in Germany's balance of payments tends to expand the German money supply, except insofar as it can be sterilized by offsetting contractionary monetary policy by Germany. When the balance-of-payments surplus becomes very large, the German authorities may experience difficulties in fully sterilizing it, particularly as the central bank runs out of domestic assets to sell and encounters limits to increasing bank reserve requirements. The result is increased inflation in Germany. The more successful the German monetary authorities are in sterilizing the balance-of-payments surplus and combatting imported inflation, the greater is the capital inflow, for two reasons: First, successful sterilization makes the interest rate higher than it otherwise would be, attracting more interest-sensitive funds. Second, because of the preceding factor, successful sterilization induces a larger balance-of-payments surplus and induces an inflow of speculative capital, seeking not so much higher interest rates as the chance of capital gain on the increasingly likely revaluation of the mark.

When the Bretton Woods system was designed, national capital markets were highly fragmented. The degree to which national money markets had become integrated by the late 1960's was unanticipated. The increase in the magnitude of potential short-term capital movements was so great that it threatened to overwhelm the ability of central banks to finance them, despite the arrangements to finance imbalances set up at Bretton Woods and reinforced by a variety of subsequent measures such as the General Arrangements to Borrow. It was as if there were a race between the capacity for international movements of liquid capital and the ability of central banks to finance such movements, a race the central banks appeared to be losing. Given national reluctance to alter exchange rates, the greater threat of losing such a race would place greater constraints upon national monetary autonomy—unless some means could be found to reduce the degree of international monetary interdependence.

The cumulative result of institutional interdependence imposed by the Bretton Woods system and structural interdependence arising from the increase in capital mobility was a degree of international monetary interdependence that was incompatible with the level of monetary autonomy sought by the governments of the major industrialized countries. This desire for a degree of national monetary autonomy is not simply the result of petty chauvinism. Major nations find it difficult to have a unified monetary policy because other aspects of their economies, particularly labor and capital markets and fiscal policies, are not sufficiently unified.

The most widespread reaction to this fundamental incompatibility of the Betton Woods system involved attempts to reduce monetary interdependence by erecting obstacles to the international movement of capital. Many countries adopted measures to control or restrict international short-term capital flows, including discouraging nonresident bank deposits by a high reserve requirement, low (even zero or negative) interest, or an outright ban on net new nonresident bank deposits; quantitative restrictions on borrowing or lending abroad by residents; special taxes on residents' interest receipts on foreign bonds; requiring interest-free deposits against foreign borrowing; and dual exchange rates for current-account and capital-account transactions.

Thus confronted by an excessive degree of international monetary interdependence, nations adopted institutional measures to reduce it. Speculative flows were more successfully deterred by some countries (e.g., Japan) than others (e.g., Germany). But in all cases their success was at best partial. The fixed-exchange-rate system established at Bretton Woods came to an end despite the rapid proliferation of capital controls in its final years.[7]

INTERDEPENDENCE AND MANAGED FLOATING RATES

Beginning in 1970, when the Canadian dollar was floated, the major currencies of the world have moved to a regime of managed floating exchange rates. The movement to flexible rates represents a step in the direction of reduced international economic interdependence. Because of greater risk from exchange-rate fluctuations, floating rates may reduce the volume of international trade, but this effect is likely to be small, because in the short run it is possible to hedge against exchange-rate risk and in the long run there is exchange-rate risk under either floating rates or the adjustable fixed rates of the Bretton Woods system. There probably has been some discouragement to trade because the adoption of floating rates significantly increased bid-ask spreads in both the spot and forward exchange markets, but the absolute size of the spreads remained small enough that the deterrent effect on international trade cannot have been very great.[8]

The primary way that floating exchange rates reduce inter-

---

7. See the survey "The Year of the Barriers," *Economist* (January 27, 1973).

8. Robert Z. Aliber, "Monetary Interdependence Under Floating Exchange Rates," paper delivered at the national convention of the Allied Social Sciences Association, San Francisco, December 1974.

national interdependence is by allowing national autonomy in monetary-fiscal policy. Under fixed exchange rates a country might find itself forced to conform to the inflationary or deflationary policies of its trading partners. Under floating exchange rates, inflation abroad, for example, would cause appreciation of a country's currency, which would allow domestic prices to remain stable while prices were rising in terms of foreign currencies. Thus, whereas fixed exchange rates tend to transmit recession and inflation from one country to another, floating rates help to insulate one country from the business cycles of its trading partners.

The assertion that a world of floating exchange rates, which had come into existence by early 1973, insulates a country from the inflationary or deflationary tendencies of its neighbors seems to fly in the face of the worldwide acceleration of inflation during 1973 and 1974. But to a large degree the simultaneous acceleration of inflation in the United States, Britain, Japan, and elsewhere is not because these countries spread inflation to each other, but because they were all reacting to the same inflationary impulses: decreased food supplies, a cartel-induced rise in world oil prices, and a classic boom in most other primary commodities. Even if floating rates insulate a country against inflationary and deflationary impulses originating abroad, no one has ever argued that floating rates can insulate an economy from *real* changes abroad affecting *relative* prices (as opposed to monetary changes affecting the general price level). Thus no conceivable adjustment of exchange rates could insulate oil-consuming countries from the adverse turn in their terms of trade engineered by the actions of the oil cartel. Inflation accelerated simultaneously in many countries because they were all reacting to the same *real* changes, which were politically difficult to absorb in a noninflationary way, given the downward inflexibility of money wages in industrialized economies. Some evidence for this interpretation of the worldwide acceleration of inflation lies in the very great differences among countries in their inflation rates, differences that depend partly on the degree of vulnerability to oil and food price increases, but mainly on national monetary policies.

Parenthetically, one stimulus to the 1973–74 acceleration of inflation may be partially attributable to the Bretton Woods system and the increased level of international capital mobility. The great rise in price of such primary commodities as copper, tin, rubber, and cotton was a classic commodities boom produced by the fact that—for the first time in years—all the major industrialized countries were in the expansionary phase of the business cycle at the same time. The resulting increase in their demand for primary commodities, combined with the fact that primary commodities tend to have highly price-inelastic short-run demand and supply, produced a big run-up in world commodity prices. Why had the industrialized countries come to have their business cycles synchronized? One plausible explanation is that by 1969 international capital mobility had become so great that in their effort to maintain fixed exchange rates countries found it impossible to maintain divergent macroeconomic policies.[9]

While the current international monetary order undoubtedly insulates countries from the business cycles of other countries to a much greater degree than did the Bretton Woods system, it nonetheless falls well short of complete insulation. That the business cycle abroad may affect income and employment of a country on a floating rate if it changes the terms of trade has long been recognized as a theoretical possibility,[10] although its practical significance probably is not great. More importantly, the present system is not one of truly floating rates, but of managed floating. Under a managed float central banks intervene in foreign exchange markets not to keep the exchange rate within certain set limits, but in a less systematic fashion, generally trying to resist trends that appear to be temporary. To the degree that they intervene to resist upward or downward trends in the exchange rate, there will be a tendency for the business cycle to be transmitted from abroad.

The third and perhaps most significant reason why floating exchange rates do not insulate countries from expansion or contraction abroad is the existence of international capital mobility. The movement from fixed to floating rates has important effects on capital mobility, but the tendency for capital to move internationally persists. The incentive to speculative international movements of

---

9. David Laidler, "The 1974 Report of the President's Council of Economic Advisers: The Control of Inflation and the Future of the International Monetary System," *American Economic Review*, 64 (1974), 541.

10. The classic article is Svend Laursen and Lloyd A. Metzler, "Flexible Exchange Rates and the Theory of Employment," *Review of Economics and Statistics*, 32 (1950), 281–299.

capital has been vastly reduced by the removal of the "one-way bet" provided by fixed exchange rates.[11] Sudden large movements of capital internationally are much less likely now. If they occur, they are likely to be for reasons other than speculation on exchange-rate changes (for example, in the form of flights of hot money because of political uncertainty or increased taxes—motives that accounted for at least part of the outflow from France after May 1968).

In its effect through the forward market, a system of floating exchange rates has a tendency to moderate international flows of capital motivated by changes in interest rates. Suppose, for example, that British interest rates rise, inducing a flow of covered-interest-arbitrage funds into Britain. The demand for forward cover of these funds will cause the forward price of the pound to fall, reducing the covered-interest-arbitrage incentive for further capital flows into Britain. Under fixed exchange rates, this self-limiting effect would be less because the expectation that in the future the spot exchange rate would be held within the officially declared range would reduce the movement of the foward rate.[12] Another consideration works in the opposite direction, however. Under the fixed-parity system, the attraction of changes in international interest-rate differentials for international capital movements was always tempered by the danger of a sudden large parity change if the investment was not hedged—and even if hedged, by the threat of the sudden imposition of exchange controls in an effort to defend the existing parity. Neither of these is a very serious danger under the existing regime of floating rates. This consideration would tend to increase the sensitivity of capital flows to changes in interest-rate differentials between countries. Whatever the net effect of these offsetting factors, it seems

---

11. A "one-way bet" arises under the fixed-exchange-rate system when a change in parities seems imminent. Since countries tend to postpone a parity change until the need for it is obvious and overwhelming, a currency that threatens to be devalued is in no danger of rising significantly in value in the near future, and a currency on the verge of revaluation is similarly unlikely to decline in value. Thus speculation can occur with a sizable gain to be expected if correct and very little loss if incorrect.

12. Of course, in times when it is widely believed that the official parity will not be maintained, the forward exchange rate may diverge substantially from the par value and be as variable as under a floating rate. At such times the speculative motive tends to swamp the interest-arbitrage motive for the international movement of funds.

clear that the international mobility of short-term capital in response to changes in interest-rate differentials will continue to be significant.

The ability of flexible exchange rates to insulate a country from economic fluctuations abroad is reduced by the existence of capital mobility. Indeed, when capital mobility exists, it is even possible that a change from fixed to floating rates may increase the degree to which the business cycle is spread from one country to another. There is some evidence that this may have occurred during the Canadian floating-exchange-rate period of 1950-61.[13] A recession, for example, would tend to be spread from the United States to Canada in the following way. As United States interest rates decline durings its recession, if the Canadian interest rate is maintained, funds flow from the United States to Canada. By itself, this flow tends to cause the Canadian dollar to appreciate. Of course, the United States recession reduces Canadian exports to the United States, which by itself tends to cause the Canadian dollar to depreciate. Whether the floating rate spreads the recession more or less than a fixed rate depends on the size of these two opposing effects. If the capital inflow increases the demand for the Canadian dollar more than the reduction in Canadian exports reduces the demand for the Canadian dollar, the net results will be an appreciation of the Canadian dollar, which will increase the recession in Canada over what it would have been under fixed rates. This seems to have been the case for Canada during 1950-61.

The preceding scenario is by no means a necessary consequence of adopting floating rates. The propagation of the business cycle occurred only because of the failure of Canadian monetary authorities to take the appropriate steps to offset it. When United States interest rates declined, the Bank of Canada should have reduced Canadian interest rates to stem the inflow of capital.[14] Thus flexible

13. Robert A. Mundell, "Problems of Monetary and Exchange Rate Management in Canada," *National Banking Review*, 2 (1964), 77-86.

14. If monetary policy alone were used to combat the international propagation of the cycle, Canadian interest rates should fall by less than United States interest rates fall. Then the contractionary effect of the capital inflow through its effect on the exchange rate would be offset by the expansionary effect of the lower interest rates on domestic spending. In this case Canada would have to accept a deterioration in its current-account balance. Alternatively, if Canada wished to keep the balance on current account unchanged, it would lower its

exchange rates allow a country to insulate its level of unemployment and inflation from fluctuations abroad, but when a high degree of international capital mobility exists, it is an insulation of a very limited sort. When no capital mobility exists, insulation is achieved automatically, but in the presence of capital mobility, insulation can be achieved only if macroeconomic policy is actively changed in reaction to developments abroad. And because of the imperfect nature of economic forecasting and the time lags inherent in the use of all macroeconomic policy tools, the insulation can never be perfect. Furthermore, while it is possible to insulate the overall level of economic activity from fluctuations abroad, those fluctuations cannot be prevented from affecting some important aspects of the economy, in particular (see note 14), the level of the current account balance and the monetary-fiscal mix.

THE CURRENT BALANCE AS AN OBJECTIVE

A useful way of viewing international monetary systems is in terms of instruments and objectives. In general, to achieve simultaneously all its policy objectives, a country needed at least as many instruments as it had objectives. In the standard analysis of a fixed-exchange-rate system, a country had two objectives, internal balance (full employment without excessive inflation) and external balance (equilibrium in the balace of payments). The fixing of the exchange rate eliminates one instrument: variations in the exchange rate. If only macroeconomic policy is available as an instrument, the country cannot expect to achieve simultaneous internal and external balance, for it has only one instrument to achieve two objectives. A solution may be found in the addition of another instrument, commonly the mix between monetary and fiscal policy. In practice, however, varying the monetary-fiscal mix may not be a sufficiently powerful instrument, or its use may be limited by legal, political, or administrative institutions, or it may conflict with other national objectives.

Viewed in terms of instruments and objectives, the contribution

---

interest rates by exactly the same amount as United States rates declined, and it must then use contractionary fiscal policy to offset the expansionary effect of the lower interest rates on domestic spending.

of floating exchange rates is to give countries an additional degree of freedom. Floating exchange rates permit the elimination of external balance as a policy objective, for it is achieved automatically by variations in the exchange rate.[15] Floating rates would keep the balance of payments automatically in balance, and supposedly the country would be indifferent whether this was achieved by a deficit on current account and a surplus on capital account or vice versa.

The problem with applying this scheme to the contemporary international financial order is that countries have not abandoned all external balance objectives, but have only changed them and made them more flexible. Countries on floating rates no longer have a balance-of-payments objective, but they have what might be imprecisely termed a *current-account objective*. Even though a country has overall balance in its balance of payments, it is not indifferent to the level of each of the separate components of its balance of payments. Here we shall express this concern as a target for the level of the current account of the balance of payments, although alternative but similar targets are equally conceivable, such as for the level of the balance of trade or the level of the exchange rate.

While the precise nature of the external objective of countries on floating rates cannot be specified, the general nature of the motivation seems clear enough. Countries are concerned about the adverse affect of large and unwarranted changes on their exporters in particular, and also on industries that compete closely with imports.[16] Countries' current-account objectives cannot be expressed as a precise level of the current-account balance. Perhaps the objective is that the current-account balance should fall within a certain range or change at no greater than a certain rate. Whatever it is, there is room for maneuver, but it is not unlimited. Changes in circumstances will, of course, change the level of the objective; a country that discovered vast oil reserves undoubtedly would change its current-account target.

---

15. Alternatively, this may be expressed by saying that the adoption of flexible exchange rates adds an instrument: variations in the exchange rate. It is essentially equivalent to eliminate an objective, keeping the instruments unchanged, or add an instrument, keeping the objectives unchanged.

16. For an excellent illustration see "Are the Swiss Enjoying Their Strong Currency? No, Not in the Least," *Wall Street Journal* (February 27, 1975).

When all countries have current-account objectives, they may be inconsistent. The current-account balance for the world as a whole must always equal zero, since a country's payments must be other countries' receipts. If the individual current-account targets for all countries do not add up to zero, it is impossible for every country to achieve its target. One way to ensure the consistency of national current-account targets is for one country to play a passive role—not having a current-account target but accepting whatever current-account balance arises from the actions of the other countries. If any country were to play such a role today, the natural candidate would be the United States. Under the Bretton Woods system the United States to a considerable degree played the passive ("nth-country") role for the balance of *payments*, but whether it did so for the current-account balance is open to question.[17] In the absence of a passive nth-country, the international monetary order must have some explicit means of dealing with the possibility of inconsistent national current-account objectives.

The question of reconciling national current-account objectives is the most significant issue related to the increased surpluses of the oil-producing countries. It now appears that the magnitude of future oil-country surpluses will be considerably less than the huge sums forecast by so many in the year following the quadrupling of oil prices. But whatever the magnitude, the oil surpluses do pose a genuine issue for the international monetary system, one that arises because of the existence of national current-account objectives. Unless the oil cartel collapses, the existence of a large current-account surplus for the oil countries as a whole seems inevitable for at least several more years. Since for the world as a whole, current-account deficits must equal surpluses, the existence of the oil-country surplus means there must be an equal current-account deficit in the other countries taken as a whole, although any particular country need not run a deficit. It is possible for one non-oil country to restore its current-account balance to what it was before the oil-price revolution; it is not possible for all. If every non-oil country myopically attempts to restore its original current-account balance, the deficit may be passed from country to country like the metaphorical hot potato,

---

17. See the comment by Robert Solomon on the paper by Whitman (note 3, above), p. 586.

but it will not go away. In the process of passing the unchanging current-account deficit around, the measures taken—excessively contractionary monetary-fiscal policy, competitive currency depreciation, increased barriers to imports—would have serious adverse consequences. There is historical precedent from the 1930's for this sort of self-destructive economic nationalism. Although there have been occurrences since the oil price revolution which might be interpreted as fitting this scenario (national measures to promote exports, some protectionist measures, contractionary monetary-fiscal policy), a serious relapse into economic nationalism has not occurred and does not appear likely.

The oil producers' collective current-account surplus continues to raise the question of the orderly determination of the distribution of the corresponding current-account deficit among the non-oil countries. It is a matter for international agreement, although it may continue to be in an informal fashion. But the distribution of the current-account deficit will not be left to the market through a floating-exchange-rate system, for that would tend to determine the distribution of the current-account deficit according to the investment preferences of the few countries with large oil surpluses, which is likely to produce an outcome unacceptable to some countries.[18]

THE ALLURE OF CAPITAL CONTROLS

As noted above (pages 67–68), various controls on capital movements were adopted during the later years of the Bretton Woods system as countries with misaligned parities attempted to defend their balances of payments against large speculative capital movements. It was widely expected that the adoption of flexible rates would bring about the dismantlement of the capital controls adopted in an effort to defend fixed exchange rates. With one important exception this has not happened. The exception is the United States, which in

---

18. Thus a country "favored" by oil-country investment managers would have an appreciating currency, increasing its current-account deficit and squeezing producers of exports and import-substitutes. This is precisely what occurred in Switzerland in the winter of 1974–75. (See above, note 16, "Are the Swiss Enjoying Their Strong Currency?") It caused the Swiss to take steps in an attempt to stem the capital inflow.

January 1974 abolished the Interest Equalization Tax and its controls on foreign lending by financial institutions and on foreign investment by United States corporations. Outside the United States, capital controls were not reduced after the adoption of flexible rates, although in a number of cases they did change form. Especially after the oil embargo, some countries switched from measures to restrict capital inflows to measures aimed at discouraging capital outflows or stimulating capital inflows.[19] On balance, it cannot be said that there has been any significant reduction in capital controls outside of the United States, and they may even have increased.

As long as a high degree of international capital mobility exists, many countries, but probably not the United States, are likely to continue to use capital controls in an effort to reduce that mobility. Although the volatility of short-term capital flows has been reduced by the abandonment of fixed parities, the potential consequences for the domestic economy of international capital movements have become greater. Under floating exchange rates, unless the capital flow is offset by a stabilizing speculative flow in the opposite direction, it will affect the domestic economy by altering the exchange rate and thereby changing the levels of demand and profitability in the production of traded goods vis-à-vis nontraded goods and reallocating resources between them. Under fixed rates, the capital flow generally does not alter relative prices, but only changes the level of official exchange holdings. When countries have current-account objectives, they have a motive to erect barriers to any capital flows that prevent the attainment of that objective. This incentive is well illustrated by the experience of Switzerland during the winter of 1974–75, when controls on inward capital flows were erected to limit further appreciation of the Swiss franc, whose rising value had greatly depressed Swiss export industries.[20]

Countries on floating-exchange rates are likely to retain some capital controls in an effort to reduce international capital mobility to increase their ability to insulate their economies from cyclical

---

19. International Monetary Fund, *25th Annual Report on Exchange Restrictions 1974* (Washington, D.C., 1974), pp. 12–15.

20. See "Swiss Take Steps to Curb Climb in Their Franc," *Wall Street Journal* (January 23, 1975), and "Are the Swiss Enjoying Their Strong Currency?"

fluctuations abroad. As explained above (pages 72–73), under capital mobility and flexible exchange rates, insulation of the domestic economy from fluctuations abroad is not impossible, but the existence of capital mobility makes it more difficult, since insulation then requires that economic policy-makers continually react to changes abroad.

The existence of international capital mobility under a system of floating exchange rates increases the potential for conflict between countries over ostensibly domestic macroeconomic policy actions, because such actions may stabilize one country at the expense of another. With floating exchange rates capital mobility makes fiscal policy by itself relatively ineffective but increases the ability of monetary policy to affect the level of domestic economic activity.[21] However, monetary policy works differently in a world of capital mobility than in a world of segmented capital markets. Expansionary monetary policy reduces interest rates and produces an outflow of capital, which causes the country's currency to depreciate, increasing exports and reducing imports. The increased demand for domestically produced exports and import-substitutes expands aggregate demand in the economy. Expansion is achieved by improving the foreign-trade balance and contraction by worsening the foreign-trade balance. Thus stabilization of the domestic economy may be at the expense of other economies. In fact, in a world of *perfect* capital mobility and floating exchange rates, there is no significant difference between expansionary open market operations and outright competitive depreciation via central bank intervention in the foreign exchange market.[22]

In reality the situation is not so extreme as this model suggests. First, if the country is so large that its own monetary policy affects the world level of interest rates, its monetary policy will stabilize its own economy only partially at the expense of other countries. Second, the fact that international capital mobility, though high, is not perfect also means that monetary stabilization is only partially

21. Robert A. Mundell, "Capital Mobility and Stabilization Policy under Fixed and Flexible Exchange Rates," *Canadian Journal of Economics and Political Science*, 24 (1963), 475–485.

22. The only difference is the trivial one that in the former case, the central bank increases its holdings of domestic assets, whereas in the latter case it increases its holdings of foreign assets.

at the expense of foreign countries. Third, it is not necessary that stabilization policy be at the expense of foreign economies at all. Just the right combination of monetary and fiscal policy, either both expansionary or both contractionary, could achieve the desired macroeconomic effect without affecting the foreign trade balance at all. Despite these three qualifications, there remains a problem of a potential conflict between nations over macroeconomic policy actions that are ostensibly domestic but in fact may achieve their effect partly at the expense of foreign countries. A country's choice of the mix between monetary and fiscal policy to stabilize its economy will determine how much its actions are at the expense of foreign countries.

In efforts to redesign an international monetary system appropriate to the new world of flexible exchange rates, much attention has focused on establishing rules for floating. In a world of managed floats, concern has centered on the possibility that management may become manipulation, as central banks intervene in foreign exchange markets not just to stabilize the exchange rate, but to push it up or down. Yet when a high degree of international capital mobility exists, something approaching this may be achieved by manipulation of the mix between monetary and fiscal policy. This possibility implies that in the presence of capital mobility, rules for floating limited to surveillance of central bank operations in the foreign exchange market may be inadequate. Since nations are unlikely to permit their domestic monetary and fiscal policy actions to become the subject of international surveillance, there will continue to exist a strong motive for the retention of capital controls aimed at reducing the degree of international capital mobility.

If all countries were of equal economic size, there would be less potential for conflict over the external consequences of a country's monetary-fiscal policy, for the repercussions of any single country's actions would be so minor and spread so widely that the effect on any other country individually would be negligible. The American economy is dominant enough, however—especially in world capital markets—that its domestic policies can have significant repercussions abroad, to which foreign countries may feel they must respond. Their response may take the form of adjusting their monetary-fiscal policies, in which case they find themselves forced to follow changes in United States macroeconomic policy—the same situation that was widely resented under the Bretton Woods system. Alternatively, foreign countries may seek to have influence on United States monetary-fiscal policy decisions, but they are unlikely to be very successful. Their third option is to seek to reduce the vulnerability of their economies to changes in United States policy by using capital controls to reduce the degree of international capital mobility.

The United States is much less likely to utilize capital controls than other countries because of the fundamental asymmetry of the situation. The United States is not nearly as much affected by the monetary-fiscal policy actions of other countries as they are affected by similar United States actions. In addition, the United States has a highly developed capital market which sells its services to the rest of the world; capital controls would handicap the operations of this market. Thus it is not surprising that within a year after the end of the Bretton Woods system the United States dismantled its system of capital controls. As an issue for United States foreign economic policy, the issue of capital controls probably will involve United States reactions to the use of capital controls abroad, although the question will always be colored by the possibility that the United States may itself wish to adopt some form of capital controls. In addition, it is conceivable that the United States might some day be asked by foreign countries to participate in the operation of an international system of capital controls.

Future capital controls systems are likely to be more symmetrical than those which prevailed under the Bretton Woods system. Because they were adopted under a fixed-exchange-rate system with greatly misaligned parities, those controls generally were asymmetrical—that is, they restricted either capital outflow (in the case of countries that had overvalued currencies, such as the United Kingdom) or capital inflow (in countries with undervalued currencies, such as Germany and Japan). In the new world of more flexible rates, countries will seek some insulation from both capital inflows and capital outflows, if they are equally adverse to foreign-induced appreciation or depreciation of their currency.

CAPITAL CONTROLS: THE ISSUES

The existence of national current-account objectives, and the possibility of their inconsistency, requires some degree of international monetary cooperation in the management of flexible exchange rates. With flexible exchange rates a nation could manipulate its current-account balance in any of three ways: (1) direct intervention in foreign-exchange markets, (2) varying the mix of monetary and fiscal policy, and (3) manipulation of its capital controls. A reconstructed international financial system for the new world of managed floating exchange rates must have means for dealing with all three of these possibilities. Discussions of new international monetary arrangements have tended to concentrate on (1). It was suggested above (page 79) that a probable approach to dealing with (2) was to reduce its impact through the adoption of capital controls to reduce capital mobility.

In a system of flexible exchange rates, changes in capital controls may be used to induce changes in the current-account balance. In the absence of official exchange-market intervention, either the current account or the capital account will be automatically determined as a residual once the other is determined. Thus manipulation of the current account may be achieved indirectly by manipulation of the capital account. For example, capital controls to deter capital inflows and stimulate capital outflows would produce an increased deficit on capital account, depreciation of the currency, and an increased surplus on current account. Such possibilities imply that any new international financial system must provide for some surveillance of capital controls, as well as of official exchange-market intervention.

It is important to distinguish between *changes* in capital controls, whose purpose is to affect the current-account balance, and the existence of a given level of capital controls, whose purpose is to reduce capital mobility, to increase the level of friction on both inward and outward movements of capital. The international financial system must find means to limit the use of the former. But the latter is likely to be a fact of life to which decision-makers in the area of foreign economic policy must adapt.

Controls on international movements of short-term capital are not ephemeral occurrences of a fixed-exchange-rate system in decline. In a world of flexible exchange rates they can be expected to persist and to be of potentially greater consequence than when fixed rates prevailed. The design of a post-Bretton-Woods system requires a more systematic adaptation on the part of international economic policy-makers to the reality of capital controls. To arrive at a position on the issue of capital controls, many questions must be resolved.

Will capital controls work? Capital controls hinder the movement of capital from lower-return to higher-return activities. Money is, however, highly liquid and, like other liquids, seeks its own level. When one channel is dammed up, funds may simply flow through other channels. When controls block capital flows through bank loans or deposits, the flows may take place through nonbank financial enterprises, the bond market, changes in the "leads and lags" on trade credits, changes in intracorporate transfer prices between subsidiaries of multinational corporations, etc. As money managers discover new means of circumventing controls, the controls are extended gradually from relatively harmless, easy-to-enforce controls to more complicated and inefficient measures. Perhaps the most important case of this is the possibility that controls over short-term capital flows may have to be extended to long-term capital movements because of the ease with which short-term capital movements may be achieved by means of long-term instruments. Capital controls are further limited because changes in capital flows may occur through actions that are passive and thus cannot feasibly be controlled at all. (For example, an increase in the net capital outflow may occur if domestic residents simply borrow less abroad than they otherwise would have.)

Thus it must be determined whether there is a built-in tendency for capital controls to deteriorate into impotence. Controls are likely to be less effective, the stronger the incentive to evade them. This sets a limit to the size of differentials between national interest rates. If the potential for evasion is so great that this maximum differential is small, capital controls will be relatively ineffective in permitting much national monetary autonomy. Research is necessary to determine the potential effectiveness of capital controls.

Do the benefits of controls justify the costs?[23] Government

---

23. For a first step in the direction of comparing benefits and costs,

restrictions on international capital movements generally have not incurred the same opprobrium as interferences with other forms of international transactions. Although the Articles of Agreement of the International Monetary Fund require free convertibility of funds obtained on current account, they permit most forms of capital controls.[24] The classic economic argument against capital controls is that they inhibit the movement of capital from locations where its productivity is low to locations where its productivity is high, thereby reducing world efficiency. Against the classical position, it is argued: (1) Because of national differences in taxation and capital market regulation, national differences in the private return to capital may not correspond closely to national differences in the social productivity of capital. (2) Compared to other forms of international capital movements, short-term capital movements are motivated more by factors other than international differences in the productivity of capital. (3) Since international trade in goods and services is at least a partial substitute for international movement of capital and other factors of production, the maintenance of reasonably free trade should keep the costs of restrictions on capital movements reasonably low.[25]

Other, more indirect, costs of capital controls are possible. Scarce resources, especially highly skilled manpower, will be devoted to finding means of evading the restrictions, while governments must devote scarce resources to countering these attempts at evasion. Restrictions on short-term capital flows may interfere with

---

applied to United States restrictions on capital outflows, see Norman S. Fieleke, "The Welfare Effects of Controls over Capital Exports from the United States," *Princeton Essays in International Finance*, No. 104 (Princeton University, May 1974).

24. One important measure to deal with short-term capital flows—dual exchange rates for current-account and capital-account transactions—is technically in violation of the IMF Articles of Agreement, which prohibit multiple exchange rates.

25. Thus it is not surprising that some prominent economists have advocated the adoption of measures to reduce the international mobility of liquid capital. For example, James Tobin, *The New Economics One Decade Older* (Princeton, N.J., Princeton University Press, 1974), pp. 84–92, and F. Modigliani, "International Capital Movements, Fixed Parities, and Monetary and Fiscal Policies," in Jagdish Bhagwati and Richard S. Eckaus, eds., *Development and Planning* (Cambridge, Mass., The MIT Press, 1973), pp. 239–253.

international trade in goods and services by hindering short-term trade credits and making them more expensive.

In a world of more highly flexible exchange rates, international short-term capital movements have an important role to play in preventing excessive instability of exchange rates. Frequently, exchange-rate variations achieve the appropriate changes in the current-account balance only after a period of time, during which interval the current-account balance may even react perversely, putting further pressure on the exchange rate.[26] For example, depreciation of a country's currency may cause its current-account balance to worsen temporarily, and in the absence of an improvement in the capital-account balance bring about further depreciation of the currency. As the currency depreciates, however, the expectation of an ultimate improvement in the current-account balance (hence an appreciation of the currency) will bring about an inflow of short-term capital, improving the capital-account balance and producing an improvement in the overall balance of payments despite a possible decline in the current-account balance. Thus international short-term capital flows will often be necessary to stabilize exchange rates in the absence of official intervention. The loss or reduction of this stabilizing effect must be considered a cost of capital controls. Policymakers must make a choice among three variables: capital controls, exchange-rate instability, and official intervention. It is a question not of either-or but of degree: An increase in exchange controls of a certain degree of restrictiveness, for example, implies greater exchange-rate instability and/or greater official intervention in any of a great variety of combinations. Research is necessary to determine the tradeoffs between these three options.

What form of controls? The variety of possible capital-control measures is almost limitless, but the most significant options may be grouped broadly into three categories: (1) quantitative restrictions, (2) measures that act directly upon the rate of return to international capital movement, and (3) dual exchange rates.

Quantitative controls on capital movements or other things usually earn the disapproval of economists because they generally

---

26. This is because the "success" of a depreciation or appreciation depends partly upon high elasticities of demand for exports and imports, and elasticities are greater in the long run than in the short.

are uneven and distortionary in their impact, because they often create inequitable windfall gains, and because they thwart the signals given by the price mechanism. The attraction of quantitative capital controls for policy-makers is that—if they work—they would permit the precise adjustment of the volume of capital flows, whereas the end result of other types of measures, even if perfectly enforced, is more uncertain. On the other hand, quantitative controls thwart capital movements that might help stabilize flexible exchange rates. Quantitative capital controls may be administered either by regulating net foreign-exchange positions or by regulating foreign-exchange transactions, the former being administratively easier but probably also easier to evade.

Measures directly acting upon the return to capital movement include mainly taxes of various kinds, such as the Interest Equalization Tax recently eliminated by the United States. Conceivably, such a tax might be made variable, to be adjusted perhaps according to the state of the balance of payments and exchange-rate movements, but discretionary variability may lead to suspicion abroad that it might be used for unwarranted manipulation of the exchange rate. An interesting variation would be a uniform-percentage tax on all capital-account spot currency *transactions*.[27] Such a tax would discourage capital flows more, the shorter their duration—an advantage because long-term capital flows occur less in response to transitory phenomena and represent less of a threat to national monetary autonomy. The major drawback of taxes on international capital movements is that although they may reduce the average volume of capital flow, unless the taxes are so high as to eliminate the incentive to international capital movement, they do not prevent a temporary, large capital movement in response to a change in the difference between national interest rates, since international capital flows have the nature of a stock adjustment. By the same token, however, they do permit movements of capital that will help to stabilize exchange-rate variations.

A system of dual exchange rates has received increasing attention in recent years.[28] Generally, the division of the exchange market

---

27. See Tobin, p. 89.

28. See, for example, J. Marcus Fleming, "Dual Exchange Markets and Other Remedies for Disruptive Capital Flows," *International Monetary Fund Staff Papers*, 21 (1974), 1-27.

has been between current- and capital-account transactions. However, a wide variety of divisions is possible. One appealing division would be between basic-balance transactions, on the one hand, and short-term capital flows, on the other, thereby separating hot-money flows from long-term capital movements. There may be practical problems, however, in keeping these two markets apart. A dual exchange-rate system has some of the advantages of both quantitative restrictions and taxes. Like quantitative controls, it can achieve fairly precise control over the magnitude of capital flows. As with tax measures, the price system is left free to operate within the limits set by the separation of the two exchange markets. However, dual exchange rates may be easier to evade than the other two types of controls. It seems probable that a system of dual exchange rates, both floating, will not be successful because the current-account exchange rate will tend to be unstable.[29] Hence, if such a system were to be adopted, it would require a considerable degree of exchange market intervention, possibly as part of a renewed international financial system. One variation that has been used is a fixed exchange rate for the current account combined with a floating capital rate.

What are the interactions with other issues? The issue of capital controls is inevitably involved with any steps that may be taken toward European monetary integration, much as United States–European negotiations with respect to international trade barriers were affected by the formation and expansion of the European Economic Community.

The issue of capital controls interacts closely with the issue of the multinational corporation. As is well known, the spread of the multinationals has been one of the prime forces increasing the mobility of short-term capital. Any effective system of short-term capital controls inevitably will infringe upon the freedom of action of the multinational corporation. Will this seriously hamper the functioning of the multinational corporation, or will it be only a minor irritation? Might controls on short-term capital flows even

---

29. This is because of the need for stabilizing speculative capital flows during the interval between a change in the exchange rate and the resulting correction of the current-account balance. Under freely floating dual exchange rates, the current and capital exchange markets are sealed off from each other, so that, say, a depreciation in the current-account rate would not bring about the necessary speculative capital inflow.

benefit the multinationals by taking some of the political heat off them, since one argument often made against them is that they cause excessive volatility of short-term funds?

What approach for United States foreign policy? When the preceding questions have been resolved, the United States may develop a position on the adoption of capital controls. The issue has many dimensions. Should the United States itself adopt capital controls? If so, what kind? Should the willingness of the United States to adopt capital controls be affected by whether other countries do? Will capital controls, insofar as they handicap international banking and the multinational corporation—two areas in which the United States predominates—effectively discriminate against United States interests? Should the adoption of capital controls abroad be encouraged or discouraged by the United States, or should no position be taken? Are some forms of capital controls that may be adopted abroad more acceptable than others?

If capital controls do come to be widely adopted, will it be desirable to establish some form of international agreement on their use? If so, what form should this take? Informal agreement among central bankers? International agreement on rules of good behavior in the operation of capital controls, perhaps including prohibitions on certain forms of capital controls? International operation of a single system of capital controls?[30] Should there be a prohibition on discriminatory operation of capital controls, or would it be acceptable for certain countries to have lower barriers on capital flows between each other than with other countries?[31]

---

30. Suppose, for example, that some countries, but not all, adopted a one percent tax on capital flows. Flows between countries, only one of which had adopted the tax, would be taxed at one percent, whereas flows between countries, both of which had adopted the tax, would be taxed at 2 percent, or twice as high a rate. Most countries probably would consider this sort of discrimination as an undesirable consequence of their desire to achieve greater monetary independence. It could be avoided by international operation of the capital control system.

31. For example, between the United States and Canada or among the members of the European Community. It is an open question whether this will work at all. If it can, there is the second question of whether it is desirable.

SUMMARY AND CONCLUSIONS

One of the most important developments in international finance during the past two decades has been a great increase in the international mobility of short-term capital. During the waning years of the Bretton Woods system of fixed exchange rates, this high degree of capital mobility greatly magnified the strains on the international monetary system arising from the fundamental incompatibility of national desires for macroeconomic autonomy and an excessive unwillingness to alter exchange parities. During the Bretton Woods years countries increasingly resorted to measures to control or restrict capital mobility, but they were insufficient to prevent the collapse of the Bretton Woods system and the emergence of flexible exchange rates among the major industrialized countries.

Despite a widespread expectation that controls on short-term capital movements would be dismantled after the advent of flexible exchange rates, capital controls have not been significantly reduced outside the United States. Under a system of flexible rates, except for the case of the United States, countries are as strongly motivated to maintain capital controls as they were before, and perhaps more so. The primary reason for a country to adopt flexible exchange rates is to achieve a greater degree of autonomy in macreconomic policy. But while such autonomy can be achieved under floating exchange rates, it is more difficult to attain, the greater the level of international capital mobility. Hence, countries seeking greater autonomy in monetary-fiscal policy will resort to measures that reduce international capital mobility.

The existence of national objectives for the current-account balance and the possibility of conflicts between the current-account targets of different countries provide a second and related motive for the use of capital controls. When international capital mobility is high, one country's stabilization policy may be at the expense of other countries' current-account objectives. Since it is extremely unlikely that any country would acquiesce in any international arrangement that would limit its sovereignty over its domestic stabilization policy, it is likely that national economic policy-makers will defuse the potential conflict by the use of capital controls to reduce the level of capital mobility.

These considerations suggest that capital controls are not a transitory phenomenon, but are likely to become widespread and enduring in the new world of managed flexibility of exchange rates. In future efforts to establish international arrangements for the new world of managed flexible rates, questions of capital controls may occupy as important a place as those of official exchange-market intervention. When exchange rates become more flexible, international arrangements to deal with capital controls become more important, because of the danger that they may be manipulated to achieve changes in a country's current-account balance at the expense of other countries. Under fixed rates, capital controls had less potential for conflict because they did not greatly affect the current account or the exchange rate and because their use to combat speculative capital flows was usually desired by both the countries experiencing that inflow and those experiencing the outflow.

In the future, capital controls are likely to be an integral and important issue in international monetary negotiations. National policy-makers will need to develop a systematic approach to capital controls as a probably permanent aspect of national policies in the area of international economic relations. There is much that we still do not know about capital controls and their effects, but in the future it is likely to become more and more important that we learn.

EDITOR'S NOTE

Precisely what role multinational corporations do or should play in the international system is a hotly disputed topic. Some view the MNC as a new international actor that threatens to displace such traditional actors as nation states; some see the MNC's as behind-the-scenes manipulators of the foreign policies of nation states; some regard MNC's as potentially useful tools with which foreign-policy makers can pursue their goals; and others regard MNC's as stimuli to international friction. After noticing such viewpoints, Professor Ringbakk orients his essay toward the MNC as a force to be reckoned with in world politics, and simultaneously deepens our understanding of the nature of MNC's while identifying United States foreign-policy implications of these organizations.

This is not simply a matter of updating traditional hackneyed arguments about the relationship between business and government in America. Most of the growth of MNC's has occurred since World War II, Ringbakk argues, and we should be wary of extrapolating such trends into the future. Size, stage of maturation, and international environment must be considered in examining the future of MNC's.

The big policy question arising from Ringbakk's discussion is whether the United States should try to provide leadership in moving the world toward a new international economic order. Surely questions such as what kind of international economic order is desirable and feasible from the standpoint of American foreign policy and how MNC's fit into such an order should be on the minds of United States foreign-policy makers during the next few years.

IV.
Multinational Corporations and Foreign Policy

Kjell-Arne Ringbakk

> It became clear that almost every economic
> policy had profound foreign policy implica-
> tions.*

A new world economy is emerging in which international trade
in goods and services is being replaced by international production.
In this new world economy the nation state is no longer the optimal
economic unit. Political and economic units are no longer synony-
mous, and we observe how far-reaching forces for change are creating
new relationships and institutions in the international system. The
traditional view of sovereignty, a world of nation states, and the
concept of the nation as the appropriate political *and* economic unit
are being challenged by new economic and geopolitical realities.

The multinational corporation is one reflection of these international forces for change. It is a symptom and an effect rather than
a cause. The multinational corporation has grown out of the new
environment. Though antecedents can be traced back to the Colonial
era, the greatest portion of the multinational corporate growth has
taken place during the past 25 years.[1] Multinational corporations as

---

*"Kissinger on Oil, Food, and Trade," *Business Week* (January 13, 1975),
p. 66.

1. For a discussion of the evolution, see Paul J. McNulty, "Predecessors of
the Multinational Corporation," *Columbia Journal of World Business*, 7 (May–
June 1972), 73–80. Boydan Hawrylyshyn, "The Internationalization of Firms,"
Journal of World Trade Law, 5 (January–February 1971), 72–82. *Business History Review*, 48 (Autumn 1974) features a series of articles on the spread of
multinational enterprise. Mira Wilkins in *The Maturing of Multinational Enterprise*

of the mid-1970's have grown in size and scope to the point where they represent a significant subset in the international system.[2]

Foreign-policy issues increasingly arise from the internationalization of production, from the flows of foreign direct investments, and from the behavior of multinational corporations. Traditional theory has become insufficient to analyze the new reality, but no new workable theory of the emergent world economy has been developed. More attention must therefore be devoted to understanding the changes and conflicts in the system. In this connection Peter Drucker argues that "to fight the symptoms in lieu of a cure has always been tempting. It is therefore entirely possible that the multinational will be severely damaged and perhaps even destroyed within the next decade."[3]

The aim of this paper is first to show why foreign-policy makers should be concerned with MNC's; second, to review how international trade is being replaced by international production; third, to assess the possible future of MNC's; and, finally, to identify some major foreign-policy issues. The paper is not solutions-oriented; rather it is intended to provide a backdrop against which issues may be identified.

One student of foreign policy has provided a partial rationale for including multinational corporations in the foreign-policy equation.

For the first time, foreign policy has become global. . . . Today, statesmen face the unprecedented problem of formulating policy for well over a hundred countries. . . . what used to be considered domestic events can now have world-wide consequences.

The revolutionary character of our age can be summed up in three general statements: (a) the number of participants in the international order has increased and their nature has altered;

(Harvard University Press, Cambridge, Mass., 1974) traces the rise of American multinationals between 1914 and 1970 and provides comprehensive statistics on their size and importance.

2. *Multinational Corporations in World Development*, United Nations, ST/ECA/190 (New York, 1973). Raymond Vernon, *Sovereignty at Bay* (New York, Basic Books, 1971).

3. Peter F. Drucker, "Multinationals and Developing Countries: Myths and Realities," *Foreign Affairs*, 53 (October 1974), 133.

(b) their technical ability to affect each other has vastly grown;
(c) the scope of their purpose has expanded.

Whenever the participants in the international system change, a period of profound dislocation is inevitable.[4]

While Kissinger may have had macro players and nation-states in mind, it is evident that multinationals are part of the new international order in which foreign policy is formulated and practiced.

As of the beginning of 1974, more than 300 corporations worldwide had attained annual sales volume in excess of one billion dollars. Most of these are multinational corporations, some with affiliates in twenty or more countries.[5] The leading multinational corporations operate primarily in oligopolistic market structures, and they frequently dominate important sectors of home and host countries. Analysis of the large multinationals shows that high investments in technology through research and development, in marketing including advertising, and in efforts to create process and product differentiation help maintain their market power, hence their oligopolistic position. Oligopoly means fewness and interdependence, therefore an important source of conflict between the large corporations and the nation state.

The size, dominance, and strength of these corporations, it is argued, represent a threat to national interests and to the sovereignty of nation states.[6]

The United Nations study asserted that "the manifold operations of foreign-based multinational corporations and their pervasive influence on the host country must be regarded as a challenge to national sovereignty. The challenge has, moreover, economic, social,

---

4. Henry A. Kissinger, *American Foreign Policy* (Expanded Edition, New York, W. W. Norton, 1974), p. 53.

5. We will use the term "foreign direct investment" to denote the case where the investor owns part or all of a company and where the investor is involved in managing its operations. The term "multinational corporation" is used to denote the case where a company controls assets in two or more countries. This follows the definition adopted by the United Nations in its *Multinational Corporations*, pp. 4–5, 118–121.

6. J. N. Behrman, *National Interests and Multinational Enterprise* (Englewood Cliffs, N.J., Prentice Hall, 1970).

political and cultural dimensions which are frequently inseparable from one another."[7]

The United States participation in the transition to international production is highly significant, since 60 percent of all foreign direct investments in the noncommunist world have been made by United States-based corporations. In addition, 10 percent of all foreign direct investments have been made in the United States by foreign companies. Thus, the United States has an interest in 70 percent of the world's foreign direct investment, which was estimated to exceed $160 billion as of the beginning of 1973.[8]

Of the dozen largest multinational corporations in the world in 1973, 10 were United States-based. Consolidated sales for these ranged in 1973 from a high of $35.8 billion for General Motors to a low of $8.4 billion for Gulf Oil. The average for the largest twelve was $15.8 billion, up more than 20 percent from 1972. If these companies were to grow at 10 percent a year in real terms, by 1980 GM's sales in 1972 dollars would be $65 billion and Gulf's $13 billion, and the average for the top twelve $28 billion. Although this is unlikely to happen, we anticipate that conflicts will continue to arise from the size and power the large multinational corporations are amassing.

Looking at the performance and size of the 500 largest United States industrial corporations, the majority of which are multinational, we observe the following: In 1973 they employed over 15,580,000 workers, or 76 percent of all employed in manufacturing in the United States. Their total 1973 sales exceeded $667 billion, which was 65 percent of sales of all U.S. industrial corporations. The 500 earned 79 percent of all profits earned in manufacturing. Sales for the 500 group increased 19.6 percent over 1972, while profits increased 39 percent.[9]

In addition to the giant MNC a new generation of mini-multinationals is emerging as a part of the ongoing internationalization process created in the new world economy. In contrast with the

---

7. *Multinational Corporations*, p. 46.

8. *A Note on the Scope and Growth of Foreign Direct Investment*, Harvard Business School, 4-373-082, revised July 1974. Since these estimates are understated because of the use of book value figures and other data deficiencies, the actual figure is probably closer to $300 billion. Foreign direct investments have been growing at a rate of 10 to 20 percent a year.

9. For performance data, see *Fortune* (May 1974).

giants, these smaller companies are likely to display different behavioral characteristics. Being smaller, more specialized, and less visible, they may seek to take advantage of opportunities in transfer pricing or currency speculation which the large by now have begun to shy away from. To the extent that these smaller companies exert less self-restraint in areas such as these, they may run into the conflicts with host country interests which the large MNC's have been accused of in the past.

Recent statistics show that United States companies are still actively pursuing internationalization strategies. According to one survey carried out in 1974, 556 United States companies invested overseas in 848 different ventures in 1973, an 8 percent increase over 1972.[10] This survey further shows that new establishments, as contrasted with expansions and licensing, accounted for 77.8 percent of the total number, that 60 percent of the new establishments were in manufacturing, and that companies with sales below $500 million accounted for 48 percent of all new establishments in manufacturing in 1973—all of which supports the point that *small to medium-sized companies increasingly are joining the MNC ranks.*[11]

The multinational corporation, however, is not purely a United States phenomenon. Data for the 300 largest non-United States industrial corporations reveal even more rapid growth, much of it internationally, than that of the 500 United States companies discussed above. From 1972 to 1973 sales for these 300 increased 34 percent and profits 91 percent.[12] In terms of absolute size we note the emergence of giants and supergiants. In 1973, 17 United States and 15 non-United States companies had sales above $5 billion. Thirty-nine United States and 40 non-United States companies had sales in excess of $3 billion. And if we look at the so-called billion-dollar league—companies with sales above one billion—we count 167 United States and 145 non-United States corporations.

Until the early 1970's multinationals sustained annual sales increases of 10 percent or more as compared with 7.5 percent for

10. John B. Rhodes, "U.S. New Business Activities Abroad," *Columbia Journal of World Business* (Summer 1974), pp. 99–105.

11. See also John R. Roach, "The Mini-Multinationals," *The Conference Board Record*, 11 (February 1974), 27–31.

12. For detailed performance data on the largest non-United States corporations, see *Fortune* (September 1974).

international trade and around 5 percent for most advanced economies. A primary driving force behind the high multinational corporate
growth has been the emergence of a world market, the development
of similar demand patterns in different countries, and the rise of
what Peter Drucker has labeled "the global shopping center." A
consequence of this higher growth has been concentration of economic power among multinational corporations at the expense of
national firms and institutions. In the process many criticisms have
been levied against the multinationals. These corporations have
become surrounded by misunderstanding, suspicion, mysticism, and
even fear.[13]

By way of summary we can identify a number of features
regarding multinational corporations.

• Multinationals are not a homogeneous group. Rather, they are
heterogeneous, diverse, and very different in important respects. This
must be understood when seeking to judge or more importantly control multinationals and their behavior.

• Multinational corporations are not an American phenomenon.
European-based companies started international operations in raw
materials extraction, commodity acquisition, marketing, and manufacturing before their American counterparts. In recent years Japanese corporations have also aggressively expanded their operations
outside Japan, frequently through joint ventures.

While basically apolitical in motivation the MNC exerts power
influencing host as well as home communities leading to potentially
serious conflicts. In exceptional cases MNC's have also involved
themselves in politics—at times with grave consequences and strong
reactions. The case of ITT has attracted much attention to the "bad
behavior aspects" of MNC's.[14]

The more recent case of United Brands paying bribes to Honduras government officials to avoid export taxes on bananas will spell
trouble for other multinationals. The so-called Bananagate Affair

---

13. For one exposé of the alleged misuse of multinational power, see
Richard J. Barnet and Ronald E. Muller, *Global Reach: The Power of the Multinational Corporations* (New York, Simon and Schuster, 1974).

14. See "Mission Impossible," *Times* (April 2, 1973); "ITT's Brazen
Behavior," editorial, *International Herald Tribune* (March 24–25, 1973); and
Anthony Sampson, "How Not to be Multinational," *Vision* (February 1973).

caused political upheavals in Honduras and new strains between host countries and foreign investors.[15] According to some, this bribe was paid in response to pressures put on United Brands.

In the case of Gulf Oil, top management told the United States government it was compelled by politicians in a foreign country to pay $4 million in two successive cash "contributions" in order to stay in business there. Gulf's chairman testified that as much as $700 million was at stake and that the company was in fact hostage to that country. Judging from the *Wall Street Journal* account, Gulf was pressured to pay or risk the loss of corporate assets.[16] What these examples show is that the MNC's are not neutral actors in the international system.

• Multinationalization has not been confined to big firms only. A review of statistics reveals that a large number of European and Japanese, as well as American, corporations that operate in two or more countries are medium to small in size. Many of these have fewer than 1500 employees.

• Multinational corporations are found not only in manufacturing but in different primary and tertiary economic activities as well. Many of the large raw materials ventures are multinational, as are increasing numbers of service industries.

In view of the discontinuities and radical upsets characteristic of the multinational corporate environment during the early 1970's, it seems that multinational corporations are in a period of transition and that their long-term future is by no means clear.

As an increasingly important and largely independent actor in the international system, the multinational corporation clearly must be taken into account in foreign-policy formulation and implementation. Through their extensive cross-border operations multinational corporations create economic and other side effects having a direct bearing on foreign policy.

The public reactions against MNC's worldwide have been strong. As of the mid-1970's, countries all over the world were looking at

---

15. Stephen Sansweet and Mike Tharp, "Bananagate Flap: Calm on the Surface. Hondurans Are Ready for Political Turmoil," *Wall Street Journal* (April 14, 1975).

16. Jerry Landeuer, "Gulf Oil Admits It Paid $4.2 million to Officials Abroad to Shield Assets," *Wall Street Journal* (May 2, 1975).

how to regulate MNC's. Host countries were bringing increasing pressures on MNC's to "localize" and to be more responsive to the needs and demands of the host community. Some of these pressures inevitably will result in conflicts with the home or other host communities.[17]

These conflicts raise the issue of the limits of jurisdiction. For the purely domestic corporation there is no problem regarding jurisdiction, but when the domestic corporation begins to expand internationally, conflicts emerge. Under the concept of sovereignty it is accepted that the host country unilaterally can decide the terms of a foreign direct investment through negotiation with the foreign investor. The host can accept or reject the new investment proposal; it can bargain for the terms most in harmony with national objectives and interests. The outcome of the bargaining process depends in large measure on the relative strengths of the host versus the investor.

It is also widely accepted that the host country has the right to terminate the investment contract provided sufficient compensation is offered to the investor. While agreement as to what constitutes fair or sufficient compensation may be hard to establish, the principle seems clear. A case in point where foreign investors are faced with the demand to renegotiate basic terms is the Andean Common Market (Bolivia, Chile, Colombia, Ecuador, Peru, and Venezuela), where so-called "fade-out" regulations require foreign firms operating in the market to divest 51 percent of subsidiary equity within 15 years.[18]

In addition, as part of international business it is accepted that the investor must conform with the laws and regulations of the host country. Legally, the corporate charter for a subsidiary or affiliate is granted by the host country.

The problems arise when policies of home and host governments

---

17. Robert Samuelson, "America Turns Against Its Own Multinational Giants," *Sunday Times* (March 11, 1973); Richard E. Mooney, "Regulating the Multinationals: Fair Play or Anarchy?" *New York Times* (August 26, 1973); "The EEC's Plans for the Multinationals," *Vision* (April 1973), p. 63. For an elaboration of the conflicts between home and host countries and how the oil multinationals were caught between, see James E. Akins, "The Oil Crisis: This Time the Wolf is Here," *Foreign Affairs*, 51 (April 1973), 462–490.

18. "Learning to Live with Expropriation," *Business Week* (July 10, 1971), p. 34.

are at odds. The United States position appears to have been the following: Corporations headquartered or operating in the United States are expected to conform with United States laws, including antitrust laws.[19] Since foreign subsidiaries of United States companies in the eyes of United States authorities are part of the United States corporation, the subsidiaries must also conform with the United States laws.

If the United States initiates, for instance, a trade embargo on a country, United States corporations usually are explicitly instructed not to trade with that country. However, another country where United States subsidiaries are located may not share the same policy and carry out trade with the embargoed country. That host country may then put pressure on the United States subsidiaries to export, while the United States government seeks to prevent it. Cuba is one case where trade embargoes have been in effect since 1961. Today we can see that "many Latin-American countries have ignored their embargoes with Cuba or dropped them. Most recently, the Argentine subsidiaries of General Motors, Ford, and Chrysler have started to ship hundreds of millions of dollars worth of trucks, buses, autos, and farm implements to Cuba." [20] Likewise, Canada has opted to trade with Cuba and has strongly pushed United States-owned subsidiaries in Canada to aid in the effort.[21] Unable to comply with conflicting demands, the subsidiary does not know to whom it should be responsible.

From a United States point of view, the answer may appear obvious. However, the logic of insisting that United States subsidiaries in foreign countries are to conform with United States laws amounts to stating that United States laws are to be operative worldwide. This extraterritorial reach of United States law clearly is not in harmony with the tenets of sovereignty.[22]

---

19. For an elaboration of principles and reference to various cases, see, e.g., William W. Bishop, Jr., *International Law* (Boston, Little, Brown, 1962).

20. H. J. Maidenberg, "Visions of Cuba Trade Again," *New York Times* (October 6, 1974).

21. "Canada Steps Up Cuba Trade As U.S. Stance Softens," *Business International* (March 21, 1975), p. 91.

22. Seymour J. Rubin, "The International Firm and the National Jurisdiction," in Charles P. Kindleberger, ed., *The International Corporation* (Cambridge, Massachusetts, MIT Press, 1970).

Several foreign-policy issues emerge as we look at foreign direct investments and the multinational corporation. What will be the United States position when host countries place increasing demands on United States foreign direct investors to behave in ways which are in conflict with United States interests or policies?

What will be the United States position vis-à-vis foreign direct investments in the United States? Will the United States be as open for such investments as was Europe, for instance, in the 1950's and 1960's? How will the United States react to foreign dominance of key sectors of the economy? These are more than academic issues since the foreign direct investments in the United States, which by the mid-1970's were estimated by the Department of Commerce to approach $20 billion, are likely to grow very rapidly during the second half of the decade.[23] World Bank calculations in 1974 showed that the oil producers stood to collect $650 billion in revenues by 1980 and $1300 billion by 1985, representing the greatest transfer of wealth in history. By early 1975 these estimates had been scaled down and significantly modified. Still, for 1974 the OPEC countries enjoyed a surplus of about $60 billion that were discretionary and available for investment, aid, and the like. For the remainder of the 1970's substantial surpluses will be realized by many Middle East oil-rich countries. Given the conservative investment attitudes on the part of these countries, we can expect that Europe and the United States will be key recipients of the portfolio and direct investments likely to be made with petrodollars in the years ahead. The United States needs a policy to cope with these and other investment demands.

Still another reason why foreign direct investments and multinational corporations are of interest to foreign-policy makers is that these corporations are important instruments for the implementation and accomplishment of foreign policy. It can be argued that the behavior and performance of multinational corporations increasingly will influence the success of foreign policy.

For example, the offer of the United States to help the Middle East to develop capability for nuclear energy depends on the posses-

---

23. Some experts estimate that total direct investments in the United States by 1200 to 1400 foreign-owned companies is 4 to 5 times as much as these Commerce Dept. figures.

sion of relevant technologies. The quality of the offer also depends on having the necessary delivery system. United States multinationals will have to be called upon to carry out a number of the economic activities of these foreign-policy transactions.

Traditionally we have looked at the multinational corporation as a transfer agent of capital, products, management, and technology. Increasingly, technology in terms of both hardware and software requires large investments, long lead times until commercialized, and sizable markets and volumes to pay off. Technological progress in the years ahead will become more rather than less important to solve the problems facing the world in areas such as development, industrialization, food production, resource depletion, ecology, and the like. Since technology to a large extent is developed in the private sector, the multinational corporation by virtue of its size and investment in research and development is central to the technological progress. An emergent policy issue related to technology transfers is how much freedom United States corporations have in selling their technology abroad, particularly where it was paid for by government through, for example, defense contracts.

In general, the multinational corporation has the transnational management capabilities and transfer systems required for the delivery of components or total industrial systems. To the extent that some countries, like France or Japan, engage in large-scale bilateral deals to secure access to resources and in the process offer macro solutions and industrialization under the guidance of government planning, it may be difficult for the United States to retain its old posture and policies. Furthermore, with the emergence of communist and state-owned multinational corporations the international competitive climate and conditions in world-resources and world-use markets are changing.

The election of Labor to a majority position in the United Kingdom elections October 10, 1974, was in part based on a campaign promise of further nationalization of British industry. In recent elections in other European countries, notably France and the Scandinavian countries, nationalization of banking and manufacturing industries was a key issue for socialists and laborites. To the extent large non-United States based MNC's are nationalized, how will the United States react to their investments and operations in the United States? Also, what will it mean to privately owned United

States companies seeking to compete with these? If nationalized MNC's become an instrument of government policy, what will it do to the equilibrium and dynamics of the international system?

In order to assess how multinationals can be an important element in the foreign-policy equation, a review of the evolution to date will be useful.

International trade has almost always been subject to control and regulation. Policy-makers have frequently accepted loss in economic welfare as an acceptable cost to obtain political or other benefits. Such a cost-benefit analysis in the minds of policy-makers has not been very difficult to justify. The "costs" of interfering with completely free trade have meant foregoing long-term expected gains produced in an international economy attaining equilibrium based on comparative advantage concepts. The benefits, on the other hand, were generally related to such short-term issues as support for industries or regions in distress, securing employment, shoring up the balance of payments, or quid-pro-quo deals with other nation-states. Since the benefit side was so much more visible in the equation, and also politically more powerful, we can appreciate the rationale for restricting free trade.

This long tradition of regulating trade is now being tested. The internationalization of production and the evolution of MNC's have produced new institutions challenging the authority of national policy-makers. A review of the evolution of multinationals shows why.

The Rise of Multinationals[24]

Under the umbrella of colonialism a number of European companies established overseas affiliates or subsidiaries as early as the beginning of the last century. Much of this internationalization was geared to resource exploitation and trade between countries and continents. Companies such as Unilever, the East Asiatic Company, Dunlop, Shell, and the like were founded at a time when the transportation and communications systems were slow, unpredictable, and very inadequate. The management style adopted of necessity

---

24. The reader familiar with the evolution of United States big business and multinationals may want to skip to page 113.

came to reflect these realities. These early multinationals therefore were highly decentralized, the subsidiaries were autonomous, and were managed by executives who often would spend their whole career in the field. These subsidiaries tended to adapt totally to local conditions. This is not to say that operating under a colonial umbrella did not represent conflicts. In looking at the early multinational corporation, however, we observe a style that is significantly different from that which has evolved post-World War II—the time when the majority of the United States multinational corporations grew up.[25]

The United States MNC Phenomenon

Historically, we may describe the evolution of United States business as follows:[26]

1. *The rise of big business* (1850 to World War I). After a start around the middle of the century, the rise gained momentum as of 1880. This period saw the large immigration, the railroad boom, and the population of the West all help to create new markets. Entrepreneurs responded to the emerging opportunities, founded corporations, and developed new technologies that have served as the foundation of United States economic growth well into the twentieth century. Large amounts of European capital were imported as part of this growth process.

Although some foreign direct investments were made by United States companies in this period, particularly in Canada and Great Britain, they were of marginal importance. The United States market offered sufficient prospects for growth to make international expansion of secondary importance to most United States managers. Most

---

25. See Lawrence G. Franko, "The Origins of Multinational Manufacturing by Continental European Firms," *Business History Review*, 49 (Autumn 1974), 277–302. John M. Stopford, "The Origins of British-Based Multinational Enterprises," *Business History Review*, 48 (Autumn 1974), 303–335. For an account of individual companies, see Charles Wilson, *The History of Unilever* (London, 1970), W. J. Reader, *Imperial Chemical Industries: A History* (London, 1970), and F. C. Gerritson, *The History of Royal Dutch* (London, 1953).

26. This section draws in part on Alfred D. Chandler, *Strategy and Structure* (Cambridge, Massachusetts, MIT Press, 1962).

of the initial foreign direct investments were aimed at securing raw materials.

At the turn of the century United States foreign direct investments stood at about $750 million. The annual growth rate of such investments until World War I was less than 10 percent. As of the beginning of World War I, 90 percent of United States foreign investments were portfolio, as contrasted with direct, investments.

2. *Diversification and growth* (World War I to World War II). Having overbuilt before World War I and facing the upsets created by the War, United States business until the early 1920's focused on consolidation and rationalization.[27] In this period scientific management, Taylorism, and time and motion studies were employed to reduce costs and increase efficiency. The business orientation was primarily internal and domestic.

The subsequent growth of the economy before the depression led to new expansion. First, companies sought to fill out their major product line. Next, they developed new products, frequently sold to different and unrelated markets. It was a period of growth and diversification. To the majority of firms the overseas markets continued to be relatively unimportant for direct investments. As Mira Wilkins has pointed out, however, many United States companies did become multinational during the 1920's. As of 1929 she identifies 50 United States-owned multinationals with both market-oriented and supply-oriented direct investments abroad.[28] Already these multinationals were a source of foreign policy problems: "When Europeans berated or acted adversely toward American investors *in Europe*, sometimes American business protested to the Embassy or to Washington." [29] As of 1929 the book value of United States foreign direct investments was $8 billion. Nearly half of the manufacturing subsidiaries outside the United States were located in Canada and the United Kingdom.

The 1930's were characterized by virtually no increase in United States foreign direct investments, and the rate dropped to less than one percent. During this period international trade and

---

27. Ibid., pp. 386–387.
28. Wilkins, pp. 143–145.
29. Ibid., p. 159.

business were influenced by the depression, competitive devaluations and great uncertainty, another world war, and the dominance of international cartels.

3. *Exports and international marketing.* After World War II, Europe lay in ruins and lacked capital, foreign exchange, and the necessary institutions for reconstruction. At the end of the War and with the beginning of the Marshall Plan (1948), Europe and other foreign economies began to recover. United States firms possessing the prerequisite technologies, products, and supply capacity became an important part of the reconstruction effort. United States firms were eagerly invited into Europe as well as other countries, since they were perceived as an integrated part of aid, reconstruction, and future prosperity. United States products and technology were seen as an intricate part of the economic development solution. Although this point may be obvious, it is important to keep in mind in view of the changes in attitudes which have since taken place vis-à-vis American companies and their overseas operations.

In the late 1940's and early 1950's United States firms found a ready export market in Europe, part of which was aided by the Marshall Plan and part being a function of the development of the European economies. United States firms gradually came to depend on exports to overseas markets. In industries with a high break-even point these incremental sales had significant impact on profitability. Companies therefore began to commit themselves more to overseas markets. Organizationally, this was expressed by first the appointment of an export manager and next the formation of an international division responsible for international marketing.[30]

As overseas markets continued to expand, the economic feasibility of overseas production improved. This set the stage for international production, which came to replace home-country production and traditional exports business.

In parallel during the late 1940's and early 1950's, United States needs for minerals, energy, and raw materials triggered significant direct investments in order to obtain the supply of these resources. Until 1958 a large portion of the United States investments overseas were in the petroleum industry for exploration and production in

---

30. Gilbert H. Clee and Wilbur M. Sachtjen, "Organizing a Worldwide Business," *Harvard Business Review*, 42 (November–December 1964), 55–67.

Latin America and the Middle East, and for refining and marketing in Europe and Japan.

This was the period where the gap was the greatest between the United States and the rest of the world in technology and management.[31]

4. *The multinational era* (mid-1950's to mid-1970's). By the mid-1950's the problem surrounding the "dollar shortage" had led to a greatly overvalued United States dollar vis-à-vis other currencies. In 1958 European currencies became a central vehicle for international trade and business. As the dollar became overvalued, exports from the United States became increasingly difficult. United States companies found, however, that the same dollars could now buy a relatively larger amount of foreign exchange, hence foreign assets. A number of forces in the international system contributed to make foreign direct investments a substitute for international trade.[32]

The expansion overseas by United States corporations entailed a geographic expansion based on products, technologies, and methods already developed and tested at home. Subsidiaries were set up in different countries to supply the local markets. Few of the initial foreign direct investment decisions were motivated by the prospects for low-cost imports to the United States or large-scale exports to third countries. As such, the subsidiaries and the investments in general were geared to satisfy the host community. Contrary to textbook arguments, these investments were not meticulously planned and they were not part of an integrated worldwide corporate strategy. Instead, companies reacted opportunistically to a set of unique circumstances.

During the early phase of the multinationalization process, United States headquarters played a strong strategic but weak administrative role. Decisions were made at headquarters as to which country to invest in, what product lines to emphasize, what size investments to make, and the general parameters for the new operations. After that much of the responsibility for managing current

31. John H. Dunning, "The Future of the Multinational Enterprise," *Lloyds Bank Review*, 113 (July 1974), 15–32.

32. Neil H. Jacoby, "The Multinational Corporation," in *The Multinational Enterprise in Transition*, A. Kapoor and P. Grub, eds. (Princton, New Jersey, Darwin Press, 1972), pp. 21–52.

operations was vested in the hands of subsidiary management. During the early stages of internationalization almost all the senior executives had their background in the United States home market, which continued to be so overwhelmingly important that it attracted most of their attention. Headquarters management at this stage had little international experience and its involvement was therefore marginal in day-to-day international decision-making control.

For reasons cited above the number of relatively independent subsidiaries grew. The typical corporation realized healthy expansion overseas, with prospects for attractive results and returns. The host countries prospered, too, with the infusion of capital and technology which foreign investments represented.

It is important to keep in mind that *for the short run the foreign direct investment represents a cost to the investor which he is willing to bear in light of expected longer-term returns.* The investor will therefore calculate the present value of short-run costs and investments against the present value of medium-run to long-run returns. *For the host country the cost-benefit picture is reversed.* The host in the short run receives most of the benefit through the infusion of capital, technology, management, and new activities stimulating the economy and contributing to the national welfare. Since much of the host's decision-making is political rather than economic-rational, medium- to long-run costs are usually underestimated or frequently not estimated at all. This helps in part to explain why many host countries become disenchanted and want to renegotiate the investment terms about the time the investor is getting the maximum benefits.

Until the early 1960's, specialization and complementarity received relatively little attention. For this reason, intracompany trading did not take on as important dimensions as they have since. The concern at the outset was getting established in different national markets.

The Drive Toward Maturity

By way of summary, United States MNC's have tended to evolve through a discernible set of stages in their internationalization. It may be useful to think of these as constituting a cycle where each stage represents a unique set of problems and challenges. The following summarizes the basic stages:

1. *The domestic company.* Management shows no concern with foreign markets or operations. All sales are to the home market.

2. *Spot export.* Demand from overseas is satisfied through occasional sales either directly to the customer or through intermediaries such as export houses or brokers. No initiatives for exports are made by the manufacturer. The home market is always served first. If shortages occur, the foreign customers are the first to be cut off.

3. *Regular export.* The manufacturer makes the first commitment to foreign markets by cultivating continuing export sales. At this stage an export manager is usually appointed; he reports to the domestic sales manager. Although of marginal importance, overseas sales begin to be explicitly factored into the budgeting and profit-planning process.

4. *International marketing.* Increased sales overseas tend to require greater investments in international marketing operations. Sales offices and branches are usually set up overseas in key markets. The product may be somewhat adapted to overseas market requirements. The export manager is usually replaced by an international division. At this stage greater commitments are made in terms of people and money to serve the overseas markets. As volume increases, international business becomes more important in considerations such as production scheduling, product development, cash flow planning, and profit contribution. In industries with a high breakeven point, the international sales may *de facto* make the difference between profits or losses.

5. *International production.* The manufacturer makes another major commitment to the foreign markets by establishing manufacturing facilities outside the home country. The rationale for this decision may be multifold: (1) defense against local producers in the export markets, (2) the costs, including transportation and possibly tariffs, making exports uncompetitive, (3) desire for participation in the higher growth realized overseas, and (4) the so-called bandwagon effect. During this stage the manufacturer begins to develop permanent relationships with important foreign stakeholders such as unions and employees, customers and channels of distribution, banks and the financial community, and governments and new host communities.

Initially "domestic" and "international" tend to coexist within the organization, but as the geographic expansion continues, management begins to view the world as the market. With the adoption of such a global perspective, the term "home market" loses some of its meaning. The United States organizationally becomes part of the North American region and is theoretically treated on a par with other regions, such as Europe or Australasia. Investments in the United States are made in light of global strategies and opportunities.

We may compare the recent period of free international production with the period of free international trade experienced some two centuries earlier. Free international production was possible because most subsidiaries were relatively small, the multinationals themselves were in the process of evolving and went largely unnoticed, and the foreign direct investments were a relatively small component of a country's gross national product.

Since the mid- to late 1960's we note significant changes in the evolution and size of the large multinational corporation. In many industries the investment process by now has played itself out, and multinational corporations have completed the entry into most geographic areas of interest. The United Nations study undertaken in 1973–74 shows that the world's twenty-five largest multinational corporations were on the average involved in thirty-two countries. The equivalent number for the ten largest United States multinationals was forty countries.[33]

Two examples illustrate the evolution of United States MNC's. The first is Minnesota Mining and Manufacturing Company (3M).[34] Between 1951 and 1972 3M's overseas net sales increased 44 times, to nearly $800 million; assets increased 91 times to more than $800 million; and exports from the United States increased 29 times to over 100 million. In 1972 more than one third of 3M's total sales were generated internationally. Describing the international expansion, 3M's chairman states:

It was, of course, a very different world market from that which we confront today. Europe and the Far East were still

---

33. *Multinational Corporations.*

34. This example is based on an article by 3M's chairman and chief executive officer, Harry Heltzer: "The World Is the Business of American Business," *Columbia Journal of World Business*, 2 (Spring 1973), 27–32.

largely under the shadow of World War II. The Marshall Plan was in full force and 3M jobs and products began to play a role in the revival of world industry and commerce. Not all overseas subsidiaries showed profits immediately, but investment was small in relation to total assets and growth was strong from the start—as much as 33% in 1955 alone. In 1956, overseas sales topped $50 million. It had taken 3M 40 years to develop a comparable volume in the United States. By 1957 all of 3M's overseas companies were squarely in the profit column. In 1959, worldwide operations were shown on a consolidated basis for the first time in our annual report—a big step toward a truly international outlook and a burying of the "them and us" dichotomy.

Our non-U.S. subsidiaries financed themselves as independent companies whenever possible, and in the currencies of the countries in which they operated. Much of their growth then, as now, came from local reinvestment of retained earnings.

Operations abroad have allowed us to participate in many overseas markets which formerly had been closed to U.S. exports because of trade barriers, and have allowed us to compete effectively in other markets by virtue of being on the scene. . . .

The key to 3M's growth and its prospects for more of the same is that it has become a worldwide company, serving customers in every corner of the globe. No single market in which we are engaged accounts for more than 5% of sales—and each of these markets is highly competitive. A substantial percentage of sales is of products new on the market in the last five years, so improvisation, innovation and new ideas are highly valued. Our research investment was $96 million in 1972, compared with $4.8 million in 1951. During the last five years 3M has invested $400 million in research and development and $575 million in plant construction, a total exceeding $975 million. One-third of this investment, vital seed money, was made possible by 3M's sales abroad. . . .

Overseas we employ over 30,000 people and we are no exception in having had a positive impact. As a multinational company we go to great lengths to cooperate with regional development plans of host governments urging industry to areas of high employment.

The 3M case shows how quickly the company has grown dependent on international markets and production. The momentum if kept up will continue to produce dependencies and relationships of importance to home and host country alike. As an actor in the international system, an MNC such as this will not and cannot be neutral in regard to United States foreign-policy planning and implementation.[35]

The second example of the evolution of a United States multinational is IBM, which conducts its business in 126 countries outside the United States.[36] Maisonrouge of IBM makes these points.

To be truly international, it seems to me, a company should meet these five criteria:
- It must operate in many countries at different levels of economic development.
- Its local subsidiaries must be managed by nationals.
- It must maintain complete industrial organizations, including research and development and manufacturing facilities, in several countries.
- It must have a multinational central management.
- It must have multinational stock ownership.

. . . In the last three years alone, IBM has spent some $2 billion on R&D, the equivalent roughly of half the corporation's net earnings over that period. This need for massive R&D, in turn, impacts our organizational needs, manpower requirements and philosophy of ownership.

For example, it is imperative that our laboratories be located in an advanced industrial environment, for we need a critical mass of scientific and highly skilled manpower. For economic and competitive reasons, our plants must be near our chief markets—the world's industrialized countries. . . .

There was a time when a company could anticipate reasonable, even robust growth within the borders of its home country. If it could also sell its products in one or two other countries,

35. K.-A. Ringbakk, "The Corporate Planning Life Cycle—An International Point of View," *Long Range Planning* (September 1972), pp. 10–20.
36. Jacques G. Maisonrouge, "The Mythology of Multinationalism," *Columbia Journal of World Business*, 9 (Spring 1974), 7–12.

fine. But its primary market was its home country. That time has gone forever, and for several good reasons.

First, certain new social, economic and political facts of life exist. Common information made instantly available to the peoples of the developed countries, for example, has generated the same economic appetites, aspirations and demands. . . .

Second, there has been a growing need to rely on larger markets to support the increasingly sophisticated developmental work characteristic of modern business. . . .

Thirdly, such technological achievements as the jet airplane, satellite communications and computers have made it possible for a company to control far-flung enterprises.

Assessing the evolution, Maisonrouge says:

Twenty-three years later, IBM Corporation grossed $11 billion, $5.14 billion of it overseas, and employed more than 274,000 people worldwide. Within a quarter of a century, therefore, IBM's gross grew over forty-fold, its overseas turnover one-hundred fold, its global population, nine-fold.

IBM's international chief executive concludes: "the inescapable conclusion is that we did not become multinational because we were big; but rather that we became big as a result of going multinational. And what is true of IBM is generally true of other MNC's."

Overseas, IBM's success has not always met with the same kind of enthusiasm. In Europe, governments have found it desirable and necessary to support an international consortium to develop a European computer-industry alternative. In the European Economic Community, an antitrust suit has been filed against IBM charging it with illegal marketing and competitive practices. Corporate information disclosed in the antitrust suit filed by the Telex Corporation reveals much about IBM's strategy and power.

Because many of the documents contain details of IBM's foreign operations and trade negotiations, there is some concern that they may create diplomatic waves, especially in Europe and Japan. IBM is extremely sensitive to its foreign relations. The records show, for instance, that IBM planned three intelligence centers in Europe and Japan to gather and evaluate information on overseas competitors. The minutes also discuss various strategies for maintaining 100% IBM ownership of its overseas operations. While there is no indication of wrongdoing, the internal memos tend to have a high-handed tone that could be politically harmful if taken out of context.[37]

Business Week goes on to observe:

> IBM's raw power comes through clearly in these documents, and some believe that this may frighten customers away from competing producers. Others feel that customers will bridle at the 30%-plus profit margins that IBM makes on some of its products, and will switch to less expensive gear. Many worry that IBM World Trade Corp.'s pretax margin goals of about 30% will inflame foreign governments and may prompt them to take restraining actions that could be detrimental to all multinational computer makers.[38]

The cases of 3M and IBM are success stories supporting the contention that the MNC's are in large measure a recent phenomenon. Their high growth and present dominance suggest, however, that their future is not likely to be more of the same. Specifically, such high-growth MNC's may have their own built-in forces for restriction and limits to growth.[39]

Just as laissez-faire and free international trade came to an end in an earlier period, we can foresee the period of free international production coming to an end in the decade ahead.

Multinational Corporations 1975–1980 and Beyond

In a world of multifold change, for policy-planning to be effective it is necessary to work with *alternative futures*. Through re-iterative forecasting, systematically building into the process different

---

37. "Inside IBM's Management," *Business Week* (July 14, 1973), p. 47.
38. Ibid., p. 47.
39. See, for example, Stephen Hymer, "Is the Multinational Corporation Doomed?" *Innovation*, 28 (1972), 10–17.

assumptions and viewpoints, we can gain a more complete understanding of likely futures. Forecasters and decision-makers can no
longer rely simply on projections and the use of point probabilities.
Instead, sensitivity analysis has to be performed to test the power
and applicability of policy alternatives. In a world characterized by
such profound change, contingency policies and plans gain in importance.[40] The following assessment is meant to contribute one set
of assumptions and viewpoints that may be useful in the overall
policy assessment and planning process.

A number of forces for change at work externally as well as
internally suggest that a mere extrapolative evolution of the MNC is
highly unlikely.[41] It is erroneous to assume that the multinational
corporations in 1980–85 will be like the multinational corporations
in 1970–75, just more so. Instead, we have to consider emerging
processes and potential discontinuities which contribute to changing
the course of events.

A basic argument we will put forward is that the MNC's evolve
through a life cycle and that the largest, well-established ones as of
the mid-1970's have reached a stage we refer to as maturity. By
maturity we understand a state where the corporation has completed
its major geographic expansion—that is, it has entered and established
operations in national markets holding the greatest potential. This
means that additional expansion will come from further marketing,
product development, and other innovations rather than by establishing additional beachheads and doing more of the same in new countries.

We envision MNC's as evolving through the maturity stage and
into an *anational* stage characterized by such multiple influences as
fragmentation, stagnation, retraction, and diminution of headquarters control. As subsidiaries and regional operations become
relatively self-sufficient, they may continue to prosper but without
strong corporate headquarters direction and control.[42]

------

40. "Corporate Planning: Piercing Future Fog," Special Report, *Business
Week* (April 28, 1975).

41. Professor Perlmutter has predicted that some 300 supergiant firms will
totally dominate international business by 1985. This seems an increasingly unlikely outcome. Howard V. Perlmutter, "Super-Giant Firms in the Future,"
Wharton Quarterly, 3 (Winter 1968).

42. The explosive growth in OPEC countries since 1973–74 may at first

A number of multinational corporations are in the process of entering the anational stage, in which conflicts between home and host countries, between headquarters and subsidiaries, between different host countries, and between different subsidiaries have begun to emerge. This new situation will require a fundamental reassessment of the *purpose* of the multinational corporation. The geopolitical shifts and international discontinuities of the early 1970's have produced a fundamental reformulation of the rules of the game. When asked, "What business are you in?" or "What are your objectives and strategy?" the answers in the 1980's will be substantially different from those to date.

It is our contention that the large United States companies which started their international production more than a quarter century ago, or before, by now have reached the maturity stage. Along with this change, the managerial mental set has also grown multinational, and this has a direct bearing on the criteria employed and the decisions made.

By focusing on the financial side of this internationalization process, we can see how extensive the evolution has been. Leading United States corporate stocks are commonly listed on half a dozen European exchanges, as well as the Tokyo exchange. Multinational corporations have borrowed extensively in the Eurobond and Eurodollar markets. In response to this need, United States commercial banks have gone through a parallel internationalization process. In 1960 eight United States banks had 131 foreign branches. By the end of 1972, 108 United States banks (an increase of 1250 percent) had a total of 627 foreign branches. Between 1960 and 1972 total foreign assets of United States banks' foreign operations rose by 1245 percent, from 7.7 billion to 103.6 billion. Furthermore, foreign assets as a proportion of total assets of all insured United States banks rose from 3.01 percent in 1960 to 14.4 percent in 1972.[43] It is worth noting that during this twelve-year period a number of United States

---

suggest that significant new geographic expansion still lies ahead. However, the terms for doing business is countries such as Venezuela and Iran support our argument that free international production is coming to an end. "What the Third World Wants," *Business Week* (October 13, 1975), pp. 56–58. "Venezuela: A Study in Third World Strategy," *Business Week* (October 13, 1975), pp. 59–60.

43. For a set of statistics, see *Multinational Corporations in World Development*, esp. pp. 130–137.

banks became full-fledged multinational corporations in their own right—also driving toward maturity.

The Eurodollar and Eurobond markets grew very rapidly from the mid-1960's, reaching a level of over $132 billion by 1972. As such the international capital market expanded in response to the financing needs of multinational corporations. Analysis of sources and uses of United States funds in the early 1970's shows that the capital outflow from United States parents amounted to less than 10 percent of total sources for overseas subsidiaries. As these overseas affiliates have reached maturity, net income, depreciation, and funds obtained abroad have increased to nearly 90 percent of all sources of funds.

This supports the notion that managers in United States multinational corporations increasingly have come to define their responsibility to a multinational group of stakeholders.[44] Analysis of these stakeholders reveals that the majority may be foreign. A number of multinational corporations realize more than 50 percent of sales outside the United States. Over half the customers are therefore non-United States. The foreign content of production, assets, or employment in many cases are over half of the corporate total. Hence in the majority of host communities where production takes place, owners, lenders, or employees are non-United States.[45] When we combine this with the fact that most of the subsidiary debt and equity are raised outside the home country, we begin to get a measure of where in the MNC life cycle a given corporation finds itself.

Based on these measures, we can see that many so-called *United States*-MNC's are in the process of transcending their maturity stage. Managers recognize this, and we can see it reflected in their behavior. International banking is a case in point of an industry having gone through a very rapid evolution. "For years, bankers could see only the dazzle of international banking: new markets, lush profits, and the glamour of having branches in far-off capitals. But then came 1974 like a cold wind in August, bringing massive and disruptive

---

44. The concept of the stakeholder influences on modern management is well summarized in Charles C. Burck, "The Intricate 'Politics' of the Corporation," *Fortune* (April 1975), pp. 109–112.

45. For a set of statistics, see *Multinational Corporations*, esp. pp. 130–137.

petrodollar flows, ghastly losses in foreign currency trading, and threats of major loan defaults by both private and government borrowers. Suddenly banking abroad has taken on a new cast—a different style of business for what is a different marketplace." [46] Some banks having experienced serious difficulties overseas have simply reduced or withdrawn from foreign operations. Others are seeking new strategies to generate income while avoiding undue exposures. Two new trends are fee-based income and project-financing, where the banks are involved in financing vast projects such as chemical plants, pipelines, or minority projects (ibid., p. 102). In either case the banks will be working much more closely with such stakeholder groups as customers, governments, suppliers, and host communities.

In the course of 1974 I had the opportunity to interview executives from multinational oil companies in the United States and Europe. At that time I learned that these international executives believed it was their responsibility to minimize the effects of the oil embargo that has been imposed on certain countries. While the members of the EEC experienced strained relations when some countries figuratively "disowned" The Netherlands, the large multinational oil corporations used their sophisticated computer-based models to distribute equitably the reduced supplies of oil. This helps explain why a country such as The Netherlands was not hurt more severely by these shortages.

This leads us to the issue of nationality and allegiance of companies. In recent years MNC's have made increased use of joint ventures, hence accepting less than 100 percent ownership in subsidiaries. Interviews with United States managers reveal that they have come to accept the use of joint-venture strategies to enter new markets such as Japan or Iran. In many instances the government of the host country or government-owned institutions are the joint-venture partner. These partners enter into the joint venture with objectives which frequently are different from those of the foreign investor. In the case of the government partners, national objectives and macro considerations predominate. These commonly relate to the acquisition of new technology, avoiding foreign dominance of

---

46. "The Swinging Days Are Over Overseas," *Business Week* (April 21, 1975), p. 98.

certain sectors of the economy, fostering regional development, or supporting growth and employment in the country. Profits per se are rarely the prime motivating force.

The foreign investor on the other hand is guided by economic and micro objectives. He is willing to accept the loss of control as the price of entry. The net result is that the joint venture is subject to pressures of the host country which the foreign investor may be unable to withstand or control. If a technology, say nuclear energy, has been transferred from the United States parent to such a joint venture and the government in the joint-venture country wants to sell the technology to a third country, there is very little the United States company can do to prevent it from happening.

In sum, many United States and non-United States multinational corporations are maturing and have overseas affiliates and subsidiaries that are full-fledged companies in their own right. If not on a national level, then on a continent-wide or regional level, they have fully integrated operations. A United States multinational corporation may have subsidiaries in Europe which individually or jointly could be self-sufficient. They perform their own research and development and their own production and marketing as well as such auxiliary functions as staffing, sourcing, financing, and the like. Thus the European part of many United States multinational corporations is largely independent and able to stand on its own feet, producing both new challenges for management and new intra-MNC strains.

Intra-MNC Strains

A change in management style whereby more *centralized* multinational corporate planning is done can be observed in many MNC's. This is beginning to create new intra-corporation strains. As national subsidiaries grow into full-fledged companies in their own right, subsidiary management seeks increased autonomy and control. Subsidiary managers in charge of country operations are frequently referred to as "kings" or "rulers." National managers typically are responsible for the performance of subsidiaries or national affiliates and have enjoyed substantial autonomy. The accepted notion has been that authority should be commensurate with the level of responsibility. This practice is in effect being renegotiated when corporate management seeks to maximize the efficiency of the total corporate system through the imposition of top-down rules and policies.

What is good and appropriate from a subsidiary point of view frequently is not in the best interest of the corporate total. In search of maximum efficiency or optimal allocation multinationally of corporate resources, central management has to superimpose decisions on subsidiary management. Although this may be appropriate from a corporate point of view, these decisions frequently do not sit well with subsidiary managers. Comparative differences in management values, cultures, and styles contribute to intra-MNC's pulls and strains.

Over the past several years I have had the opportunity to work with and observe managers in a large number of corporations. Based on this experience, I identify different kinds and sources of strains and conflicts. As demands and requirements are placed on affiliates or subsidiaries from headquarters, some adopt a minimum-response stance: carrying on business as usual but doing the minimum necessary to comply with the new requests. Some simply take a wait-and-see attitude, to find out how important the new corporate requirements are and how serious top management is on instituting change. In some instances this may be because of unwillingness to comply; in others it is because of the inability to do so. The introduction of multinational, organized, corporate-planning systems is a case in point. The imposition by top management of new planning requirements on subsidiaries has frequently created a set of such conflicts. Multinational, organized, corporate planning represents a change in management. The need to state assumptions and to identify how decisions are made in terms of objectives and decision criteria and the need to employ formal approaches to decision-making, have not been well received by many executives. In the area of organized corporate-planning systems, MNC's have experienced various problems in getting the activity started. In many instances internal conflicts have ensued when subsidiaries and affiliates have not complied with headquarters demands.[47]

The questions of top-down versus bottom-up decision-making

---

47. K.-A. Ringbakk, pp. 10–20.

and who should be responsible and involved in various kinds of decisions are at the heart of the conflict. Corporate management seeking improved performance from the multinational corporate system as a whole will want subsidiaries to operate according to corporate-wide criteria and strategies. This requires subordination, which many subsidiaries in turn find hard to accept. It is interesting to note that some regulations considered or applied by host governments may work in favor of subsidiary management and support their desire for autonomy.[48]

Most companies having entered Japan have done so via the joint venture route and their experience tells them non-Japanese business approaches do not work well in Japan. Managerially, success in large part depends on the ability to manage the subsidiary or joint venture in a Japanese style. Discussion I conducted with nearly 50 executives in Japan in 1974 supported this point: The Japanese culture and business practices are so pervasive and well established that substantial conformity by the outsider is required to be successful. This means that multinational corporations entering and operating in Japan have to accept that the Japanese companies will behave differently from the rest of the system. Direct transfers of management practices and strategies to Japan are not successful. Multinational corporation management has to accept a split corporate personality. However, this often is in conflict with the desire on the part of United States managers to obtain uniformity and similarity in their management system.

In less developed countries we observe that management within subsidiaries frequently identifies less with headquarters than with other peer groups. In such countries managerial talent is attracted from a small educated elite, and they sometimes appear to have a split loyalty. On the one hand, they work for the multinational corporation subsidiary and are expected to conform to its needs and to its management system. On the other hand, they ideologically and culturally associate with national objectives and aspirations. Some

---

48. For example, the Australian government in 1973–74 made use of a variable deposit clause causing Australian subsidiaries to be cut off from the free international financial flows with the remainder of the MNC. The consequence has been that these subsidiaries have been forced to develop greater self-sufficiency and hence independence in financial matters.

come to see the subsidiary as an instrument of host-country development and begin consciously or unconsciously to make decisions with that point of view in mind. In the developing country the political side of doing business is relatively more important than in the industrialized countries. Since the interaction with ministries and government officials is much more intense and more of an ongoing process, managers in such subsidiaries become further exposed to and cognizant of the national side of the equation. This also influences their behavior.

In sum, as corporations have become more international in orientation and as subsidiaries have been set up in different countries, the MNC affiliates have become an integral part of the host-country industrial structure. The initial entry decisions have usually been strategic, concerning such matters as where the facilities should be located, what technology and processes should be employed in light of costs and availability of resources, what the scale of operations and the size of investments should be, and what degree of integration should be sought. The long life of modern manufacturing assets and the specialized nature of plant and equipment have been important considerations affecting the decisions.

Once foreign operations are established, management no longer has the option to switch production to low-cost areas. With high break-even points and pressures from multiple stakeholder groups, management is forced to operate the existing units at the most economic levels, meaning close to capacity. Closing plants, rationalizing product lines, and changing locations virtually ceases to be an option for the company. Vested interests on the part of employees, governments, host communities, suppliers, lenders, and the like contribute to the pressure put on management to extend the life of investments and to continue local operations. When the needs of the host country so dictate, pressures are also put on the subsidiary to reinvest earnings in the country, to diversify, and to channel more of the corporate growth back into the host country. Host governments rely on frequent renegotiations of contracts with foreign investors to induce them to invest more, to become more like indigenous companies, and to develop what amounts to further allegiance to that country rather than elsewhere. Subsidiary management in a case like this is bound to experience conflicts with headquarters or other parts of the MNC system.

While the intra-multinational corporation strains may not appear significant, they do represent a factor that will make it increasingly difficult to behave in completely unified ways. Internal dissent will potentially lengthen decision processes, will reduce MNC synergies, and may represent a negative force in the MNC system. In areas like Canada, Scandinavia, and Australia, where national sentiment has turned against multinationals, some subsidiary managers have begun to look at how to behave in light of increased independence from the multinational corporate system. The external forces discussed in the following section will in many cases reinforce the above argument that multinational corporations in the future will behave less like unified systems, and that subsidiaries and affiliates will become more independent just as the multinational corporation at large will grow more anational.

External Pressures and Restraining Forces

This section reviews some forces for change which may have the effect of restraining, altering, or halting the expansion of multinational corporations. The most important are host country demands and pressures and the general forces of nationalism. Growing nationalism worldwide has begun to influence governments in their regulation of international business. This phenomenon can be observed in less developed as well as more developed countries. As one result, host-country governments have become much more active in negotiating with foreign investors not only the terms of entry but also ongoing operations. Intensified host-country influence and demands are emerging as a global phenomenon.

For example, in 1968 as drilling in the North Sea proved large oil deposits, the Norwegian government insisted on participation in any discoveries on terms that were virtually without financial risk to the government. A Norwegian spokesman stated that the government's policy "is simply one of getting the best possible return from the country's natural resources." "Our aim," said the spokesman, "is to find a ceiling—the best offer that the oil companies are willing to accept."[49]

---

49. Quoted in Harold Burton Myers, " 'Blue-Eyed Arabs' Scramble for the Riches of the North Sea," *Fortune* (June 1973), pp. 140–145 et seq.

As of the early 1970's, host countries were employing a number of strategies to maximize their returns from foreign direct investments. As attitudes and bargaining strengths shifted, host countries appeared more successful than in previous efforts. Both developed and developing countries have been imposing more stringent requirements on foreign firms to gain a larger share of benefits.[50] Bergsten argues that "host-country efforts are now far more likely to succeed because of fundamental shifts in the world economic and political environment that have put many host countries in a far stronger position than before."[51] He goes on to say that foreign firms "can no longer dictate, or even heavily influence, host-country policies as they may have done in the past; the *dependencia* syndrome, under which foreign and domestic elites collude against the national interests of host countries, is rapidly disappearing."[52]

The most radical changes in the relations between MNC's and host countries have taken place in relationship with OPEC members. In the span of a few short years the multinational oil companies have lost much of their control over production facilities, over production scheduling, and over pricing strategy. The oil-producing nations first insisted on part ownership of the MNC production subsidiaries in their countries, followed by a remarkably rapid drive for absolute ownership and control. However, by mid-1975 many of the oil-producing nations backed off from their most extreme demands, recognizing that they could not accomplish their development strategies without help from the oil companies.

The same multinational oil companies have met with new regulation and challenges in the consuming countries also. Several countries have sought national participation in the marketing of oil through state-owned oil companies. Many of these same countries have closed important bilateral deals to secure oil from, for example, the Middle East. When the heads of countries such as France and Iran close deals in a magnitude of $3-5 billion, the strategic initiative has been lifted from the corporate to the national level.

---

50. C. Fred Bergsten, "Coming Investment Wars?" *Foreign Affairs*, 53 (October 1974), 135-152.

51. Ibid., p. 137.

52. Ibid., p. 138.

In discussing the future of the multinational oil companies a senior planning executive observed:

> Our legitimacy in the past was based on our ability to provide technology, move finance, manage across borders, and to move oil. As of now control over the ability to move oil is less important. At the same time other institutions have grown up capable of handling the financial side.
>
> That leaves management and technology. This by the way is not unique to the oil industry. If we in the future can provide services on the basis of management and technology, the MNC is an ideal institution. Our future therefore depends on the quality of the management services and the technology we can provide.[53]

Venezuela is a case in point. As of January 1, 1975, she nationalized the iron ore industry, involving United States Steel and Bethlehem Steel. On the occasion of the nationalization Venezuelan President Carlos Andres Perez addressed his countrymen:

> We have nationalized the iron industry, not to withdraw it from international cooperation, but to deliver it to the construction of an independent and authentically sovereign fatherland, struggling for a world where international justice will open a path for the well-being of the peoples that are oppressed, subject to exploitation or denied their right to the self-determination, not only of their sovereignty but also of their own national destiny. We have nationalized the iron industry to transform it, in Venezuela, by Venezuelan workers, for the benefit and well-being of our countrymen, and to place the fruits of our labor at the service of the whole of mankind.
>
> We have acted with serene responsibility. Venezuela cannot assume in these crucial moments of its life unnecessary risks that might lead us to adversities and anxieties we do not have to suffer. We owe it not only to ourselves but to the very fate of Latin America.

---

53. Interview conducted by the author in 1974 as part of a study of multinational planning and strategy.

The decisions to nationalize the iron industry, as well as that of oil, not to allow ourselves to be manipulated from the great financial centers of the world, and to set just prices for our raw materials and basic commodities, are supported by the vast majority of our people as conduct inspired by the nationalist and Latin American conscience of Venezuela.[54]

Late in 1974 Venezuela also offered to make some of the surplus oil revenue available to other Latin American countries, in order to cross-subsidize agricultural crops and commodities.

In late 1974 Jamaica moved to nationalize the bauxite industry. This followed an earlier decision to increase by 800 percent the tax United States aluminum companies paid on Jamaican bauxite.[55]

The example set by OPEC has stimulated similar resource cartels elsewhere. The International Bauxite Association is now feared by some companies as much as OPEC.[56]

The significance of these developments to the evolution of multinationals is clear. First, MNC's are increasingly hard pressed to protect or hold on to existing property in various resource-rich countries. In the face of nationalization or outright expropriation, repercussions will follow which the foreign-policy makers must be attuned to.

Second, MNC's are under pressure to produce more value added in the resource-rich country, and they are required to export more semi-manufactures and finished goods. This will influence the MNC relationship with other host countries and with the home country if it disturbs existing export markets or if imports begin to replace existing production.

Finally, foreign direct investments are less welcome and MNC's are no longer able to fill the traditional role of bridging resource

54. As quoted in "The Venezuelan Views," advertisement in special international section, *New York Times* (January 26, 1975), p. F75.

55. "The Caribbean: Moving in on Foreign Resource Companies," *Business Week* (November 30, 1974), pp. 38–39.

56. For an assessment of the prospects for resource cartels, see C. Fred Bengsten, "The New Era in World Commodity Markets," *Challenge* (September–October, 1974), pp. 34–42. For a discussion of the United States dependence on raw materials imports, see Donald B. Thompson, "Our Dependence on Imported Materials," *Industry Week* (October 7, 1974), pp. 32–38.

markets with use markets. This may cause some MNC's to over-commit themselves to the resource-rich countries in terms of capital and technology transfers. That in turn will contribute to shifting some of the international business decisions from the corporate level into government hands.

In general, a conflict between the sovereign state and the multinational corporation is coming to a head where the conflict resolution seems to lie in greater give and accommodation on the part of the multinational. In the past, multinational corporations could threaten to locate investment and production elsewhere if terms were not met. In the 1970's this is becoming increasingly impossible, in part because the MNC's are already established in the most important markets. Host countries, either alone or in concert, are demonstrating stronger political and economic nationalism. As a consequence, multinational corporations have lost much of their bargaining power. Canada is one country where the terms for foreign investment have been rapidly changing. Over 50 percent of Canadian manufacturing industry is foreign-owned. This is very much resented, and there is increasing evidence that Canadian control is becoming a primary objective. "A fundamental economic objective of Canada is the development of industry that is both innovative and Canadian controlled. Without innovation there is no economic growth. But without Canadian control, the viability of the country as a sovereign state is at risk."[57]

The United Nations hearings on MNC's conducted in 1973-74 brought out the fact that important stakeholder groups such as home countries, host countries, labor, consumer interests, and even the multinational corporations themselves are concerned about the "fundamental new problems (that) have arisen as a direct result of the growing internationalization of production as carried out by multinational corporations."[58] The United Nations outlines several conflicts between the sovereign state and the multinational corporation:

---

57. Harold Crookill and Leonard Wrigley, "Canadian Response to Multinational Enterprise," *Business Quarterly*, 40 (Spring 1975), 58.

58. *The Impact of Multinational Corporations on Development and on International Relations*, United Nations, ST/ESA/6 (New York, 1974), p. 26.

Most of the problems connected with multinational corporations stem from their distinctive transnational features in a world that is divided into separate sovereign States. As we have observed, multinational corporations have developed important capacities which can be put to the service of world development. Yet, these same capacities can also be used in ways which may conflict with the interests of individual States. While Governments pursue a variety of economic and non-economic objectives to advance the welfare of their citizens, the chief goals of multinational corporations like those of all business enterprises, are profit and growth. The differing objectives of nation-States and multinational corporations suggest that their respective decisions will not always be in harmony with each other.

The exercise of direct control over the allocation of one country's resources by residents of another—forcefully expressed to us by representatives of developed and developing countries as a matter of considerable political concern—makes the task of harmonizing varying interests and the promotion of the public good by Governments especially complex. Advances in communications technology allow many multinational corporations to pursue global strategies which, rather than maximizing the profits or growth of individual affiliates, seek to advance the interest of the enterprise as a whole. Lack of harmonization of policies among countries, in monetary or tax fields for example, allows multinational corporations on occasion to utilize their transnational mobility to circumvent national policies or render them ineffective. It is in this context that countries may find their national sovereignty infringed upon and their policy instruments blunted by the operations of multinational corporations.

In the process of conducting their normal business activities, multinational corporations make decisions which may have far-reaching consequences for the societies in which they operate. They affect patterns of consumption and the direction of innovation; they orient technological change and investment; and they own or produce most of the basic commodities used in industry and commerce; intentionally or unintentionally, they can affect political processes of both home and host countries.

Decisions on the allocation of resources, with respect to what, how, and for whom to produce, are usually made by corporate planning mechanisms situated in a few industrial countries. The size and scope of the larger multinational corporations make it possible for a few large firms to control substantial shares of local and sometimes world markets. Because of this, and their transnational flexibility, they can engage in export market allocation, price discrimination, and transfer pricing, place stringent conditions on the transfer of technology and patents, and enter into cartel agreements that reduce competition.[59]

This U.N. report argues that multinational corporations are in such a strong position that a special U.N. commission on multinational corporations ought to be established to promote a series of international agreements to regulate them. It also recommends that a special U.N. office should be set up to collect and analyze information on multinationals in order that regulation at the international as well as the national level could be facilitated. The U.N. study in general presents a picture of multinational corporations portrayed as powerful agents able to upset the international system, hence able to turn tensions to personal corporate gains.[60]

One writer's reaction to this was "the United Nations report is obviously a time bomb ticking in the wings at least as far as the investment future of the multinational corporations is concerned.—It looks like the heyday of their growth is past. Multinationals have more danger signs looming on their investment horizon than at any time since World War II."[61]

The developments whereby host governments are negotiating more aggressively with multinational corporations is a sign of things to come. Host countries having experienced success, and reinforced by the so-called demonstration effect, have begun concentrated efforts to redress whatever imbalances the multinational corporations are perceived as having at least in part created.

The following list suggests the kinds of demands host countries are placing on foreign direct investors:

---

59. Ibid., p. 30.

60. See *Multinational Corporations*, chapter 3, pp. 42-74.

61. John F. Lyons, "Multinationals: Reaching the Outer Limits?" *Financial World* (October 17, 1973), p. 39.

• Increased exports to improve the foreign-exchange and balance-of-payments position.

• Reduced imports of components, parts, and supplies where local suppliers can be used or developed.

• Demand for increased value-added on exports. Reduced exports of basic raw materials. Further backward integration and the buildup of more integrated production units in the country.

• Reduced use of expatriates at all levels. Development and employment of locals for technical, skilled, and managerial positions.

• Subordinating corporate strategy to host country objectives and adjusting to national plans, although at the expense of synergies and efficiencies in the multinational corporation system.

• Demand for assistance and aid to help with balance-of-payments deficits and to help develop the infrastructure. (As a case in point, Brazil in 1974 put pressure on Japan to provide aid in addition to the heavy stream of foreign direct investments from Japan.)

• Fostering indigenous competition. Government is lending increasing support to local companies to counterbalance the multinational corporations. In Europe this has taken the form of support for transnational mergers as well as specific support for industries such as aerospace and computers to match the United States challenge.

In general, as investments mature, the romance declines, perceptions change, and there is a new questioning as to the value and contribution of foreign investments and MNC's. This, combined with a changed capability on the part of the host country, has begun to produce added pressures for more select investments, sharing of ownership, and local management and control. Host countries have improved their bargaining power and are making more effective use of it. We expect this to continue.[62] Subsidiaries and affiliates of multinational corporations increasingly are found to adjust and adapt

---

62. *Dun's*, "Canada: A New Chile in the North?" (June 1973), pp. 84–85. John C. Culver, "Foreign Investment in the United States," *Foreign Policy* (Fall 1974), pp. 157–164. D'Arcy O'Connor, "Moving In: Britain's Burmah Oil Expands Role in U.S., Alarms Some Critics," *Wall Street Journal* (October 14, 1974).

to host-country demands even if these are in conflict with home-country-or corporate objectives (which has already begun to happen).

As multinationals have come under an attack that is fostering suspicion, scrutiny, and increased regulation, management, becoming more cautious, has begun to make extra effort to accommodate new demands. Whether all the charges levied against MNC's are true or not, management frequently has to go out of its way to prove its innocence.

In conclusion, national welfare and economic activity will grow much more closely interrelated in the years ahead. Home and host countries have already become more directly involved in international business and trade. The many bilateral deals recently concluded are one example of this.

The relative freedom MNC's have enjoyed during the past two decades will be constrained and subordinated to home and host country regulations.[63] The period of free international production has passed. In the years ahead some MNC functions will be rendered superfluous as governments engage in more economic planning and as economic transactions are decided between governments and heads of state. MNC's will experience further loss of facilities as host countries demand control over local industries. The recent takeover of production facilities by OPEC countries and others point to the intent and desires on the part of host countries. The nationalization of major industries in Great Britain, for example, shows this can happen in developed home countries as well.

The beginnings of an uneasy relationship between nations and MNC's can be observed today. It is producing new tension and conflicts. In the short run unilateral actions are likely to predominate whenever the home or host country perceives them to be in its best interest. The MNC will be faced with demise if it fails to adapt, adjust, and modify its behavior to meet these new demands.[64]

---

63. See Stefan H. Robock, "The Case for Home Country Controls over Multinational Firms," *Columbia Journal of World Business*, 9 (Summer 1974), 75–79.

64. Joseph S. Nye, Jr., "Multinational Corporations in World Politics," *Foreign Affairs*, 53 (October 1974), 153–175.

Foreign Policy Issues

A number of foreign-policy questions and issues can be raised in connection with MNC's. While few clearcut foreign-policy options readily emerge, it is possible to single out areas where policy-makers need to direct their attention.

First, in today's world of international production and multinational corporations, worldwide inflation, conflict surrounding the availability and price of resources, and a host of interdependent complex problems, better international economic leadership is needed. A group of distinguished writers have argued that 1974 was largely lost and that "there is barely enough time for a quiet sorting out of the interacting influence of trade, prices, aid, and investment." [65]

The United States as a leading economy, as the most dominant home and host country for foreign direct investments and MNC's, and as a major exporter and importer has to get its own options and policies straight. For the United States policy-makers this raises some questions: What international economic posture can and should the United States develop for the future? What economic linkages do we want to foster for the 1980's and beyond? What export base should we prepare? What imports will we be dependent on and how do we secure these in the years ahead? In general, we need to determine what strengths to build on and what general strategy to follow.

The United States has the opportunity to take initiatives which will influence the world economy as a whole, international trade and production in general, and the United States position within this. The United States is *de facto* so important that *what it does or does not do* may produce equally significant responses in the international system. While these points may be self-evident and obvious, they need to be said, because United States foreign-policy behavior does not reflect this fact. "The evident gaps in all our traditional foreign-policy arrangements plainly show that the U.S. needs to develop a new strategy, adapting old traditions to the new problems of a new age." [66]

---

65. K. Farmanfarmaian, A. Gubowski, S. Okita, R. V. Roosa, and C. L. Wilson, "How Can the World Afford OPEC Oil?" *Foreign Affairs*, 53 (January 1975), 222.

66. A. James Reichley, "Foreign Policy in an Era of Interdependence," *Fortune* (April 1975), p. 157.

This points to the importance of choosing *objectives* for future United States policy. Policy-makers have to take into account the asymmetrical position of the United States in which United States exports are only 5 percent of the Gross National Product but 15 percent of International Trade. Domestic choices have far-reaching international consequences, whether desired or not. Controls imposed on, for example, agricultural exports will, in the short run, produce long-term reactions in the international system. What objectives are adopted will depend in large measure on who is responsible for formulating them.

That brings us to the next point. United States foreign economic policy generally is formulated and implemented in a suboptimal fashion. The process seems to be inadequately managed and lacking in coordination and integration. On the issue of East-West trade departments such as State, Commerce, Treasury, Agriculture, and the Federal Reserve, special units, as well as the White House and Congress, have all been actively involved in the process. That raises the question whether the involvement can be improved through a central strategic-planning body. Can corporate-planning experiences from private enterprise be applied to bridge gaps, avoid overlaps, and secure a more orderly approach to foreign economic-policy formulation and implementation? This may be part of a larger question regarding the benefit of better planning at the national level. If such planning has proved useful in managing large enterprise, can some of the experiences be transferred to foreign economic-policy planning?

With regard to the United States as a host country, the following kinds of questions have to be dealt with: How freely can foreigners invest in the United States? Can they take over such major companies as Exxon, General Motors, and IBM, or will the capital placement be regulated? Will private and public investors be treated equally? Will European, Mid-East, Japanese, and communist investors be treated equally? Will all sectors of the economy be open to foreign direct investments? Will takeovers, joint ventures, and projects started from scratch be treated the same way? What will be the limits on foreigners wanting to enter? What criteria are to be applied? Who will develop and who will enforce these criteria?

The United States has been and continues to be a very attractive country for foreign investors. There are multiple reasons for this: large markets, sophisticated technology, advanced manufacturing and marketing systems, support and incentives provided by state and local authorities, as well as general stability. The reduced value of the dollar and the depressed stock market provide added incentives at least at this point in time. Given the desire on the part of outsiders to enter the United States, questions like the ones above have to be answered.

From the point of view of the United States as a home country to MNC's, important policy questions also arise. Many have been identified in this paper. The following suggest the kinds of issues policy-makers will have to address:

How free will United States companies be in their future international expansion in terms of transfers of capital and technology? Will the United States government support United States-based MNC's if there is increased nationalization and pressure for "localization"? What will be the United States response when foreign companies receive government support and United States companies can no longer compete as in the case of Pan Am? To what extent will export bans and quotas imposed on United States companies result in long term restrictions elsewhere? As resource-rich nations seek control over facilities established and owned by United States-MNC's, what will be the United States response? How can MNC's be made to behave globally in line with home country interests? As MNC facilities or executives are "kidnapped" or held for ransom, what is the United States responsibility? How can wrongdoings and misbehavior on the part of MNC's be regulated?

The behavior of MNC's has come under severe scrutiny and attack during the past years. Many nations have taken unilateral measures to regulate the MNC's. This could lead to loss of economic welfare and it will create new upsets in the international system. This raises another set of questions: What regulation is necessary? Should the United States support a code of conduct for MNC's? Should the U.N. proposals for a commission on MNC's be supported or should the United States take the initiative to multilateral negotiations leading to a general agreement on MNC's à la GATT? What should be done to prevent unilateral actions leading to overregulation while at the same time preventing MNC's from wrongdoings?

The most specific recommendation we can make is to invest more in strategic analysis and planning to identify and establish priorities among the critical questions. Specifically we would like to *recommend that a strategic long-range planning effort be launched to*

• clarify United States foreign economic policy objectives;

• develop a better understanding of the driving and restraining forces shaping the world economy;

• identify alternative options open to the United States and assess the cost-benefit of these;

• formulate a set of strategies to be followed by the United States vis-à-vis the world economy at large, in multilateral negotiations in general, and toward foreign direct investments and multinational corporations in particular.

Policy-makers to date have been frustrated by the paucity of data and measures on the scope and nature of MNC's. The strategic long-range planning recommended here is premised upon *ongoing* analysis and surveillance of major forces for change to gain an adequate understanding of opportunities and challenges relative to United States strengths and capabilities. Specifically, the quality of the planning effort will depend directly on the quality of the inputs. The inputs are of two kinds: information and people. Although specialist staff can be used, it is imperative to involve the senior policy-makers from the outset. What we are advocating is a policy-making group made up of the true "line executives" and headed by the President or the Vice President of the United States.[67] The Policy Planning Staff in the State Department in James Reston's view is well staffed and used. However, the scope of its authority by definition is limited to the authority of State.[68]

This recommendation is based on the argument that the posture

---

67. Since I wrote the first version of this chapter for the State Department, in the fall of 1974, this notion of national planning has received some support: "The Need to Plan for Economic Policy," editorial, *New York Times* (February 23, 1975); "Time for Economic Planning," editorial, *Christian Science Monitor* (March 3, 1975); "Diverse Group Advocates Economic Planning for U.S.," *New York Times* (February 28, 1975).

68. James Reston, "The Policy Planners," *New York Times* (February 19, 1975).

adopted by the United States will significantly affect the international system in the years ahead. To keep a low profile and do nothing may not be in the United States interest—it may not even be a viable option. This paper has shown that the issues of foreign direct investment, multinational corporations, and international trade are highly interdependent and too significant to treat lightly. We believe a strategic-planning approach to foreign economic-policy formulation is one way to deal with the complex issues involved.

EDITOR'S NOTE

For some the "new international economic order" is a goal to be sought (or avoided). For others it is a reality to be adjusted to. For all it symbolizes the third world's continuing search for improved economic status.

Bargaining with multinational corporations and bargaining about special marketing arrangements for their exports are two issues that will be prominent in third world policies during the next five years. Professor Mazur examines these issues in the context of the call for a "new international economic order" and identifies some implications for American foreign policy.

V.
The Developing Countries in the World Economy: A Question of Bargaining Power?

Michael P. Mazur

Something seems to be happening to the economic relations between the developing countries and the developed countries. In the spring of 1974 the United Nations adopted a "Declaration on the Establishment of a New International Economic Order," which proposed measures for the reordering of economic relationships between the less developed countries (LDC's) and the developed world.[1] In that declaration the "new international economic order" was a goal, not a current reality and perhaps not even a future likelihood. Some observers have suggested, however, that because of major changes in the world economic environment a realigned relationship between the LDC's and the developed world either is already upon us or is fast closing in.[2]

The concept of a new international economic order does not have the same meaning to all who envision it. And frequently, as in the U.N. declaration, the concept is so all-encompassing, and occasionally ambiguous, that it is difficult to perceive its essential features. Nonetheless, it is possible to discern one predominant theme. In the years of greatest optimism about the prospects for development of the LDC's, primarily the 1950's and early 1960's, development was widely conceived to be a harmonious venture of cooperation between developed countries and LDC's. It was expected

---

1. For the text of the declaration see *UN Monthly Chronicle*, 11 (May 1974), 66–84.
2. See, e.g., C. Fred Bergsten, "The Response to the Third World," *Foreign Policy*, 17 (Winter 1974–75), pp. 3–34.

that the developed countries—at relatively little cost to themselves—could start the LDC's on a trajectory of self-sustained growth, which would ultimately have beneficial feedback effects on the developed economies. These overly sanguine hopes were not fulfilled.

Coming in the wake of the inevitable scaling down of hopes for fast and painless LDC development, the vision of a new international economic order apparently rejects as unrealistic the idea of development as harmonious and mutually beneficial to developed and less developed countries alike. It would be putting it too strongly to say that the concept of a new economic order sees the development process as an adversary relationship between the LDC's and the developed world, but there is a heightened stress on the position of LDC's in relation to the developed countries and on measures to redistribute wealth from the developed countries to the LDC's.[3] The new emphasis can be seen in the preoccupation with the "widening gap" between LDC's and developed countries, the hopes for cartels among LDC raw material exporters to emulate the apparent success of the OPEC (Organization of Petroleum Exporting Countries) oil cartel, and the stress on trade concessions from the developed countries to the LDC's. The new emphasis was strengthened not only by the success of OPEC, but also by the widespread acceptance, rightly or wrongly, of the concept of imminent "limits to growth."[4] If world economic growth were to reach a limit, economic growth of the LDC's could be only at the expense of the developed countries.

Even before this view of a reordered world economy gained currency, it was recognized that some of the most important relationships of the LDC's with the developed world were at bottom bargaining relationships. This was particularly true for LDC relations with multinational corporations. But it was the success of OPEC in increasing the price of oil that brought the concept of LDC bargaining power to the forefront of the thinking of LDC's about their development prospects.

Two of the most important issues in LDC relations with the developed world, both of them integral parts of the concept of a new

---

3. A similar analysis has been made by John P. Lewis, "Oil, Other Scarcities, and the Poor Countries," *World Politics*, 27 (October 1974), 65–70.

4. Donella H. Meadows et al., *The Limits to Growth* (New York, Universe Books, 1972).

international economic order, are the relations of LDC's with multinational corporations and the pricing of LDC primary product exports. For both of these issues the question of bargaining power is paramount. This paper examines these two issues in the context of bargaining power.

I. THE DEVELOPING COUNTRIES AND THE MULTINATIONAL CORPORATION

The rapid proliferation of the multinational corporation (MNC) confronts national governments with vital questions of public policy, but the nature of these problems differs between developed countries and LDC's. In the developed countries the primary problem is the challenge to national economic sovereignty posed by an institution which by definition spans more than one national jurisdiction. The MNC may use its ability to transfer resources and activities between countries to reduce the degree to which it is subject to any national jurisdiction. It may attempt to evade the regulations of one government by using affiliates in countries with less stringent requirements. This possibility may cause a nation to extend its jurisdiction to the point where it comes into conflict with that of another state, as in the case of extraterritorial application of United States antitrust law and trading-with-the-enemy acts. The ultimate threat to national economic sovereignty is the possibility that nations, in an effort to attract the MNC, will compete against each other in offering concessions to such an extent that national regulations shrink to impotence. This would tend to reduce the nation-state toward the level of economic sovereignty of an American state or Canadian province.

For the developed countries, the most important specific problems posed by the MNC probably are those of antitrust policy, government measures to attract foreign direct investment, and corporate taxation. Because the United States has the most stringent antitrust laws of any major economy, conflicts of national sovereignty may arise when the United States extends its jurisdiction to the subsidiaries abroad of United States MNC's or through the United States subsidiaries of foreign MNC's to the parent firm abroad. To attract MNC subsidiaries to locate in particular countries, governments may grant various forms of tax relief and direct or indirect subsidies, whose end result may be not to change the location of MNC activity, but to eliminate most of the benefit that might have accrued to host-country governments, as different countries simply bid up each others' offers. Taxation of the profits of MNC's is complicated by the possibility that MNC's may transfer profits, as recorded in their accounting statements, from one country to another by manipulation of intracorporate payments. These issues, important as they are or may become for the developed countries, are not currently the most important ones for the LDC's.

It is widely recognized that foreign direct investment is carried out mainly by firms in oligopolistic industries—that is, industries concentrated in the hands of a few firms.[5] This fact does not mean that the entry of an oligopolistic MNC into an LDC economy necessarily reduces competition in that economy. In fact, there is a general presumption that the entry of the new MNC competitor will increase competition, although this is not always the case. Nor does it mean that antitrust legislation is a key issue in LDC relations with the MNC, as it is for the developed countries. The LDC's are not much threatened by the extension of antitrust legislation from MNC home countries into the jurisdiction of the LDC's, mainly because indigenous firms of the LDC's have little chance of restraining trade in the markets of the developed countries. There is also little chance of conflict of antitrust laws, because the LDC's for good reason make very little use of them. In LDC's, where the optimum scale of plant in many industries is large relative to the small local market, it is counterproductive to use antitrust policy to create a more competitive structure. Other measures, particularly tariff policy, must be used by LDC governments to limit the exploitation of monopoly power.

The real significance of the oligopolistic nature of MNC's lies in the pattern it imposes upon LDC government dealings with MNC's. The relationship between MNC and LDC frequently is one of bilateral monopoly or bilateral oligopoly. It is a bargaining situation

---

5. The pioneering study is Stephen H. Hymer, "The International Operations of National Firms: A Study of Direct Investment," unpublished Ph.D. dissertation, Massachusetts Institute of Technology, 1960. See also Richard E. Caves, "International Corporations: The Industrial Economics of Foreign Investment," *Economica*, 38 (February 1971), 1–27.

with typically a wide range within which the bargain may be struck.[6] The essence of the bargaining situation is this: For an MNC contemplating entry into an LDC, the minimum return on investment necessary for it to be willing to make the investment often is well below the maximum rate of return the LDC government would be willing to allow it in order to attract the investment. It is this gap between the minimum acceptable to the MNC and the maximum allowable by the LDC over which the bargaining takes place. The oligopolistic character of most MNC's contributes to a bargaining situation, because if the firms did not have some market power, competition among firms would drive the rate of return on the investment down to the minimum acceptable to the firm. The bargaining situation is more pronounced in LDC host countries than in developed host countries, because the MNC often faces less competition from indigenous firms in the LDC.[7]

For a bargaining environment to exist between LDC and MNC, there must be limitation of competition not only on the part of the MNC's, but also on the side of the LDC's, for if there existed a great deal of competition among LDC's to attract MNC investment, the competition would drive the returns received by the LDC's from MNC investment down toward the minimum acceptable to the LDC's, leaving little scope for bargaining between MNC's and LDC's. It is widely believed that such a high degree of competition among LDC's exists. For example, a major U.N. study of the role of MNC's in the developing areas claims: "The most urgent point at issue among the developing countries is that of competition among themselves for foreign investment."[8] But the degree of competition among LDC's to attract MNC investment varies according to the nature of the investment and according to the tariff policies of the

---

6. The prevalence of the bargaining environment in MNC-LDC relations has been stressed by Charles P. Kindleberger, *American Business Abroad: Six Lectures on Direct Investment* (New Haven, Yale University Press, 1969), pp. 149 ff. See also Constantine V. Vaitsos, *Intercountry Income Distribution and Transnational Enterprises* (Oxford, Clarendon Press, 1974), esp. chapter VII.

7. A bargaining situation does not mean that there is necessarily a process of direct face-to-face negotiation. It may involve simply the stating of terms by the LDC followed by an MNC decision to invest or not to invest.

8. United Nations Department of Economic and Social Affairs, *Multinational Corporations in World Development* (New York, 1973), p. 90.

LDC's. For a substantial part, and perhaps most, of MNC investment in LDC's, competition among LDC's is limited, and a true bargaining environment prevails.

Three major types of MNC investment in LDC's may be distinguished: (1) raw materials extraction, (2) production for sale in the LDC home market, and (3) production for export. The bargaining element is great almost always in the first case, frequently in the second case, and rarely in the third case. In the case of MNC investment in raw materials extraction, the bargaining element in LDC-MNC relations usually is highly visible. The possession of natural resources almost always puts the LDC government into a bargaining position because every natural resource endowment is in some respects unique and produces some differential rent over which bargaining may take place. In most cases of MNC production for the LDC home market, the bargaining element is likely to prevail, because LDC's are not very competitive with each other for such investment. Where a national market is protected either by natural barriers such as transport costs or, more commonly, by quotas or tariffs, so that it is infeasible for an MNC to produce in one LDC for export to another, LDC's are not in competition for each others' markets.[9] Since high levels of protection have been widespread among LDC's, competition among LDC governments for MNC investment to produce for the LDC market probably has been more the exception than the rule. Competition among LDC's for MNC investment is likely to be the greatest in the case of investment in production of manufactures for export to the developed countries.

The prevalence of a bargaining relationship between MNC's and LDC governments has important implications for LDC policy toward MNC's. It means that LDC governments must deal with MNC investment on an individual or sectoral basis. Unlike the developed countries, they cannot rely on the forces of competition subject to

---

9. If the supply of MNC investment funds available for investment in the LDC's were fixed, LDC's would find themselves in competition with each other for that fixed sum. However, this surely is not the case for MNC's producing for the LDC home market. For them, investment in the LDC's represents only a small fraction of their total investment. An additional investment in an LDC could easily be financed by diversion of funds from investment in the developed countries or by raising additional funds, and would not have to be at the expense of another LDC.

legislation of general applicability to bring about a satisfactory result because competitive forces are weak. The terms of the bargain must be changed to fit the circumstances, which may vary widely depending on the nature of the investment. What may be very generous terms for an MNC in one industry may deter desirable foreign investment in another sector.

Negotiations between an LDC government and an MNC will not be solely over the division of the benefits from the MNC investment, but also over the form in which the benefits are taken. The LDC government may have a variety of goals in addition to its receipt of tax or royalty payments, such as local equity participation in the MNC subsidiary, a high domestic resource content in the output of the subsidiary, a high level of exports by the subsidiary, or rapid advancement of nationals to managerial positions in the subsidiary.[10] The rational LDC government will accept a trade-off of one of its goals for another. The terms on which the MNC will trade one of these constraints on its actions for another will be different for different MNC investments. For example, an MNC establishing a subsidiary producing solely for the LDC home market will be more willing to accept local partners than if the subsidiary were exporting, because the MNC parent desires complete control of pricing and marketing strategy of the exports to prevent the LDC subsidiary from competing with other branches of the MNC's operation. Thus the fact that LDC governments typically have more than one objective in their negotiations with MNC's provides a second motive for LDC governments to deal with MNC investors in terms of case-by-case negotiation.

There is a third reason why LDC governments, more than developed country governments, will seek to deal with foreign direct investors on a basis of individual negotiation. One of the most frequently acknowledged differences between LDC's and developed countries is the much greater degree of market imperfections in LDC's. Because of lack of information, small numbers of participants, or institutional constraints, market-determined prices in LDC's

---

10. It is arguable whether the LDC government should have such supplementary goals. In some cases, such as the promotion of exports, the LDC government may be confusing means and ends. But in this context it is the existence of these goals, not their appropriateness, that matters.

frequently are poor guides to optimal resource allocation. Where LDC governments are unable or unwilling to improve the functioning of these markets, they frequently seek second-best solutions that at least partially compensate for the distortions in resource allocation that arise from market imperfections. In effect, the government overrides the signals given by the market mechanism in instances where these signals are likely to lead to especially serious misallocation. The government's intervention often is on a case-by-case basis and as a practical matter must be limited to only the most important cases of potential distortion. Since foreign direct investments tend to be among the larger enterprises in an LDC economy, they are especially subject to government intervention on these grounds.

The case-by-case approach can readily be seen in the dealings of LDC's with prospective MNC investors. In the case of mineral exports, the main item of negotiation will be the level of royalty payments; whereas in the case of production for the LDC home market, it will be the level of tariff protection. A variety of additional measures, such as tax holidays and tariff remittances on imported equipment or components, may be used to adjust the terms in favor of the foreign investor. The return to the investor may be reduced by other measures, such as local content requirements, joint-venture requirements, mandatory export quotas, and restrictions on the repatriation of earnings.[11] Screening of prospective foreign investment, such as now exists in Canada and Mexico, is another device for dealing with foreign investments on a case-by-case basis.

The LDC's naturally are eager to improve the terms on which they are able to make bargains with foreign investors. It is not a question of setting tougher terms across the board, for this may drive away desirable foreign investments. Rather, the LDC's would like to set tougher terms for the MNC investments that will not be deterred by them, while allowing more generous terms for desirable foreign investments that otherwise would be deterred. Of course, in setting

---

11. Although these latter measures change the terms of the bargain, that is not their primary purpose, which is to induce MNC's to act in particular ways. It has been argued that the complex system of incentives and disincentives used by many LDC governments is highly inefficient, but that is another story. See Grant L. Reuber, *Private Foreign Investment in Development* (Oxford, Clarendon Press, 1973), pp. 128–32.

different terms depending on whom they are bargaining with, the LDC governments are acting no differently from the MNC's themselves, who, for example, will extract more generous terms for investment in a country with a small domestic market than in a country with a very attractive domestic market.

The relationship between LDC's and MNC's has begun to emerge as an issue of foreign policy. The underlying question of LDC-MNC relations is the issue of bargaining power. Many LDC's feel themselves to be in an unduly weak bargaining position vis-à-vis the MNC's. In a negotiating situation, the MNC often is perceived to have a very great advantage over the LDC in information and expertise. This formulation of the issue leads to proposals to strengthen the negotiating capability of LDC governments by such measures as the establishment of a centralized negotiating agency in each host country and the provision of technical assistance to train LDC negotiating personnel. Measures to increase disclosure of information by MNC's and to gather and analyze information on MNC's would also contribute to improving the negotiating posture of the LDC's, although they would serve other purposes as well. Another proposal to improve the LDC bargaining position involves "taking the package apart." Foreign direct investment involves an international transfer of a combination of resources, mainly capital, technology, and management. Some observers believe that LDC's acquire these more expensively in the form of foreign direct investment than if they obtained them separately, by borrowing capital, licensing technology, and hiring management. There are strong opinions on both sides of the issue, but neither side is well supplied with evidence as yet.[12]

If this view of the relations between MNC's and LDC governments is accepted, it has important implications for the conduct of American foreign economic policy on the issue of the MNC. Actions by parent countries or international organizations to affect directly the *terms* of bargains struck between MNC's and LDC governments

---

12. For an optimistic view of the prospects for "unbundling" see C. Fred Bergsten, "Coming Investment Wars?" *Foreign Affairs*, 53 (October, 1974), 138. For a less sanguine assessment see Charles P. Kindleberger, "U.S. Policy Toward Direct Investment with Special Reference to the Less Developed Countries," in *United States International Economic Policy in an Interdependent World* (Washington, U.S. Government Printing Office, 1971), II:343–344.

will be counterproductive. Each negotiating situation is unique. Outside parties cannot be expected to know the circumstances of a negotiating situation nearly so well as the direct participants. Furthermore, if an outside party influences the terms of the bargain, it may be placed in the very undesirable position of being held responsible if one of the direct participants comes to feel that the terms were unsatisfactory.

Rather than seeking measures which change the terms of MNC-LDC bargains, policy-makers in the United States and other MNC parent countries and in international bodies should support measures which improve the *environment* of negotiations, particularly measures to increase the competence of LDC policy-makers and the information available to them. It might appear that measures to improve the negotiating capacity of LDC's without similar measures to assist the MNC's necessarily involve a gain for the LDC's at the expense of the MNC's, but this is not true. An improvement in the LDC level of skills and information may on occasion benefit both parties to the negotiation. For example, it may reduce the number of instances in which an LDC sets terms so stringent that a desirable foreign investment is deterred.

In the bargaining environment each foreign investor's situation is unique. The implication is that United States policy on the treatment of its corporations' subsidiaries abroad cannot be based very greatly upon the principle of nondiscrimination. Discrimination is the very essence of the bargaining environment. Conceptually, a distinction may be made between justifiable and unjustifiable discrimination, but when the bargaining atmosphere is as pervasive as it is in LDC-MNC relations, the distinction will be extremely difficult to carry out in practice.

There have been a number of proposals for formal international agreements to harmonize national policies toward the MNC, such as a code of national conduct enforced by an international agency or a GATT-style agreement on the MNC. Some such arrangement has much to recommend it for developed countries. But it is one of the implications of the analysis offered here that LDC's are unlikely to adhere to any such arrangement, for it will limit their flexibility in setting terms with the MNC's without giving them many offsetting benefits.

Bargaining between an LDC government and an MNC cannot be

thought of as a once-and-for-all action limited to the original decision of the MNC to enter. Unforeseen circumstances and a shifting power balance between MNC and LDC may bring about some renegotiation of terms. The LDC government will concern itself with the total bargain struck over an extended period, rather than simply with that part of the bargain arranged at the initial entry of the MNC. Given this possibility for renegotiation, one suggestion has been that LDC's may improve the negotiating environment by establishing at the initial negotiations the institutional framework within which subsequent renegotiations will be carried out.[13]

Generally, the passage of time strengthens the hand of the LDC at the expense of the MNC, for the obvious reason that once the MNC commits resources to the LDC, the withholding of those particular resources is no longer a bargaining weapon available to the MNC. However, the efforts of LDC's at renegotiations are restrained by the possibility of deterring subsequent MNC investment. Substantial renegotiation of terms is much more common in extractive than in other industries, for two reasons: (1) Resources discoveries suddenly and drastically alter the MNC profit picture, leading the LDC to press for renegotiation. (2) In many LDC's the extractive industry is very large relative to the rest of the economy, so that the benefits to be obtained by the LDC from squeezing the MNC's in that sector far outweigh the costs entailed in deterring future investments by those and other MNC's. In recent years the process of renegotiation has been especially visible in the oil-producing countries, but it has been important elsewhere as well.[14]

Sometimes LDC demands for renegotiation have arisen from their dissatisfaction with terms arrived at in the past by MNC's bargaining with unsophisticated and uninformed representatives of the LDC's. Such notoriously one-sided negotiations still shape many persons' mental picture of LDC-MNC relations even now as the situation is being radically transformed. The well publicized sophistication and expertise of the managers of the OPEC oil cartel is only

---

13. Vaitsos, p. 141.

14. For a good portrayal of the complexity and fluidity of LDC-MNC relationships in an extractive industry see Theodore H. Moran, *Multinational Corporations and the Politics of Dependence: Copper in Chile* (Princeton, N.J., Princeton University Press, 1974).

the most visible example of the rapidly increasing willingness and ability of LDC governments to drive hard bargains with foreign investors.[15]

The inherent difficulty of determining the taxable profits of MNC subsidiaries magnifies the problems of LDC governments trying to extract a larger share of the benefits from foreign direct investment for the host country. The problem in determining the taxable income of one unit of an MNC's empire is that intracorporate payments (interest, royalties, management fees and transfer prices) may be manipulated to reduce accounting profits in high-tax jurisdictions and increase them in low-tax jurisdictions.[16] The problem exists in the developed countries as well as the LDC's, but the solution differs. In the developed countries the necessary measure is improvement in administration. Because of the complexity of establishing the appropriate payments for intracorporate transfers, the task of enforcement is extremely difficult, but for the developed countries it is probably not intractable.

In most LDC's the scarcity of administrative talent and the need to employ the available talent in tasks more important for development means that accurate estimation of the taxable income of local MNC subsidiaries is probably not a practical possibility. Recognizing this, LDC's sometimes levy a corporate income tax on some artificially constructed profit figure.[17] A similar approach has been

---

15. See, e.g., Richard J. Barnet and Ronald E. Müller, *Global Reach: The Power of the Multinational Corporation* (New York, Simon and Schuster, 1974), chap. 8.

16. It is questionable whether a very large volume of MNC profits escapes LDC taxation in this way. MNC's in most LDC's do not have much incentive to shift taxable income from LDC's because of provisions for crediting foreign profits taxes paid abroad, because LDC profits taxes often are no higher than in the parent country, and because of restrictions on the ability of MNC's of the United States to use tax havens enacted in the 1962 tax law. The manipulation of intracorporate payments is perhaps most often used not to reduce LDC taxes payable but mainly to transfer profits out of a country with stringent exchange controls or limitations on repatriation.

17. One method that has been used is simply to assume that taxable income is some predetermined, arbitrary percentage of invested capital. The well known technique of oil-producing countries is to levy a tax on "income" calculated by using an artificial "posted price." These are income taxes in name only, the former actually being a kind of capital levy, the latter essentially a specific

proposed in a United Nations study, which suggested a "factor-formula" method comparable to that used by the states of the United States.[18] In most instances, some such approach is likely to be much more workable for the LDC's than the exceedingly difficult approach of trying to reconstruct the "true" profits of local subsidiaries.

One proposal to improve LDC bargaining power vis-à-vis the MNC is the formation of agreements among LDC's to restrain competition among them to attract MNC investment. Such action is likely to achieve its goal only insofar as the LDC's really are in competition with each other for MNC investment. In the past an important part of MNC investment in LDC's has gone into production for an LDC home market that was highly protected by tariffs and other trade barriers. For MNC investment of this nature, competition among LDC's is negligible. The lower their trade barriers, the more countries are placed in a position to attract MNC's. When trade barriers are low, it is easy for an MNC to supply one country's market with goods produced elsewhere. In view of this, it is not surprising that national competition for the location of industries has been especially intense among the countries of the European Common Market.

LDC's have been turning away from the strategy of import-substituting industrialization behind high trade barriers as the drawbacks of such a strategy became more apparent. As they move toward promotion of manufactured exports, frequently produced by the subsidiaries of MNC's, the LDC's come more and more into competition with each other to attract MNC's. Agreement among LDC's to restrain such competition is in effect a form of cartel arrangement and is subject to the usual problems of any cartel. The larger the number of members, the greater the incentive of any individual member to cheat on the cartel; and if substantial cheating

excise tax. The reason for designing them to look like income taxes is to take advantage of the provisions in the MNC's home country for crediting the payment of foreign income taxes against income taxes payable at home. Taxes other than corporate income taxes would be treated as deductions from income rather than the more favorable tax credits.

18. United Nations Department of Economic and Social Affairs (above, n. 8), pp. 90–91.

takes place, the cartel is destroyed. There are too many LDC's with the potential to export manufactures to the developed countries for an agreement restraining competition among them to be very effective. Where such agreements may be effective, and perhaps absolutely necessary, is among the members of customs unions formed by groups of LDC's. For example, the Andean Group, a customs union of six South American countries, has established common requirements for foreign subsidiaries producing for sale in more than one member country. The desire to restrain competition among LDC's to attract MNC investment might even be a motive for LDC's to form customs unions, as opposed to more general trade liberalization.

LDC's exporting some primary commodity and facing MNC's with market power may gain by joining together to improve their bargaining power vis-à-vis the MNC's. Such a strategy is not generally an easy one because of the problem of reconciling the interests of countries with widely varying ability to produce the commodity. In any event, the greatest hopes for gain from association among countries exporting a primary commodity rest not upon redistributing income to the exporting countries from MNC's, but from ultimate consumers. In the case of OPEC's oil-price increases, for example, OPEC's gains were at the expense of the ultimate consumers of oil, with gains or losses to the MNC oil companies being only marginal and incidental to the whole process. Had OPEC's gains been limited solely to extracting more of the oil companies' profits, the maximum that OPEC could have gained would have been only a small fraction of the increase in revenues actually achieved.

For perhaps the majority of LDC primary commodity exporters, association is intended primarily to improve their bargaining power at the expense of the ultimate consumer rather than the MNC. For some primary commodity exports, the role played by MNC's is not very important, or the MNCs' lack of market power leaves little-monopoly profits to be extracted. In other cases, as in the oil industry, the existence of the MNC's actually may facilitate the formation of a successful cartel among the producing countries.[19] Moran has argued that in their own self-interest nationalized copper industries "must carefully learn to exploit the consumers in the industrial

19. M. A. Adelman, "Is the Oil Shortage Real? Oil Companies as OPEC Tax-Collectors," *Foreign Policy*, 9 (Winter 1972–73), 69–107.

countries exactly the way the multinational corporations do."[20] Even where the division of profits between MNC's and LDC primary-product exporters is a critical issue, the nature of final consumer demand will play a vital role, for it will greatly affect the ability of MNC's to resist the LDC's or to pass on LDC exactions to the final consumer. Thus for LDC primary commodity exporters the critical question of cooperative agreements is one of bargaining power vis-à-vis the ultimate consumer.

II. COMMODITY CARTELS AND INTERNATIONAL COMMODITY AGREEMENTS

OPEC's apparent success inevitably has encouraged imitators. Cartelization efforts have been stepped up in such products as copper, tin, bauxite, phosphate, coffee and tea. According to Bergsten, this is just the beginning of a "new era in world commodity markets," in which commodity cartels will "mark a major new factor in both international economics and world politics."[21] But are attempts by LDC's to exploit "commodity power" likely to meet with much success? There are strong reasons to be skeptical.

The potential success of an exporters' cartel depends on the characteristics of the market for the individual product in question. It is fruitless to discuss the prospects for cartelization of raw materials in general; it must be done on a case-by-case basis for each commodity. Even so, there are some general reasons to think that cartels in many commodities will be much less successful than the oil cartel. Many products—including rubber, natural fibers, and cocoa—face competition from synthetic substitutes. Some metals face competition from such synthetic substitutes as glass and plastics, in addition to competition from other metals and from scrap. For agricultural products the danger of entry into production by countries outside the cartel is often especially great.[22]

---

20. Moran, p. 244.

21. C. Fred Bergsten, "The New Era in World Commodity Markets," *Challenge* (September-October 1974), pp. 34–42. See also his "The Threat from the Third World," *Foreign Policy*, 11 (Summer 1973), 103–124.

22. Also, where an export crop is produced by many farmers, the govern-

These general considerations suggest that while cartels may be successful for some commodities, the formation of export cartels is unlikely to bring about a large across-the-board increase in the prices of most primary commodities. In 1973 and early 1974, when prices of most primary commodities were rising rapidly, it was easy for many people to believe that all primary products were becoming increasingly scarce and that the bargaining power of their producers was steadily increasing. However, the rise in most commodity prices, aside from oil and food, was a cyclical phenomenon caused by the coincidence of the expansionary phase of the cycle throughout the industrialized world. In the short run such a worldwide boom tends to cause greater inflation in the prices of primary commodities than of most other goods and services, because of the lower short-run elasticities of demand and supply for most primary commodities. The decline in many commodity prices which began in 1974 is evidence of the important role played by cyclical factors. Will commodity prices soar again during the next upturn in the business cycle? One reason to think that future commodities booms will not be as pronounced as that of 1973–74 is that the adoption of flexible exchange rates by the major industrialized countries makes it less likely that their business cycles will be so closely synchronized as they were in the era of fixed exchange rates.

The only way to determine the prospects for success of primary product export cartels is to examine individually the prospects for each commodity. Several studies have surveyed the prospects for success of cartels in a wide range of primary commodities, with the general conclusion that producers of most primary commodities are unlikely to be able to approach OPEC's success.[23] This essay will not

---

ment may be unable to resist the political pressure to pass on to farmers a sizable part of any price increase, which will lead to the accumulation of surpluses unless the government is able to enforce production controls. If large and growing national surpluses are allowed to overhang the market, they will exert very heavy pressure on the cohesion of the cartel. The cartel would need to destroy or internationalize the surpluses, both of which have their problems.

23. Bension Varon and Kenji Takeuchi, "Developing Countries and Non-Fuel Minerals," *Foreign Affairs*, 52, no. 3 (April 1974), 497–537. Raymond Mikesell, "International Collusive Action in World Markets for Nonfuel Minerals," U.S. Department of State, Bureau of Public Affairs, Economic Policy Series 5, no. 4, 1974. Ibid., "More Third World Cartels Ahead?" *Challenge* (November-

attempt to evaluate the prospects of cartel success for all important commodities exported by the LDC's, which would be a major research undertaking. Instead, we shall use the example of two commodities to suggest why more comprehensive studies have reached generally negative conclusions about the prospects for many commodity cartels. To illustrate the problems in forming successful export cartels, we shall examine two important and related primary commodities frequently cited as good candidates for cartel action: bauxite and copper.

At first glance, bauxite would appear to have good prospects for cartelization. The ten members[24] of the International Bauxite Association (IBA) account for 75 percent of world bauxite production. Although aluminum competes with many other products, including iron and steel, copper, tin, platic, and glass, a rise in the price of bauxite will not result in much substitution of these products for aluminum, because the cost of bauxite is less than 10 percent of the cost of aluminum. A doubling in the price of bauxite will raise aluminum prices less than 10 percent. Compared to many other metals, a cartel in bauxite has the advantage that currently scrap provides a relatively small fraction of total aluminum supplies.

The real obstacle to bauxite cartel success lies not so much on the demand side of the market as on the supply side. Aluminum is one of the most plentiful materials on earth, comprising 10 percent of the earth's crust. And more importantly from an economic point of view, bauxite and nonbauxitic sources of aluminum are available widely outside the cartel countries at costs not much greater than costs within the cartel countries. This is the all-important difference between oil and bauxite. Marginal costs of oil production outside OPEC are higher and rise rapidly as production is expanded, whereas outside the bauxite cartel there is a virtually limitless supply at low and only gradually rising marginal cost. The noncartel supplies include not only existing reserves of high-grade bauxite, but lower-grade

---

December 1974), pp. 24–31. Ernest Stern and Wouter Tims, "The Relative Bargaining Strengths of the Developing Countries," paper delivered at the national convention of the Allied Social Sciences Associations, San Francisco, December 1974.

24. Jamaica, Surinam, Guyana, the Dominican Republic, Haiti, Ghana, Guinea, Sierre Leone, Yugoslavia, and Australia.

bauxite that would become economical at a modest increase in bauxite prices and abundant nonbauxitic sources of aluminum, such as clays. Extraction processes for nonbauxitic sources of aluminum already are known, and a large rise in bauxite prices would be likely to stimulate further development of these processes.

In addition, it probably will not be difficult to discover large new reserves of high-grade bauxite. There are many areas of the world where the probability of finding large reserves of high-grade bauxite is high. As long as bauxite from existing known reserves was cheap and plentiful, there was little interest in looking for more, but a cartel-induced rise in bauxite prices could bring about some quick discoveries.

Because it would take time to switch to alternatives to bauxite supplied by the IBA countries, the bauxite cartel does have the potential to increase prices over the short run. But short-run gains may be at the expense of very large long-run losses, in that the response to a rise in prices may be to induce changes that are irreversible. If the price rise causes improvements in the technology of extraction from nonbauxitic sources of aluminum or development of new sources of bauxite outside IBA, these will not be reversed by a subsequent lowering of prices by IBA.

The bauxite-exporting countries have begun their efforts to raise prices at the wrong time. Aluminum is used principally in producers' and consumers' durable goods, transportation, and construction. Because these industries are highly cyclical, the demand for bauxite is cyclical. The world recession, which began in 1974, by cutting the demand for aluminum has reduced the bargaining power of bauxite exporters just when they were becoming more intent on exploiting it. When the resumption of world economic growth restores the demand for bauxite, the members of IBA may find their bargaining power much eroded by actions taken by the aluminum companies during the slump in demand. Aware of IBA's intentions, the aluminum companies have stepped up research into extraction from nonbauxitic ores and exploration for bauxite in countries outside IBA.[25]

The copper exporters' cartel (CIPEC, the acronym for its French

---

25. "Bauxite Official Finds Organizing's No Cinch for 10-Nation Group," *Wall Street Journal*, April 23, 1975.

title)[26] also faces great obstacles in trying to raise monopoly profits through increased prices, but they differ from the problems faced by the bauxite group. CIPEC's problems lie not so much on the supply side of the market as on the demand side.[27] Copper faces much competition from substitutes, particularly aluminum, but also steel, zinc, lead, and plastics. In addition, scrap is an important source of competition, providing about 30–40 percent of world annual com-sumption. Competition from substitutes is much more serious for copper than for bauxite, because copper ore is 40 percent of the cost of the primary metal, whereas for bauxite the figure is under 10 per-cent, so that a rise in the price of copper ore will induce much more consumer resistance than an equal percentage rise in the price of bauxite ore. These two very different percentages have another important implication as well. Since copper and aluminum compete closely, it has been suggested that the bauxite and copper cartels raise their prices jointly to prevent substitution between them. But to prevent switching from copper to aluminum, the percentage increase in bauxite prices would have to be four times the percentage increase in the price of copper ore. Since the prospects for a lasting increase in bauxite prices are so greatly limited by the wide availability of supplies, the prospects for joint cartelization in copper and bauxite seem quite poor.

The difficulty in enforcing a cartel in copper would be greater than that of the OPEC oil cartel. Because a significant part of copper output is marketed by producing-country governments rather than by large, easily taxed firms, it is easier for a country that cheats on the cartel to escape detection. But even if the cartel could hold together, it would be unlikely to increase its revenue significantly for any extended period by raising its price: there would be too much competition from other materials, scrap, and non-CIPEC production. According to a World Bank study, the demand for CIPEC copper has nearly unitary elasticity in the short run and considerably greater

26. Composed of Zaire, Zambia, Chile, and Peru.
27. There is not nearly so much copper in the earth's crust as bauxite, and compared to bauxite, the cost of extraction rises more sharply from higher-grade to lower-grade deposits. This is not to say the CIPEC has no problems on the supply side, for its members account for only about 40 percent of world produc-tion and a little over half of world exports. One of CIPEC's current goals is to add other producers to the group.

than unitary elasticity in the long run.[28] Thus even if the CIPEC countries could act together to raise prices, it would not increase their earnings significantly in the short run and would reduce them significantly in the long run.

The apparent success of the OPEC cartel does not appear to foreshadow a general realignment of bargaining power between producers and consumers for other primary commodities. Cartels may be successful for some individual commodities, but for most commodities they are unlikely to achieve much. For some commodities, cartelization could be made to work if the producers succeeded in getting the cooperation of the consuming countries in enforcing a commodity agreement, as, for example, the United States has cooperated in the International Coffee Agreement. Such measures have been a central part of the proposed dialogue between producers and consumers of raw materials. Several speeches by Secretary of State Henry Kissinger in May 1975 intimated that the United States might accede to some such arrangements.

United States cooperation in an agreement that raised the price of an imported commodity would constitute an indirect form of foreign aid, the transfer taking place by means of higher prices paid by United States consumers to foreign producers. As such, it is not a very attractive form of aid, for several reasons. It is financed by what amounts to an excise tax on the commodity in question, a form of taxation that is often regressive and would not ordinarily be chosen as a means to raise government revenue. The distribution of aid among countries is haphazard, depending on whether a country produces a product covered by a commodity agreement or not. It tends to freeze production into existing patterns and to encourage production by high-cost producers. Some primary products are produced by developed countries as well as by LDC's, and it may prove impossible to exclude the developed countries from the benefits of the aid. Some, perhaps most, of the aid will accrue to private producers of the primary product, much of it to be used for nondevelopmental purposes. The primary advantage of this indirect form of aid in the

---

28. Cited in Mikesell, "International Collusive Action," p. 12, n. 1. Of course, a price increase that reduces volume so much that CIPEC's short-run total revenue remains unchanged still increases CIPEC's short-run profits somewhat, insofar as production costs are reduced by the cut in volume.

eyes of the recipient, and a drawback in the eyes of the donor, is that the donor has little or no control over the use of the aid. Related to this is the fact that this indirect form of aid presumably would not be subject to the annual budgetary review process in Congress, a virtue to those who stress the slow and cumbersome nature of the foreign-aid review process but a drawback to those who emphasize the value of annual surveillance.

On balance, from the viewpoint of the United States and other aid donors, the disadvantages of indirect foreign aid via price-increasing commodity agreements seem to greatly outweigh the advantages. If foreign assistance is to be given, direct foreign aid is much the preferred form. It is not difficult, however, to think of reasons why this apparently inferior form of aid has drawn increasing support from the LDC's. One reason is the normal preference of transfer recipients, hardly unique to LDC's, for transfers to be received in a disguised form, which makes it easier to imagine that they are earned receipts. Also, while it is appropriate for donor countries to think of different forms of aid-giving as alternatives, it is not so for recipient countries, which lack control over the volume of aid and therefore, unlike the donors, cannot assume that a decrease in one form of aid will be matched by an equal increase in aid in some other form. The OPEC oil price increases and the experience of the 1973–74 commodities boom also probably contributed to heightened LDC interest in price-increasing commodity agreements, but the beginnings of greater LDC support for such agreements considerably antedate those events.

There is another reason, of greater significance to United States foreign policy, for the intensification of LDC support for price-increasing commodity agreements. The LDC's, not without cause, increasingly have despaired of the prospects for aid in conventional form. Since the early 1960's the aid effort of the United States, and of the developed countries in general, has been diminishing. The nominal value of aid stagnated, while its value in real terms has declined because of inflation, a shift from grants to loans, and increased tying of aid to imports from donor countries.[29] As a percentage of GNP in the donor countries, the decline in real aid-giving

29. Jagdish N. Bhagwati, *Amount and Sharing of Aid* (Washington, D.C., Overseas Development Council, 1970), chaps. 2–3, 7.

has been even greater. The intensified efforts of the LDC's to promote the expansion of aid in unconventional forms, such as international commodity agreements, may be seen as partly their response to a decline in aid effort in conventional forms, which they feel powerless to reverse. Other forms of unconventional aid included in the declaration of a new international economic order are the linking of development aid to the creation of Special Drawing Rights and the extension of tariff preferences to LDC exports of manufactures.[30] In part, these too may be seen as second-best substitutes for aid in conventional forms. Tariff preferences for LDC manufactures are partly a response to LDC complaints, not unjustified, that the protective systems of the developed countries tend to discriminate against production activities most suited to the LDC's. As such, tariff preferences are a second-best policy; preferable policy would be for the developed countries to change their systems of protection. Since domestic political pressures in the developed countries are likely to prevent the alteration in their protective systems that is called for, tariff preferences for LDC's, already enacted by major developed countries, have a strong case as a second-best strategy.

Commodity agreements whose aim is to raise prices above their long-run equilibrium level must be distinguished from commodity agreements intended to stabilize prices around an unchanged long-run equilibrium level. While the former, if successful, redistributes income from consumers to producers, the latter entails no redistribution over the long run and may benefit both producers and consumers. It is debatable whether price instability of exported primary products is a serious obstacle to LDC development.[31]

Even if commodity price instability is sufficiently serious to warrant remedies, international commodity agreements do not

---

30. The proposed link between development aid and the creation of Special Drawing Rights has not been enacted, but tariff preferences for LDC manufactured exports have been legislated by the United States and the European Communities.

31. For a statistical study that supports the position that export price instability is not a serious obstacle to the development of LDC's generally, see Alasdair I. MacBean, *Export Instability and Economic Growth* (Cambridge, Harvard University Press, and London, Allen and Unwin, 1966). But see also the review of MacBean's study by A. Maizels in *American Economic Review*, 58 (June 1968), 575–580.

appear to be the best means to deal with the problem. A country does not need to achieve international agreement to moderate the effects of export price instability on its economy. It can use its own taxing powers, increasing taxes on its export commodity when prices are high, retaining the extra revenue for use in years when prices are low, when taxes on its export commodity should be lowered. On the international level there already exists a means of helping LDC's who have been hurt by fluctuations in the prices of their export commodities, a means that is simpler and less costly than international commodity arrangements. This is the International Monetary Fund's "commodity tranche," a line of credit available to a developing country that experiences a loss in export revenue due to a drop in its export proceeds. The commodity tranche has been little used because of its highly stringent conditions for loans, but its liberalization and expansion should not be difficult and would be preferable to international commodity agreements as a measure for dealing with export price instability.

Thus, from the standpoint of United States foreign policy, adherence to an international commodity agreement, whether its purpose is to raise prices, to stabilize them, or both, would be inferior to other means of achieving the same end. Such action could be justified only if the superior measures cannot be implemented, and not necessarily even then.

III. SUMMARY AND CONCLUSIONS

Important aspects of the economic relations between rich and poor countries increasingly are being viewed as elements of a bargaining situation. In many instances the relationship between LDC's and MNC's is one of bargaining. Where this relationship exists, the appropriate role for foreign-policy makers of the United States and other MNC home countries is to attempt to improve the bargaining environment rather than to affect the outcome of LDC-MNC negotiations. Two major trends are affecting the course of MNC-LDC relations: (1) Representatives of LDC governments are gaining in sophisticaion and expertise. (2) Many LDC's are turning away from policies of import substitution toward more outward-looking policies, which places them more in competition with each other to attract

MNC's. Unless the LDC's reach agreements with each other to restrain their competition to attract MNC investment, this trend will attenuate the bargaining element in MNC-LDC relations by reducing the bargaining power of the LDC's vis-à-vis the MNC's.

Inspired in part by the success of OPEC, the LDC's have redoubled their efforts to increase prices of their primary commodity exports. Their efforts have taken two directions, unilateral and multilateral. Unilaterally, exporting countries have been attempting to increase commodity prices by forming new cartels or strengthening old ones, but the prospects for sustained and widespread success are poor. On a multilateral basis, the LDC's have sought to enlist the participation of consumer countries in international commodity agreements. United States foreign-policy makers are facing increased demands from the LDC's to join in such agreements. However, international commodity agreements represent an inferior means of achieving the goals of commodity price stabilization and transfer of resources from the developed countries to the LDC's.

Although United States foreign policy should resist attempts to enlist its cooperation in international commodity agreements, especially if their purpose is to increase the long-run price of imported commodities, dogged foot-dragging alone would hardly be a sufficient response. There are a number of factors behind the increasingly insistent demands from the LDC's for a new international economic order and the concomitant stress on the elements of rivalry and bargaining in the economic relations between the LDC's and the developed countries. Not all the roots of the current LDC attitude are amenable to United States foreign policy actions, but some are. In particular, the decline in the United States foreign aid effort and seemingly in the United States commitment to LDC development must be seen as an important cause of the increasingly strident tone taken by many LDC representatives.

Several of the measures sought by the LDC's represent indirect and inferior forms of foreign aid. The strongest argument against such measures as international commodity agreements is that they are inferior to conventional aid. It is important that the connection be recognized between direct foreign aid and LDC proposals for commodity agreements and other forms of indirect aid. Although many LDC's may not acknowledge it, direct foreign aid is the more appropriate response to LDC aspirations for development. The LDC's need real resources, and the most helpful policy is the one that transfers the resources with the fewest adverse side effects.

The policy of the United States should be to reaffirm the superiority of direct foreign aid, but herein lies a dilemma. If United States direct foreign aid continues to be available only in niggardly amounts and often on hard terms, the argument loses its moral force. If, because of a weakening in the United States commitment to direct foreign aid, United States foreign policy spokesmen are unable to present conventional aid as a genuine alternative to inferior indirect forms of aid, their resistance to such indirect aid will lack moral authority in international forums.

The immediate danger is of a worsening in this dilemma. The oil price increase and the recession in the United States may further diminish an already waning enthusiasm for foreign aid. Although higher prices of imported oil reduce real incomes in the United States by no more than about 2 percent, and if the recession is only temporary, the temptation to plead poverty will be difficult to resist. The argument that the MDC's cannot give more foreign aid because of a poor balance of payments is specious, but it will carry great weight. It is specious because it confuses a lack of liquidity with a lack of wealth. It is like a millionaire who declines to give anything to charity because he has no ready cash, all his wealth being tied up in stocks and bonds.

The task facing United States foreign-policy makers is to reaffirm the value of direct foreign aid in two forums. To the American public, they must reassert the importance of an American commitment to the developing world. If this appeal is successful, then United States foreign-policy makers, in their dialogue with the LDC's, should defend the superiority of direct aid over indirect forms of aid, especially international commodity agreements, proposed by the Declaration on the Establishment of a New International Economic Order.

EDITOR'S NOTE

Nuclear weapons have greatly increased interdependence among nations by increasing the possibility of mutual destruction. For the average person, however, this change in the international environment is abstract and unreal; it is something one reads about but does not experience. Most of us have never seen a nuclear weapon, let alone a nuclear explosion. Food shortages, by contrast, have intruded upon the daily experience of the common man. They have given him a feeling for international interdependence that nuclear weapons can never give—unless they are used.

The Limits to Growth,[1] *which Professor Meadows co-authored, barely mentions military problems; yet it has stimulated more awareness of global trends toward interdependence than any book since Herman Kahn's* On Thermonuclear War.[2] *In this essay Professor Meadows pursues questions raised by* The Limits to Growth *and considers their implications for United States policy. Although solutions to the food-population problem lie in the long-term future, Professor Meadows argues that policy makers must address such problems in the short run in order to make long-run solutions possible. If certain of her policy proposals sound unorthodox and impractical, in a world beset by revolutionary change yesterday's utopianism may be tomorrow's realism. For some, politics is the art of the possible; for others, it is the art of making possible tomorrow that which is impossible today.*

1. *Donella H. Meadows, et al.,* The Limits to Growth *(New York, Universe Books, 1972).*

2. *Herman Kahn,* On Thermonuclear War *(Princeton, Princeton University Press, 1960).*

VI.
Food and Population:
Policies for the United States

Donella H. Meadows

I. INTRODUCTION

Two United Nations conferences in 1974, one in Rome and one in Bucharest, emphasized the necessity for every nation to confront two interlocking global problems: food shortages and rapid population growth. The World Food and Population Conferences also dramatized the extreme difficulty of formulating effective policies for dealing with these problems on either a national or an international level. The issues are complex, they involve areas of great political sensitivity, and "experts" and ordinary citizens alike express widely divergent viewpoints about the severity, causes, and possible cures of what is often called the "world food crisis." The current debate is not simply bipolar, but multipolar, as the following quotations, all written by Americans, illustrate:

> What, then, accounts for the sharp deterioration in the world balance of supply and demand in the past 3 years? . . . These events can be explained essentially as the result of transitory factors: an unusual, but not unprecedented, series of crop shortfalls in the U.S.S.R., South Asia, and North America; and the failure of the major producing and consuming countries to prepare for such an eventuality . . . . What future course of action is suggested by the experience of the past few years? . . . All that would seem to be required is a grain reserve of limited size, though adequate to meet contingencies such as those experienced in the mid-1960's and again in the past 3 years.[1]

---

1. Fred H. Sanderson, "The Great Food Fumble," *Science*, 188 (1975), 503.

The current international scarcity of major agricultural commodities reflects important long-term trends as well as the
temporary lack of rainfall in the Soviet Union and parts of Asia
and Africa. From a global perspective . . . the world is likely to
be highly vulnerable on the food front in the years ahead. The
poor nations, and the poor people within nations, are in an
especially dangerous predicament.[2]

The United States should remain an island of plenty in a sea of
hunger. We are not responsible for the rest of humanity . . .
Famine is one of nature's ways of telling profligate peoples that
they have been irresponsible in their breeding habits . . . Until
those asking for handouts are doing at least as well as we are at
reducing existing excessive population growth rates, we should
not give away our resources—not so much as one bushel of
wheat.[3]

Some scientists and publicists have seriously advocated a "lifeboat ethic", saying that nations which do not compel human
fertility control . . . are endangering the survival of our species
—hence they should be starved out of the human race by denying them food aid. This obscene doctrine assumes that men and
women will not voluntarily limit their own fertility when they
have good reasons and the knowledge and means to do so . . .
The World Food Conference dramatically signifies the true
interdependence of human beings everywhere, but it emphasizes
even more the necessity to change the selfish and shortsighted
behavior of many people in both the rich and the poor countries.[4]

If all these writers could agree upon any one thing, it would be
that there is a problem, present or potential, that requires some
action. No one seems to think that the food situation will get better

---

2. Lester R. Brown, "Global Food Insecurity," *The Futurist*, 8, No. 2
(April 1974).

3. Johnson C. Montgomery, "The Island of Plenty," *Newsweek* (December 23, 1974), p. 13.

4. Roger Revelle, "The Ghost at the Feast," *Science*, 186 (1974), 589.

if it is simply left alone. There is vast disagreement, however, about what policy would be most effective, and who should carry out that policy. Grain reserves, green revolutions, increased aid, no aid, population control, market control, agribusiness control—all are seriously advocated. In the face of such disagreement, can a national policy be designed, and implemented with sufficient diligence, to produce a perceptible result? Is there any way to resolve the many interpretations of the world food problem, to understand and analyze them, and to forge them somehow into a comprehensive and effective food-population policy?

The present controversy, I believe, arises from three major areas of difference: the *boundaries* of space and time within which the contenders view the problem, the *theories* by which they explain the causes of the problem, and the *values* underlying their respective choices of preferable costs and benefits. Each individual combines these three factors into a consistent mind-set or world-view that influences not only his policy position but also the facts he perceives as relevant and the questions he asks to elicit new information. Unfortunately, in debates about food or population policy the participants seldom state clearly the world views that determine their positions. As a result, arguments rarely address real differences, produce mutual understanding, or lead to a basis for action.

In this paper, after a brief review of some current food and population statistics, I attempt to make explicit the boundaries, theories, and values behind several different policy proposals. Since I feel that no one can view this problem without some pre-established mind-set, I will not pretend to be an objective commentator on the various positions presented. Instead I will define my own position within the same framework applied to the others.

II. THE POPULATION-FOOD SITUATION

Many nations do not take a regular census, very few have reliable vital statistics, and no uniform standards exist for measuring agricultural output, estimating the amount of product that bypasses the cash economy, or ascertaining the actual daily diets of most of the world's people. Nevertheless, any policy discussion must proceed from some perception of the present state of the problem. The following summary is based on standard statistical sources, primarily the United Nations and the United States government. All numbers are illustrative of the real situation, but not necessarily accurate.

In mid-1975 the world population was estimated at about 4 billion persons. The global population was then growing at an average rate of about 1.9 percent a year (derived from an estimated average birth rate of 3.2 percent a year, minus an average death rate of 1.3 percent a year).[5] The total increase in world population in 1975 was approximately 78 million. The rate of increase is estimated to have been 0.4 percent in 1800, 0.6 percent in 1900, and 1.9–2.0 percent only in the 1960's and 1970's.[6] This recent acceleration is due primarily to a decrease in death rate rather than an increase in birth rate.

Neither population nor population growth is evenly distributed geographically or nationally. About 80 percent of the population increase in 1974 took place in the nonindustrialized countries of the world. Perhaps 12 million persons were added that year to the population of India, 14 million to China, and a little over one million to the United States.[7] Demographic statistics for the fifteen most populous nations of the world (encompassing almost 70 percent of the global population) are summarized on the left side of Table 1. The historic trends that have led to this widely varying set of birth, death, and growth rates will be discussed under the theory of the demographic transition later in this paper.

The average human being requires about 2200 vegetable-equivalent kilocalories of food per day to survive.[8] In 1974 the total world

---

5. Population Reference Bureau, *1975 World Population Data Sheet*, Washington, D.C., 1975.

6. A. M. Carr-Saunders, *World Population: Past Growth and Present Trends* (Oxford, Clarendon Press, 1936), p. 42; and Department of Economic and Social Affairs, *Statistical Yearbook*, New York, United Nations, 1960–1975.

7. The natural increase (excess of births over deaths) in the United States population from February 1974 to February 1975 was 1.225 million. Added to that was a legal net inmigration of 395,000.

8. Food and Agriculture Organization, *Provisional Indicative World Plan for Agricultural Development*, 2 (Rome, United Nations, 1970), 491. To express dietary intake in vegetable-equivalent kilocalories, those consumed directly as vegetable matter are added to the kilocalories derived from animal products, multiplied by the number of vegetable kilocalories required to produce one kilocalorie of animal product. This number varies from 3 to 10. Thus a person

grain production was approximately 1,200 million tons, or about 300 kilograms per person (roughly equivalent to 2900 kilocalories per person per day), if it had been distributed evenly over the global population.[9] When nongrain foodstuffs are added to this total, it is clear that food production in that year was sufficient to support the world population at well above the subsistence level. Total world food output has increased slightly faster than the population over the last decade. About half of this expanded output has come from extending cultivated land and half from better yields on land already cultivated.[10] Both area and yield increases required inputs of numerous other resources. For example, the 34 percent increase in world food production from 1951 to 1966 was accompanied by a 63 percent increase in yearly expenditures on tractors (in constant dollars), a 210 percent increase in use of fertilizers (by weight), and a 300 percent increase in expenditures on pesticides (in constant dollars).[11]

The figures quoted so far have been in terms of world totals and global averages. But food, like population, is by no means evenly distributed. Some food production and consumption statistics for the fifteen most populous countries are shown on the right side of Table 1. As the table indicates, the typical American consumes about five times the grain equivalent consumed by the typical Indian.[12] Over the last decade total food output has grown at about the same rate in both the nonindustrialized and the industrialized regions of the world. In the industrialized regions this growth has amounted to a 15 percent increase in food per capita, while in the nonindustrialized regions, because of rapid population growth, average food output *per capita* has increased very slightly, if at all.[13]

---

eating 1000 kilocalories of meat per day may be consuming as many as 10,000 vegetable-equivalent kilocalories per day from that source alone.

9. Lester R. Brown, *By Bread Alone* (New York, Praeger, 1974), p. 43.

10. Georg Borgstrom, *Focal Points: A Global Food Strategy* (New York, Macmillan, 1974), p. 178.

11. Study of Critical Environmental Problems, *Man's Impact on the Global Environment* (Cambridge, Mass., MIT Press, 1970), p. 118. Fertilizer use from Georg Borgstrom, *Too Many* (New York, Macmillan, 1969), p. 27.

12. Brown, *By Bread Alone*, p. 36.

13. Food and Agriculture Organization, *Preliminary Assessment of the World Food Situation*, Rome, United Nations, 1974.

TABLE 1

Population and Food Statistics for the Fifteen Most Populous Nations

	Population (million people) mid-1975 estimate[a]	Crude birth rate[a] (births/1000 people/year) mid-1975 estimate	Crude death rate[a] (deaths/1000 people/year) mid-1975 estimate	% Population growth/year[a] mid-1975 estimate	Per capita GNP (US$) 1971 or 1972
China	822.8	26.9	10.3	1.7	160
India	613.2	39.9	15.7	2.4	110
USSR	255.0	17.8	7.9	1.0	1400
USA	213.9	16.2	9.4	0.9	5590
Indonesia	136.0	42.9	16.9	2.6	90
Japan	111.1	19.2	6.6	1.3	2320
Brazil	109.7	37.0	8.8	2.8	530
Bangladesh	73.7	49.5	28.1	1.7	70
Pakistan	70.6	47.4	16.5	3.1	80
Nigeria	62.9	49.3	22.7	2.7	130
W. Germany	61.9	12.0	12.1	0.3	3390
Mexico	59.2	42.0	8.6	3.2	740
U.K.	56.4	16.1	11.7	0.3	2600
Italy	55.0	16.0	9.8	0.5	1960
France	52.9	17.0	10.6	0.9	3620

---

[a] Population Reference Bureau, *1975 World Population Data Sheet*, Washington, D.C., 1975.

[b] Calculated from United Nations, Dept. of Economic and Social Affairs, *Statistical Yearbook, 1971* (New York, 1972), pp. 504–509.

[c] United Nations Food and Agriculture Organization, *Monthly Bulletin of Agricultural Economics and Statistics*, 23, No. 9 (September 1974), pp. 3–4.

[d] Calculated from United Nations Food and Agriculture Organization, *Production Yearbook 1972* (Rome, Italy, 1973), pp. 3–8.

[e] Ibid., calculated by dividing nitrogenous fertilizer consumption by arable land.

[f] Approximated as slightly higher (1900 versus 1820) than the figure given for calories/person/day in UN, FAO, *Monthly Bulletin of Agricultural Economics and Statistics*, 23, No. 9 (September 1974), p. 3.

TABLE 1

(continued)

	Food/person (vegetable equivalent kilocalories/ capita/day)b	Year of estimation	% Annual growth in food productionb (exponential trend, 1952-72)c	Average grain yieldd (kg./ha.)	Nitrogenous fertilizer (kg./ha.) cultivated land)
China	3750	64–66	2.3	1788 rice wheat	28.0
India	2640	68–69	2.4	1120 rice wheat	9.3
USSR	7110	64–66	3.9	1407 wheat mixed	8.4
USA	13570	69	2.0	3899 corn wheat	38.7
Indonesia	2070	64–66	2.0	2122 rice	97.8
Japan	4510	69	4.3	5497 rice	180.8
Brazil	4970	66–68	4.4	1369 corn rice	9.3
Bangladesh	1900f	70	1.6	1487 rice	4.6
Pakistan	4050	68–69	3.0	1268 rice wheat	11.8
Nigeria	2550	64–66	2.0	764 mixed sorghum	.5
W. Germany	9660	69–70	2.5	3817 wheat mixed	149.9
Mexico	4360	64–66	5.3	1376 corn wheat	23.0
U.K.	11812	68–69	2.8	4080 mixed wheat	128.7
Italy	6310	68	2.9	2955 corn wheat	65.7
France	11120	69–70	3.0	4222 wheat mixed	87.55

III. BOUNDARIES IN SPACE AND TIME

If the world food situation is considered in terms of the problems and possible solutions that might appear between now and the next harvest, the conclusions will obviously be different from those drawn by looking from now to the end of the century or beyond. A five-year policy view must center on measures that could have an effect within that time, such as grain buffer stocks, incentives to farmers, or organization of famine relief efforts. A fifty-year view would encompass an entirely different set of factors: population growth, new technologies, new ways of distributing land, labor, or food output.

Long or short time horizons can lead to differing assessments of the situation, and so can wide or narrow space horizons. Those who, by the mandates of their official duties, are concerned primarily with the United States agricultural system may be worried about a revisitation of unmarketable surpluses and falling prices. Those with a global view tend to be concerned about areas of current food shortage or about the effect of higher prices on families already spending 80 percent of their income on food.

Neither of the two extreme viewpoints, the short-term domestic or the long-term global, can be labeled incorrect. Lower prices are indeed a hardship to farmers and a disincentive to increasing production. Higher prices are unquestionably disastrous for the poorest people in all areas of the world. In the short term, population policies might be expected to have no effect and to divert resources from current needs. In the long term, a rapidly growing population may weaken or defeat efforts to improve material living standards. Each conflicting conclusion arising from a different time and space horizon may be valid within its own context.

The debate about whether narrow or wide boundaries or long-term or short-term horizons should predominate in the formulation of public policy must be resolved by the realization that neither view alone is sufficient. Just as a person walking must continually shift attention from the path immediately ahead to the far distance so as to avoid nearby obstacles without losing sight of the ultimate destination, so must a nation find a balance between broad and narrow horizons. Finding this balance may be the most difficult aspect of any political decision, especially since most political rewards and punishments depend on short-term results.

In the case of food and population, I feel that the compromise between the long and short term, and between domestic and international concerns, should be shifted more toward the long-term global view. My reasons for this preference are both pragmatic and moral. The practical necessity for a global perspective is becoming more apparent daily. All the factors that contribute to greater international interdependence—proliferation of nuclear weapons, spreading communication and transportation networks, geographic concentration of energy and mineral resources—render policies made within a national or regional context unrealistic and ineffective. The practical necessity for a long-term view arises from the long delays within food production and population growth processes. A complete global change in either food consumption habits or methods of food production would require shifts in capital stocks and social attitudes that would take decades. Population growth and stabilization are properly viewed not in decades but in human generations. The problems of agricultural shortage and overpopulation are inherently slow to develop, and they are easier to prevent than to solve once they have actually appeared. Transportation of improved seed strains by ship is cheaper than carrying famine relief supplies by helicopter. Overgrazing and erosion can be avoided rather easily, but can be reversed only at great cost. Control of a system with long delays and with high costs for correcting mistakes is impossible to achieve without a long-term perspective.

A moral concern for future generations cannot be justified logically, yet I believe that most people in most cultures feel such concern. In the words of B. F. Skinner: "Why should I be concerned about the survival of a particular kind of economic [or governmental] system?" The only honest answer to that kind of question seems to be this: "There is no good reason why you should be concerned, but if your culture has not convinced you that there is, so much the worse for your culture."[14]

The rest of this paper and its final recommendations reflect my own preference for wider time and space horizons in the consideration of food and population policies. This emphasis does not imply that short-term or domestic concerns should or will be ignored.

---

14. B. F. Skinner, *Beyond Freedom and Dignity* (New York, Alfred A. Knopf, 1971), p. 131.

Given the pressures on all social institutions, current urgent problems are not likely to go unnoticed. The short term will certainly continue to influence policy formulation, as it has in the past. In arguing for the broader longer-term view, I am confident that no argument can make that view completely dominant. I simply hope that the scale may be tipped in that direction.

IV. THEORIES OF POPULATION-FOOD INTERACTION

Four distinctly recognizable theories seem to underlie the most commonly recommended policies for dealing with the world food problem. I will refer to them as the Western Economic Model, the Environmental Model, the Socialist Model, and the Demographic Transition Model. Each will be presented here both in words and in causal diagrams, which can sometimes capture the complexity and simultaneity of mental models better than words. My goal is to outline the similarities and differences of the theories, therefore I will emphasize only what I believe to be the most important elements of each, eliminating much detail and nearly all supporting evidence. Finally, the four models will be combined into a composite that represents most closely my own view.

1. The Western Economic Model

> Price and supply fluctuations are inevitable, as long as the forces of nature—weather and pests—prevail. Price changes are the only way necessary production adjustment, to meet supply and demand changes, will come in an incentive economy . . . The whole question of food security finally comes down to the farmer and whether he will produce, whether he and his family benefit by producing, and whether he has the physical and financial tools available.[15]

---

15. Earl Butz, statement before the House Committee on Agriculture, Subcommittee on Department Operations, July 23, 1974, printed in *World Population and Food Supply and Demand Situation* (Washington, D.C., U.S. Government Printing Office, 1974), pp. 27-29.

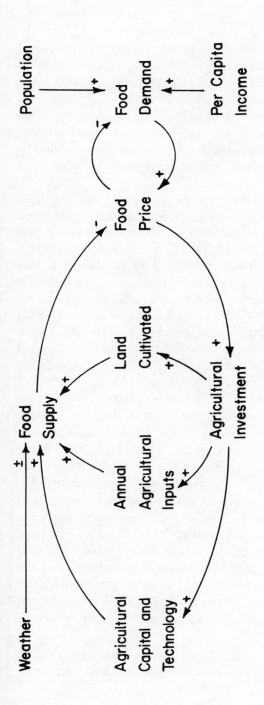

Figure 1. -- Western Economic Model

An *arrow* indicates a causal influence of one element on another. A *plus sign* (+) indicates that the influence is direct—as the element at the tail of the arrow increases, the element at the head of the arrow also increases (if the first element decreases, the second decreases). For example, as food demand goes up, food price also goes up. A *minus sign* (−) indicates an inverse relationship—as the first element increases, the second decreases; and as the first element decreases, the second increases. For example, as food supply goes up, food price goes down. The diagrams do not specify the exact quantitative relationship between elements, nor the rate of response of one element to another (the response may be instantaneous or very much delayed) but represent only rough sketches of underlying models that may be very complicated.

In the Western capitalist nations a model similar to that shown schematically in Figure 1 often forms the basis for policy. Food supply and food demand are brought into balance by the operation of a free competitive market, where food price is the central variable. If supply of any commodity decreases relative to demand, the price will rise. Higher price has two effects—it decreases demand and provides both the funds and the incentive for increased investment in agricultural production. Both these effects tend to bring supply and demand back into equilibrium.

On the supply side, investment can be allocated to any of three factors that increase production—development of new cultivated lands, increase in annual agricultural inputs (fertilizers, pesticides, energy) or increase in longer-lasting agricultural capital (tubewells, tractors, irrigation systems). Investment in research that produces new knowledge may be considered equivalent to investment in long-lasting capital. As land, agricultural inputs, and capital increase, so does food supply, eventually leading to a decrease in food price.

Several factors may interfere with regulation from the supply side of the market system. Weather adds uncertainty to the expected output, even when land, capital, and other inputs are utilized with utmost efficiency. Another complicating factor is the delay in farmers' response mechanisms. Farmers may not believe that a new higher price is meaningful and may not change their investment decisions until it has persisted for some time. Agricultural production can respond to increased investment only after one harvest cycle, at the soonest. Investment in new land or capital may not yield any increased production for several years. This response delay in the supply side of the system can produce alternate over- and under-compensation by suppliers, resulting in the well-known periodic oscillations in many commodity prices.[16]

Those who favor the Western Economic Model are usually well aware of another potential impediment to the responsiveness of the supply side of the system. As investment increases, producing more and more output, diminishing returns to any of the three factors of production may be met—that is, a given amount of additional invest-

---

16. For an extended discussion of this phenomenon, see Dennis L. Meadows, *The Dynamics of Commodity Production Cycles* (Cambridge, Mass., Wright-Allen Press, 1970).

ment might produce less and less additional output. Diminishing returns are often associated with the approach to some physical limit, such as the amount of potentially arable land in a region, or the rate at which plants can absorb nutrients from the soil. Diminishing returns to fertilizer application, for example, are well understood and often encountered in actual farming situations. On an aggregate level and over the long term, however, diminishing returns have often been offset by new technological approaches. The "miracle grains" of the green revolution continue to produce higher yields at levels of fertilizer application well above those where traditional grains reach their maximum yield. Such examples, and analysis of actual historic trends, have led many Western Economists to assume that limits to the effectiveness of agricultural investment are surmountable through the development of new technologies. Thus diminishing returns are not usually included in the Western Economic Model.

Food demand is determined by total population and per-capita food consumption. In the Western Economic Model per-capita consumption is a function of food price and per-capita income. Higher food price relative to per-capita income decreases demand. Population increase stimulates demand, unless per-capita income simultaneously falls. The demand side contains another regulatory mechanism: people demand more food when it is abundant (prices are low) and less food when it is scarce (prices are high). The demand side of the system is not perturbed by unpredictable factors such as weather, but demand may shift to reflect variation in population, per-capita income, or consumer tastes. Response on the demand side is relatively rapid, since it depends on consumer decisions, not on biological or physical processes such as crop growth or construction of capital equipment.

Since it is more rapid, demand adjustment usually plays a major role in maintaining the supply/demand equilibrium. Regulation from the demand side, however, becomes both undesirable and ineffective under one important set of conditions. When food price rises so high that a mere subsistence diet absorbs a large fraction of per-capita income, consumers have no more freedom to reduce consumption in response to higher prices—in economic terms the elasticity of demand approaches zero. Under these conditions supply shortages can be alleviated only by alterations on the supply side, or by malnutrition.

According to the Western Economic Model the interplay of supply and demand, if allowed to proceed without interference, will produce efficient allocation of resources to food production and efficient distribution of food to consumers. Policies based on this model tend to work toward freeing the market mechanism, by restricting monopolization on the supply side and by opposing government interference in the market. From this point of view, interference is only permissible if it is directed toward correcting known imperfections in market operations. Buffer stocks can help smooth out weather fluctuations. Public support of agricultural research, low-cost capital improvement loans, or better information systems can shorten response delays on the supply side. Direct donation of food would be counterproductive, however, because food aid would lower price, thereby destroying local incentive to invest in increased production capacity.

The Western Economic Model, focusing on the continuous and mutual adjustment of supply, demand, and price, represents the agricultural system as self-regulating and self-maintaining. Since, according to the model, short-term adjustments keep the system at or near a desirable equilibrium at all times, a long-term view is unnecessary. Population affects the agriculture system from the outside, but as long as population grows slowly enough, the system can accommodate it. More recently, however, many people who favor the Western Economic view have recognized that the system operates unsatisfactorily when supply is near subsistence and regulation from the demand side breaks down. Thus some free-market supporters advocate measures to slow population growth or to provide sufficient employment to the destitute to keep them in the market. In general, however, the Western Economic Model is associated with optimism and not with strong or urgent recommendations to change the food-population system. The food problem, as seen through this model, is solvable. Governmental policy need only be concerned with protection of market mechanisms, support of basic research, administration of food buffer stocks, dissemination of new technologies, and in the poorest regions widespread employment opportunities combined with family planning.[17]

---

17. For examples of this argument, see Sanderson, "The Great Food Fumble"; Thomas T. Poleman, "World Food: A Perspective," *Science*, 188

2. The Environmental Model

The land of every nation has a limited carrying capacity. The exact limit is a matter for argument, but the energy crunch is convincing more people every day that we have already exceeded the carrying capacity of the land. We have been living on "capital"—stored petroleum and coal—and soon we must live on income alone.

The harsh characteristics of lifeboat ethics are heightened by reproduction, particularly by reproductive differences. The people inside the lifeboats of the wealthy nations are doubling in numbers every 87 years; those outside are doubling every 35 years, on the average. And the relative difference in prosperity is becoming greater.[18]

From an Environmental viewpoint the economic system and the price of food are very nearly irrelevant. The emphasis falls on real physical quantities, rather than on social artifacts such as money or prices. What matters is the amount of food actually available per person, which is most simply determined by the food supply and the number of people among whom the food must be shared.

As in the Western Economic Model, the food supply is increased by capital, annual agricultural inputs, and land development (see Figure 2). However, the Environmental Model includes important limits to all these factors and therefore to the total amount of food that can be produced. Land expansion is limited by the total area of cultivable land on the earth. Capital and inputs are limited by their ultimate resource base, the terrestrial deposits of metals, phosphate rock, fossil fuels, and other nonrenewable resources. Increasing agricultural investment as a policy may increase food supplies in the short term, but only by pushing the entire system nearer to the limits and thereby making further increases in the long term more difficult. The economic concept of diminishing returns to investment in any of

---

(1975), 510, and Don Paarlberg, statement before the House Committee on Agriculture, printed in *World Population and Food Supply and Demand Situation*, p. 16.

18. Garrett Hardin, "Lifeboat Ethics—The Case against Helping the Poor," *Psychology Today* (September 1974), p. 88.

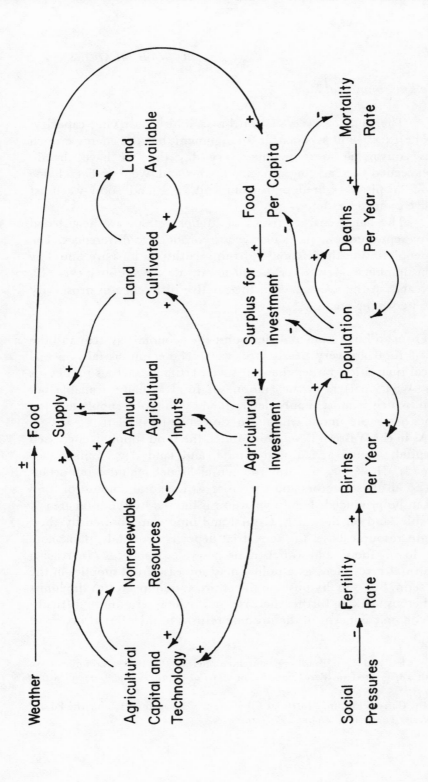

Figure 2. -- Environmental Model

the three factors of agricultural production plays a very important role in this model. Though the absolute limits may be far away, and technology may permit a closer approach to them, the cost of approaching the limits is seen to become higher and higher. In this model technology is primarily a tool for shifting the factors of production from one resource to another; it does not expand the actual size of the resource base.

Since policies to increase food output are ultimately limited in the Environmental Model, more concern is devoted to controlling the other factor in the determination of food per capita: the population. Environmentalists are aware of the tendency of human populations, like all biological populations, to grow exponentially. The number of births per year is determined by the number of people in the population and by the fertility rate. At a given fertility rate the more people there are, the more births will be produced per year. If these births are not balanced by deaths, the population will grow. Eventually the new people will produce still more births. The population will increase ever more rapidly until something happens to make the fertility and mortality rates equal, either by reducing fertility or by increasing mortality.

Environmentalists, like the Western Economists, see a natural self-controlling mechanism in the population-food system, but unlike Western Economists they do not like the mechanism they see. An increasing population tends to decrease food per capita, all else equal. A decrease in food per capita for any reason provides a social impetus to increase agricultural investment. In the long term, however, increased investment pushes the supply side of the system toward the ultimate earthly limits to food production. As those limits are approached, food production can no longer keep pace with population growth, and food per capita declines. Finally malnutrition causes death rates to rise. When mortality has risen so high that deaths balance births, the population stops growing. The natural equilibrium and the final consequence of increasing agricultural investment, in the Environmental view, is a population living near the limits of the earth, held in check by a near-subsistence standard of living.

Since no one desires this outcome, Environmentalists see the need for fairly urgent and major changes in the food-population system. Efforts to increase food supply are considered counterproductive, since more food merely increases population growth and hastens the onset of the undesirable equilibrium. A better outcome can be reached only through a decrease, or at least a stabilization, of the population. Since no one favors population stabilization by increasing deaths, the only acceptable policy must be to decrease births. The more quickly the birth rate falls, the more favorable will be the ultimate balance between population and global resources.

Therefore, the Environmental Model calls for social pressures of one sort or another to decrease human fertility. The fertility reduction policies that are advocated range from further extension of family planning[19] through various incentive or disincentive programs,[20] to "mutual coercion, mutually agreed upon."[21] Sometimes the Environmental argument is also accompanied by opposition to short-term measures for decreasing mortality (the arguments labeled "triage" or "lifeboat ethics").[22]

Environmental policies are focused on the long term and are aimed at increasing the resource/population ratio, so as to improve the standards of living and the quality of life. Thus in addition to supporting population-control policies, Environmentalists tend to favor less wasteful resource consumption habits. They promote technologies such as solar energy conversion or organic farming, which rely upon renewable, rather than nonrenewable, resources. They would encourage deliberate conservation long before the market signals the need for it through scarcity and rising prices. They seek to live within the limits of the earth rather than to try to push those limits outward.

This basically conservative world view leads to a fairly radical policy position. Since the system does not naturally seek a desirable state, large changes must be made. Sociocultural patterns should be altered to favor small families. Resource allocation decisions should not be made by short-term market forces alone. The world food

---

19. Bernard Berelson, "Beyond Family Plannning," *Science*, 163 (1969), 533.

20. Lenni W. Kangas, "Integrated Incentives for Fertility Control," *Science*, 169 (1970), 1278.

21. Garrett Hardin, "The Tragedy of the Commons," *Science*, 162 (1968), 1243.

22. Garrett Hardin, "Lifeboat Ethics," and William and Paul Paddock, *Famine-1975!* (Boston, Little Brown, 1967).

situation is a symptom of a larger problem: the material desires of the human population are approaching the sustainable physical capacity of the earth. The only solution is to stop the growth in those desires by stabilizing the human population and its material consumption.

3. *The Socialist Model*

One of the greatest outrages of the present food situation is the excuse it has provided for muddle-headed apologists for capitalism to blame it all on the "population problem" . . . The very existence of the phenomenon described as "agricultural Malthusianism" represents the greatest *potential* leap forward in the whole of human history—it holds the promise of food productivity on a scale such that *food would become so plentiful it would not be possible even to give it all away*. But under capitalism, such a development would be intolerable . . . The solution to the crisis of world food production can only be realized through its reorganization as social production for human need.[23]

If the price system is irrelevant to the Environmentalist point of view, it is anathema to the Socialists. They believe the most important human goal is the provision of enough food and other goods to meet basic human needs, regardless of price or freedom of the market. The Socialist Model contains some elements in common with the two models described previously, but with some important additions and deletions (see Figure 3).

The central focus of the Socialist Model is on distribution, primarily of the means of production (capital and land) and secondarily of the output from production (food, services, and manufactured goods). The capitalist free-market system and economic exploitation by the rich perpetuate inequities in distribution. These inequities are the cause of the present food problem. The millions of deaths due to hunger each year could all be prevented by a different economic world order.

---

23. Cliff Conner, "Hunger," *International Socialist Review* (September 1974), p. 20.

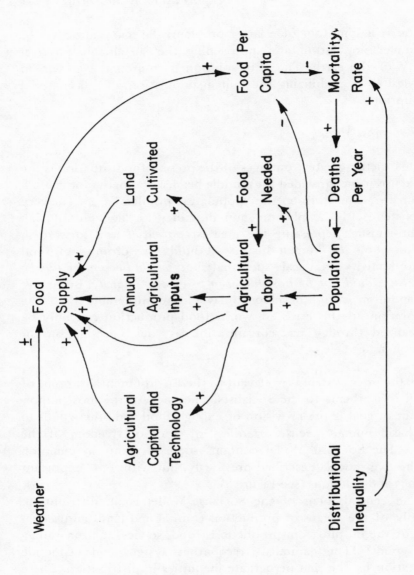

Figure 3. -- Socialist Model

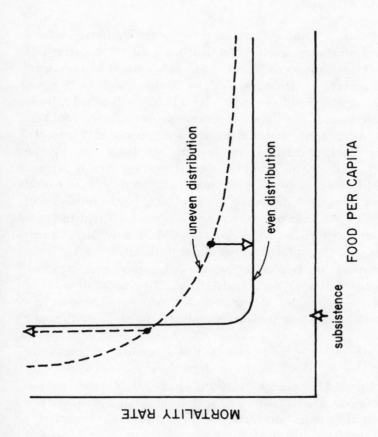

Figure 4. -- Effect of Food Distribution on Mortality

Figure 4 shows possible forms of the relationship between food per capita and mortality, each dependent on a different pattern of distribution. If distribution of food (and all other goods and services) were perfectly even, mortality would be uniformly low. If equal sharing persisted at a food per-capita level below subsistence, however, mortality would soar upward, since no one's share would be adequate for survival (represented by the solid curve in Figure 4). On the other hand, if distribution were uneven (as shown by the dashed curve) some people would die of starvation even if average food per capita were more than adequate, and some people would have sufficient diets even if the average level were below subsistence. Since the amount of food per capita available in the world today is well above subsistence, the food crisis should be solvable through redistribution. As the solid downward-pointing arrow in Figure 4 indicates, the mortality rate could be reduced, not by growing more food but by distributing it differently. "The first maxim of nautical ethics is that you don't go to the lifeboats, which will save only a few, until you've made every effort to salvage the ship for the sake of all."[24]

Environmentalists would answer this Socialist argument by pointing out that in the long term decreasing mortality rates by redistribution would increase population, which would decrease food per capita, moving the system to the left in Figure 4, toward a Malthusian equilibrium. Socialists would agree that a capitalist regime could produce this outcome, but under a socialist system of production, they maintain, the additional population would provide more labor and increase output. Food supply would grow faster than the population, and food per capita would rise. In a society truly devoted to socialist principles, population would become stabilized at a point long before diminishing returns to labor would set in. In fact, many of the socialist nations of the world are now experiencing population growth rates very near zero.

No concept of global limits appears in the Socialist model, nor does any concern for overpopulation. Of crucial importance is the addition of human labor to the factors of production. In fact the Socialist Model elevates labor to the primary factor, upon which all

---

24. Frances Moore Lappé, "Fantasies of Famine," *Harper's* (January 1975).

others depend. Since each new mouth comes equipped with two new hands, overpopulation is unthinkable. Recently some Socialist thinkers have also embraced the idea of "intermediate" or small-scale, labor-intensive technology,[25] which places even more emphasis on labor as the key to increasing agricultural output.

Policies favored by those who see the world through the Socialist Model center on economic reorganization and redistribution. Population policies are viewed with suspicion as distractions from the real issue, and perhaps as disguised genocide. Attempts to increase production under a capitalistic free market are considered exploitive. Socialists are generally enthusiastic, however, about new technologies that increase output, especially technologies that are dependent on the productive factor accessible to everyone—labor—rather than on heavy concentrations of privately owned capital. Socialists vary in the degree to which they would favor complete restructuring of the capitalist system, but most of them would agree that measures such as land reform, food aid, progressive taxation, village-level agricultural education, and alteration of international terms of trade are steps in the right direction.

4. The Demographic Transition Model

> In order to bring the birth rate down, in order to create the conditions in which people see their own interest in having smaller families, we need a continuation of economic development, particularly in the developing countries. In my opinion, it is essentially impossible . . . to expect people in these countries to behave in a way that will stabilize population . . . unless they have sufficient economic development so that they see some reason for doing so.[26]

The theory of the Demographic Transition is based upon the demographic history of nations that have undergone the industrial revolution. The historic pattern of birth and death rates for three

---

25. See E. F. Schumacher, *Small is Beautiful* (New York, Harper and Row, 1973.

26. Roger Revelle, interview with William L. Oltmans in *On Growth* (New York, G. P. Putnam's Sons, 1974), p. 185.

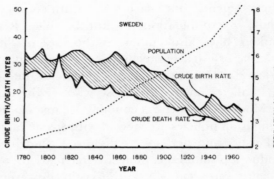

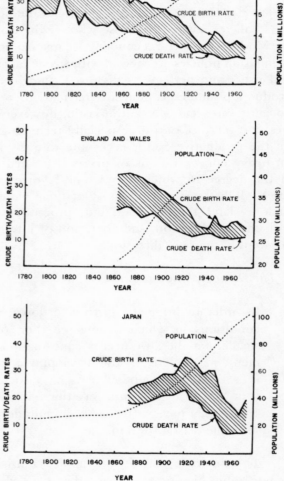

Figure 5. -- Demographic Transition in Industrialized Countries

industrialized nations—Sweden, Japan, and Great Britain—is shown in Figure 5. In all three countries the birth and death rates were once relatively high and the population growth rate was slow. As economic development slowly permitted better living conditions, more reliable food supplies, and medical knowledge, death rates decreased. In the case of Sweden, the crude death rate dropped gradually from 25 deaths per 1000 persons per year to 10 deaths per 1000 per year over a period of 120 years.

As the death rate decreased, the birth rate followed, but even more slowly, typically with a lag of thirty to fifty years behind the death rate. The widening gap between birth and death rates meant rapid population increases for many decades, as shown in Figure 5. Only in the twentieth century have the birth rates of the industrialized countries fallen to about the same level as the death rates, so that the rate of population growth is again relatively slow.

The demographic history of Japan follows a pattern similar to that of European nations, but more compressed in time. After the Tokugawa period of moderate birth and death rates and slow population growth, the Meiji restoration of 1868 effectively eliminated abortion and infanticide, which had been prevalent.[27] Both birth and death rates increased. Around 1900 these trends began to reverse. Within fifty years Japan's birth and death rates were as low as those of Europe.

The historic pattern of change from high birth and death rates to low birth and death rates, illustrated by the three graphs in Figure 5, is called the *demographic transition*. It has been observed in some form in all countries that have industrialized, although its onset, rate of development, and conclusion vary greatly.[28] Despite these variations, however, the demographic transition is the most prominent and consistent demographic phenomenon observed in the history of industrialized areas. It has therefore led to a general theory of population dynamics that is often extended to nonindustrialized nations as well. The basic

---

27. Ryoichi Ishii, *Population Pressure and Economic Life in Japan* (Chicago, University of Chicago Press, 1937).

28. Ansley J. Coale, in *Proceedings of the IUSSP International Population Conference* (International Union for the Scientific Study of Population, Liege, Belgium, 1973), pp. 53–77.

assumptions of the Demographic Transition Model are represented in Figure 6.

The Demographic Transition Model is primarily concerned with two social forces that are assumed to reduce birth rates. First, a decrease in mortality, especially infant mortality, will cause parents to perceive that they are less likely to lose a child. Since they need not have so many children to achieve their desired family size, the number of births will fall. (In historical demographic transitions, death-rate decrease nearly always preceded birth-rate decrease.) Second, an increase in all aspects of industrialization and modernization (represented in Figure 6 by an increase in income per capita) changes the perceived costs and benefits of having children. The Demographic Transition Model assumes, and many current spokesmen for the Third World affirm,[29] that large families in preindustrial societies are needed and wanted. Children are seen as inexpensive labor and as insurance for old-age protection, as well as sources of all the noneconomic, psychic, and cultural benefits associated with children everywhere. Furthermore, in nonindustrial societies children are not regarded as a burden; they do not require much space, food, education, or other material expenditures, and their care is often shared by a large extended family or clan. As a society industrializes, however, the benefits associated with children decrease and their costs increase. The family must become mobile and urbanized to find industrial jobs, so the extended family breaks up. The children, instead of working on a family farm, must become educated so that they too can qualify for the new jobs. Alternate forms of social security emerge. On balance, children are still regarded as highly desirable, but the concept of having only as many as one can afford becomes dominant.

The Demographic Transition Model holds out hope for treating both the food supply and the food demand side of the problem with the same set of policies. Increasing industrial output leads to smaller family size, and also to greater food output, through all the

---

29. See Maaza Bekele, "False Prophets of Doom," *UNESCO Courier* (July-August 1974), p. 42; interview with Mercedes Concepcion in *Ceres* (U.N. Food and Agriculture Organization, November-December 1973), p. 58; Varendra T. Vittachi, "No Future Without a Present," *Newsweek* (September 2, 1974), p. 12.

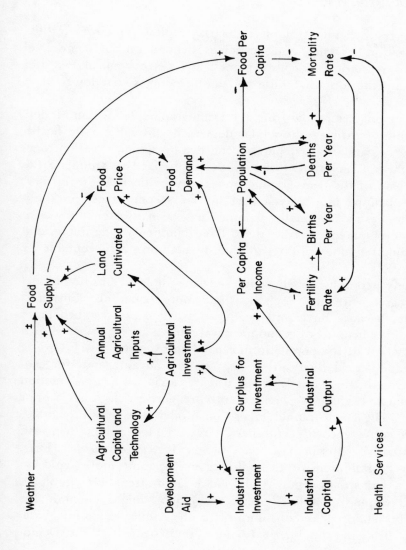

Figure 6. -- Demographic Transition Model

technologies dependent upon industrial capital. Tractors, fertilizers, irrigation systems, and pesticides depend on the same steel mills, oil refineries, assembly plants, and petrochemical factories that create the jobs that raise per-capita incomes that lower birth rates.

What policies follow from the Demographic Transition Model? First, child mortality should be decreased through public health services to start the first part of the demographic transition. Second, industrial investment should be emphasized to stimulate the second part of the demographic transition, the decrease in fertility. Family planning may play a part in this second stage, but only after the desire for smaller families has been awakened by economic development. Before then, large families are desirable, and the population does not regard family planning as acceptable or necessary.

Many people who believe in the Demographic Transition Model would agree with the Socialists that more equal distribution is desirable, because birth and death rates will decrease much more rapidly if the benefits of economic development are experienced by a large fraction of the population rather than by just a few.[30] On the other hand, equal distribution may not be advantageous for economic growth, since a rich person usually can invest a larger fraction of his income and take greater entrepreneurial risks than a poor person.[31] The Demographic Transition Model is usually thought to be more consistent with centralized, large-scale technology than with labor-intensive intermediate technology, for two reasons. First, modern capital-intensive technologies may permit more rapid increase in industrial output. And second, labor-intensive technology, with its emphasis on family-scale techniques, might maintain the desire for children as contributors to the family economic base, thereby delaying the birth-rate decrease expected in the Demographic Transition theory.

---

30. See, for example, William Rich, "Smaller Families through Social and Economic Progress," Washington, D.C., Overseas Development Council, January 1973.

31. For a refutation of this argument, see Rich, "Smaller Families," p. 34.

5. A Composite Model

The four models presented here are often viewed as mutually exclusive and basically inconsistent. For example, at the World Population Conference in Bucharest no agreement was reached between Western Economists and Environmentalists on one side, calling for population control, and Socialists and Demographic Transitionists on the other side, calling for redistribution and economic development. On other issues, such as resource conservation, the Western Economic and Environmental models would lead to very different and seemingly irreconcilable conclusions. On still others, such as the best path toward economic development, those who favor the Socialist and Demographic Transition models would probably part company. Although few people see the food problem simply through one of the models as I have described it, probably even fewer can see all these points of view simultaneously.

When informed and reasonable people consistently maintain very different models of the same underlying reality, it seems probable that no one of those models can be totally wrong, nor can any one be totally complete. Each model is probably a correct description of *part* of the real system. Much can be learned by trying to combine the important insights of all the models into a composite or holistic view. I shall present such a composite model here, starting with the Western Economic Model and adding to it important concepts from other models. A causal diagram of the Composite Model is shown in Figure 7.

The central structure of the Composite Model is the price mechanism of the Western Economic Model. The price mechanism can produce fine-scale adjustments of food supply and demand in the short term and eliminate the necessity for extremely detailed centralized planning. Relatively high food price is a signal that stimulates investment in agricultural factors of production and attracts labor to agricultural jobs, allowing increased food production, as long as reasonable marginal returns to land, labor, capital, and annual inputs can be realized.

When the assumptions of the Demographic Transition Model are added to the Western Economic Model, a reassuring picture of the total food-population situation emerges. With the market to correct supply/demand imbalances in the short term and industrial

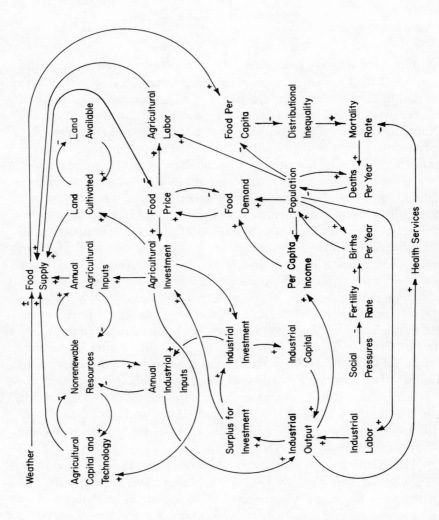

Figure 7. -- Composite Model

growth to increase supply while stabilizing population in the long term, the food problem might be viewed as a temporary problem that is about to solve itself.

For some parts of the world, over some historical periods, the combined Western Economic–Demographic Transition Model provides a sufficient explanation of what has actually occurred. Industrialization has proceeded relatively smoothly, birth and death rates have decreased, and food scarcities have been temporary or nonexistent. The diminishing returns of the Environmental Model and the distributional problems of the Socialist Model do not seem important in representing the history of these now industrialized nations. However, all nations have not followed this pattern, and future patterns need not necessarily resemble historical ones. In order to decide whether the Socialist or Environmental Models can increase the applicability of the Composite Model to the future and to the poorest areas of the world, we must examine more carefully the assumptions behind the Western Economic and Demographic Transition models and the nature of the environmental limits and distributional inequalities that might alter those assumptions.

To begin with the demographic transition, Figure 8 illustrates the historic demographic behavior of three nonindustrialized countries. Comparison with the industrialized-country transitions in Figure 5 will reveal both similarities and differences. A point-by-point comparison of the demographic situations in the nonindustrialized countries during their historical transitions and in the currently industrializing countries indicates that the Demographic Transition Model is not entirely applicable as a guide to future development patterns:[32]

32. Similar criticisms of the general applicability of the Demographic Transition Model can be found in Ansley J. Coale and Edgar M. Hoover, *Population Growth and Economic Development in Low Income Countries* (Princeton, N.J., Princeton University Press, 1958), pp. 13–17, and in Michael S. Teitelbaum, "Relevance of Demographic Transition Theory for Developing Countries," *Science*, 188 (1975), 420.

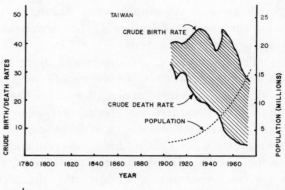

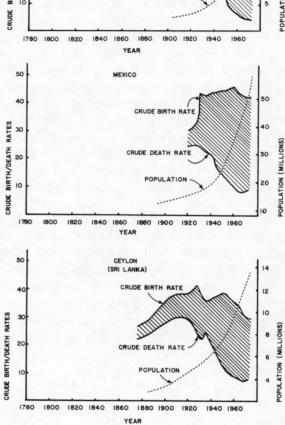

Figure 8. -- Demographic
Transition in Non-
industrialized Countries

Industrialized Countries	*Industrializing Countries*
Decreases in death and birth rates accompanied profound social change. The process of industrialization altered nearly every aspect of the family; its organization, its economic base, its importance relative to other social institutions, and the costs and benefits of having children. All major social changes take time; this one typically extended over 100 to 200 years.	The decrease in death rate has preceded, not accompanied, the deep economic and social changes that result from industrialization. Birth rates are still high and can be expected to remain high, because the traditional family structure is still basically unchanged. The completion of the economic and social development that may bring birth rates down in these countries can be optimistically expected to require at least 50 more years.
During the transition the widened gap between birth and death rates resulted in a multiplication of the preindustrial population by a factor of 4 or 5.	The populations of the non-industrialized countries have already increased by factors of 4 or 5 in this century, with much of the transition still ahead of them. Assuming rapid birth-rate decreases in the near future, these countries will experience a total population multiplication by at least 10 before their transition is complete.
In many European countries the population increase was counteracted by significant out-migration to the New World.	Many of the industrializing areas are already densely settled, and there are essentially no New Worlds left to absorb their population growth.
The maximum rate of population growth in the demographic	Typical population growth rates now are 2 to 3 percent a year in

transitions of the European countries was typically 1 to 1.5 percent a year. Sweden's fastest actual population doubling took 95 years; Great Britain's, 70 years; Japan's, 60 years.

In most European countries the transition began from a birth rate that was already moderate—30 to 35 births per thousand persons.

Because of the moderate birth rates, the fraction of the population under age 15 and economically dependent was rarely more than 35 percent at any time during the transition.

At the end of the transition, the populations of the industrialized countries are still growing. Because of their larger population bases, their annual population increments are not now greatly different from those experienced during the transition. Sweden's 1860 population of 3.5 million increasing at 1.4 percent a year produced an annual increment of 49,000 persons. Sweden's 1970 population of 8 million growing at 0.4 percent a year increased in one year by 32,000. The increase of the U.S. population in 1860 (30 million at 2.2

the nonindustrialized countries, or about twice the rates ever experienced in Europe. Mexico's last population doubling took 20 years; Ceylon's, 25 years; Taiwan's, 20 years.

The crude birth rates at the beginning of the transition are considerably higher than those that obtained in Europe—40 to 50 per thousand instead of 30 to 35 per thousand.

The population of dependent children in these countries is typically 45 to 50 percent of the total population.

percent) was 660,000; in 1970
(200 million at 0.8 percent) it
was 1,600,000.

In short, the current demographic situation in the nonindustrialized nations is not analogous to that experienced by the West
before and during its period of industrialization. Health services
generated by industrial development in the richer countries have
lowered mortality in the nonindustrialized countries and altered the
traditional relationship between the rate of population growth and
the state of industrial development. Rapid population growth slows
the rate of growth of per-capita income, literacy, and industrial
employment, retarding the social changes that seem to bring down
birth rates. The larger population demands more food. In response
to hunger and high food price, either the market mechanism or social
planning diverts output from industrial investment to agricultural
investment, further slowing industrial growth. The intrusion of
externally generated health services in the race between growing
population and growing capital can disrupt the entire development
process. The disruption could be balanced by the addition of externally generated capital as well, but only if the returns to that capital
are reinvested in the economy of the developing country, and if the
entire population benefits from the additional output generated.

When these considerations are added to the Composite Model,
the resulting theory provides both a broader description of reality
and a more uncertain forecast of the future. The model now accounts for imperfections in the market mechanism and interruptions
in the demographic transition. It predicts that industrial growth and
demographic transition could proceed much more slowly in the
future than they have in the past. This result is certainly not inevitable, but it is particularly likely if governments assume that an
automatic and effortless demographic transition will solve the
population-food problem, or if the capital-intensive approach to
development is emphasized over the labor-intensive, or if death rates
are lowered with no coordinated attempt to lower birth rates. In
other words, the Demographic Transition Model, like the Western
Economic Model, is valid only under special circumstances. Those
circumstances include a tight linkage between industrialization and
mortality, an industrial labor demand that absorbs displaced farm

workers, an internal reinvestment of the returns from capital, and a fairly even distribution of the increasing goods and services of the growing economy. Few of these conditions now prevail in the non-industrialized areas of the world. Therefore, distributional constraints, exponential population growth, and perhaps environmental constraints as well should be added to our model.

If the entire world population completes the demographic transition, so that the average global birth rate reaches replacement level by 1980-85 (a development rate that most people would consider impossible), the stationary global population would total 6.4 billion. If the completion of the transition takes until the year 2040 (perhaps more likely), the final population will total more than 15 billion.[33] That number has meaning only in relationship to the earth's carrying capacity—the number of people that could be sustained indefinitely by the ecosystem. If the carrying capacity is well above 15 billion, the Environmental Model's concepts of diminishing returns and earthly limits can be left out of the Composite Model. Policies can then concentrate on establishing the proper conditions for promotion of industrialization and the demographic transition. If an industrialized population of 15 billion would strain the earth's carrying capacity, however, physical limits should be included in the model and should influence policies derived from it.

Taking into account three basic resources—land, water, and solar radiation—a recent study has estimated an absolute maximum global food yield of 49,830 million metric tons per year.[34] This amount of food would support 217 billion persons at subsistence, or 50 billion at the consumption level of a typical European country today (10,000 vegetable-equivalent kilocalories per person per day). The study assumes widespread improvements in technology, optimum weather, perfect management, perfect distribution, no damage from insects or diseases, no limit to material or energy resources,

---

33. Thomas Frejka, *The Future of Population Growth* (New York, John Wiley and Sons, 1973).

34. P. Buringh, H. D. J. vanHeemst, and G. J. Staring, "Computation of the Absolute Maximum Food Production of the World" (Wageningen, The Netherlands, Agricultural University, 1975), p. 47.

multiple cropping, no pollution problems, and no loss of cultivable land to erosion or to uses other than agriculture. The authors of this study do not themselves believe that this output is actually achievable, nor desirable from an ecological viewpoint. Let us assume, however, that it is substantially correct, and simply reduce the limit by 20 percent to allow for weather fluctuations. That gives us an estimated upper limit, on the basis of food needs alone, of 40 billion persons living at industrialized standards of living. As shown by curve A in Figure 9, this limit would be reached, if current population growth rates continued, about the year 2075 (note that the vertical scale in Figure 9 is logarithmic). Two other population projections are shown in Figure 9; curve B illustrates a demographic transition by 2040 to 15 billion people; curve C, a transition by 1985 to 6.4 billion.

The horizontal dashed lines in Figure 9 indicate the possible positions of several other kinds of limits to the global population. The upper limit of 40 billion takes into account only land and water resources and only the food needs of the population. It assumes that energy, capital, fertilizers, and all other resources are available to the agricultural sector in whatever quantities are necessary for maximum yield, and also that arable land and fresh water are used only for food production, not for other human needs. If some other resource is more limiting than land or water, or if agricultural resources must be shared with other sectors, the real physical limit will lie below 40 billion.

Whatever economic system prevails, at some point the added cost of producing more food will be considered not worth the added gain. Resources must be used to produce other things besides food. Under any economic system and technology now conceivable, the point where the marginal cost of producing more food exceeds the marginal benefit will lie far short of the actual physical limit. Especially in an industrial society, the economic limit to food production is lower than the physical limit, simply because the list of human needs contains other items than food alone. In Figure 9 the economic limit has been set at 10 billion, a guess based on the supposition that the present global mixture of capitalist and socialist economies will support the cost of expanding cultivated land by 50 percent and global average yields

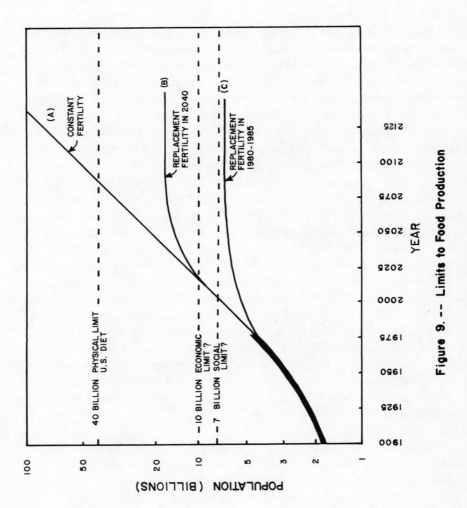

Figure 9. -- Limits to Food Production

by 400 percent over current values. A more careful study, based on considerations of availability of other resources, has actually set this limit at 7 billion.[35]

The third limit shown in Figure 9 arises from the realization that economic decisions are seldom ideal and that many human actions are based on factors other than the most rational allocation of resources to recognized social goals. This social limit accounts for misallocation of resources due to war, greed, corruption, economic monopoly, mismanagement, and resistance to change. Because all men are not of good will, and even men of good will make mistakes, resources are rarely optimally distributed to production processes, nor are final products distributed so as to maximize human welfare. Furthermore, the pressures for maldistribution and the opportunities for and costs of mismanagement probably increase as physical limits are approached. Therefore the social limit must lie somewhere below the economic limit. In Figure 9 it has been rather arbitrarily set at 7 billion. The exact positions of all the limits in Figure 9 are uncertain, and the social limit is certainly the least certain of the three. It has been estimated quantitatively here simply to indicate its position relative to the other limits.

The lower two limits in Figure 9 could be raised by social and technological improvements; the upper one could not, unless the human food supply is drawn from some resource base other than land, water, and sunlight. If the population actually reaches one of the two lower limits, the average material standard of living will begin to fall and the resource base will erode. Eventually the aggregate death rate will rise to equal the birth rate and population growth will stop, until social or technological innovations push the limit upward.

This excursion into the unknown realm of earthly limits has been deliberately oversimplified. I have ignored the vagaries of weather, markets, and international politics that complicate the calculations by imposing short-term fluctuations on the lines in Figure 9. I have not distinguished the disparate and important subregions of the earth, some of which are much closer to their

---

35. D. L. Meadows, W. W. Behrens, D. H. Meadows, R. F. Naill, J. Randers, and E. K. O. Zahn, *The Dynamics of Growth in a Finite World* (Cambridge, Mass., Wright-Allen Press, 1974).

limits than others, some of which have been able to push the social and economic limits much nearer to the physical limits than others, and some of which are approaching the limits at a much faster rate than others. Since we can never know physical or social limits exactly, the only reason for considering them at all is to ask whether any limits are conceivably near enough to be included in a policy oriented model. The estimates and arguments already presented here lead me to believe that some limits may indeed be encountered before a worldwide demographic transition can be completed. Therefore I feel that the constraints of the Environmental Model should be added to the Composite Model.

To summarize, the important concepts from the four partial models that have been included in the Composite Model are:

Western Economic Model

- price as a useful signal of supply/demand imbalances
- use of the market for short-term, incremental adjustments and detailed decision-making
- correction of deficiencies in free market operation.

Environmental Model

- importance of diminishing returns to capital, labor, land, and other inputs
- tendency of populations to grow exponentially unless constrained by physical or social pressures.

Socialist Model

- importance of labor as a factor of production
- moral and pragmatic necessity for equitable distribution
- reorganization of production through intermediate, labor-intensive, operator-owned technologies.

Demographic Transition Model

- coordination of industrial and agricultural development
- role of individual motivations in determining birth rates
- association of industrial development with declining birth and death rates.

The Composite Model leads to the following general conclusions about the future world food situation and the policies that may affect it:

- A free market mechanism is efficient in adjusting short-term supply and demand differentials. Therefore policy should strive to keep the market mechanism operating and should not duplicate its role by imposing detailed, day-by-day interferences with supply, demand, or prices.

– Important long-term forces such as population growth, systematic inequities, and resource limitations tend to push the market system into regions of inelasticity of supply or demand, so that normal adjustment mechanisms are ineffective or unacceptable. Thus policies to maintain the free market must include protection against these long-term trends.

– In all cultures children are desirable, and parents are likely to desire more than a replacement number of them. Populations will grow until some constraint brings birth and death rates into balance. The constraint may be physical, tending to raise death rates, or social, tending to reduce birth rates. Industrialization has historically caused social and economic pressures that reduce birth rates, but not necessarily to replacement levels.

– Considerable expansion of agricultural output is possible, but at a cost in terms of resources needed for other human desires. The cost increases as the level of output increases. Technological advancements may shift the cost from more limiting factors of production (historically, labor and land) to less limiting factors (historically, capital and energy).

– More people could be supported by even distribution of the earth's resources than by current patterns of uneven distribution. Distributional equality may be easier to achieve when resources are abundant than when they are scarce.

– The global resource base may not be sufficient to permit a worldwide transition to industrialization, especially given the rate the transition is currently proceeding, present consumption levels in the most highly industrialized countries, and rates of population growth in nonindustrialized countries.

– National economies today are so tightly intercoupled that even those societies farthest from their resource limits must be concerned about societies that are close to their limits.

V. VALUES AND PRIORITIES

One of the first publications of the newly formed United

Nations was the Universal Declaration of Human Rights. This document reads, in part: "Everyone has the right to a standard of living adequate for the health and well-being of himself and of his family, including food, clothing, housing, and medical care and necessary social services."[36] Similar statements of rights have been issued periodically by various organizations of the United Nations and by many national governments. One of the most recent was released at the U.N. World Population Conference at Bucharest, Romania, in August 1974: "All couples and individuals have the basic right to decide freely and responsibly the number and spacing of their children and to have the information, education, and means to do so."[37]

Declarations of rights are statements of fundamental policy goals, primary objectives that governmental policy should seek above all else. The right to a minimum standard of sustenance and the right to establish a family and determine its size are reiterated constantly in discussions of food and population policy. Yet the Composite Model of the food situation suggests that under some circumstances these two rights may come into conflict with each other, with other human goals, and with the physical laws that govern the earth. Unless by chance families choose to have on the average exactly the number of children required to balance the aggregate death rate, the right to reproduction could lead on an exponential path to the limits of the earth's resources, eventually restricting the right to sustenance. Recognition of this dilemma is by no means recent:

> When goods are increased, they are increased that eat them.
> —Ecclesiastes 5:11

> To feed a family of five
> A farmer must work like an animal

---

36. *The Universal Declaration of Human Rights* (New York, United Nations, 15th Anniversary Edition, 1963).

37. The World Population Plan of Action, *Studies in Family Planning*, 5, No. 12 (December 1974), 383.

To feed a family of six
Even a flogged animal will not work

Chinese adage[38]

Our numbers are burdensome to the world, which can hardly supply us from its natural elements; our wants grow more and more keen, and our complaints more bitter in all mouths. . . . Pestilence, and famine, and wars, and earthquakes have to be regarded as a remedy for nations, as a means of pruning the luxuriance of the human race.

Tertullian, 3rd century A.D.[39]

The pressure arising from the difficulty of procuring subsistence is not to be considered as a remote one which will be felt only when the earth refuses to produce any more, but one which actually exists at present over the greatest part of the globe.

Malthus, 1830[40]

If two important goals, such as freedom of reproduction and guarantee of sustenance, are in direct conflict, pursuing them both may waste effort, at best, and fail to achieve either objective, at worst. The essence of policy-making is the choice among conflicting goals. Choices cannot be made without reference to a theory that suggests what the future costs and benefits of a course of action might be, and to a set of values that indicates what is good, what is bad, and how various goods and bads should be balanced against each other. Even if the model or theory of the causes and consequences of the problem is agreed upon, different sets of values may lead to very different policies.

The world food problem raises some classic value questions,

---

38. Quoted in J. L. Buck, *Land Utilization in China* (Chicago, University of Chicago Press, 1937).

39. Quoted in Harrison Brown, *The Challenge of Man's Future* (New York, Viking Press, 1954), p. 30.

40. Thomas Robert Malthus, *A Summary View of the Principle of Population*, 1830 edition.

debated by many societies for centuries. Is individual freedom more important than social stability and order? Are the needs of future generations as important as the needs of people alive now? If efficiency and equity are inconsistent, which should be sacrificed? How much of a risk to survival justifies how much of an incursion on freedom, justice, or material welfare?

Models and values are certainly not independently learned or chosen. Much of the appeal of a model may stem from its congruence with a particular value set, and the model may then lead to conclusions and observations that reinforce that value set. For instance, the Western Economic Model focuses more on freedom and efficiency than on equity. The Socialist Model sets equity as the highest value, while the Demographic Transition Model emphasizes material welfare and freedom. Of all the models discussed here, only the Environmental and Composite Models suggest a risk to long-term survival and raise the problem of weighing that risk against other values that a society might cherish.

I am not aware of any way of determining a single set of values and priorities that is applicable to all persons at all times. Yet each of us readily forms an operational set of priorities that guides our choices and decisions. These individual value sets may be very different, and the differences may be undebatable. Nevertheless, discussions of policy alternatives might be enhanced if we could make our value sets explicit, not to argue their relative merits, but to increase our understanding of the various viewpoints within our society. My own primary values, in order of priority, are:

1. survival (of the total social and ecological system)
2. material welfare (up to a level of simple comfort, after which this entry goes down to the bottom of the list)
3. equity (equal access to other items on this list)
4. freedom (individual self-determination, diversity)
5. efficiency (maximum output per man-hour)

Of course I consider all five of these goals important and worth pursuing. However, my mental model suggests that striving for efficiency could undermine all four of the other values, a sacrifice I would not be willing to make. To me individual freedom would be meaningless without the first three items on the list; I would give up my personal freedom, if necessary, to obtain survival, material sufficiency, and equity. Equity in poverty does not appeal to me, so I would seek basic material welfare before distributional justice. Survival seems to be necessary before any of the other values can be enjoyed. I would not tolerate a very high risk to total social or ecological survival for any reason, even for one of the other values on the list.

My value set is included here not because it is the best or only defensible one, but because I would like to show what a value set looks like, and because my own policy recommendations depend on my ordering of value priorities. Some of the policy-relevant conclusions that seem consistent with my value set are:

– The long-term survival of human society and the stability of the natural system upon which human society depends should be the highest goal of any policy. Therefore risks to the total system should be minimized, including implicit dependence on as yet unproven technologies.

– According to my value set, the costs of social change are more tolerable than the costs of physical destruction of resources or of environmental integrity.

– Short-term sacrifices, especially material sacrifices, to preserve long-term stability are justified. In accordance with the goal of equity, sacrifices for the future should be borne disproportionately by the privileged of today.

– The quality of human life is more important than the quantity, and material sufficiency is more important to quality of life than is the freedom to have more than two children. Therefore, the right to sustenance has a higher priority than the right to reproductive freedom.

– Several important aspects of quality of life cannot be measured in strictly economic terms. Therefore decisions should be made on a broader basis than simple economic cost-benefit analysis.

– Industrialization is a means to one end that can improve the quality of life, namely material welfare. It may not be the only means to that end, and it is not an end in itself.

– In the interests of preserving individual freedom and diversity, intervention by centralized government should be minimal. Intervention is justified only to preserve the three values prior to freedom: survival, basic material welfare, and equity.

VI. PRIMARY POLICY CONSIDERATIONS

In the remainder of this paper I will attempt to translate these idealistic value statements into general guidelines for United States food and population policy. I shall assume throughout this discussion that the primary purpose of food-population policy is to solve the problem of world hunger, not to gain national or personal political power or to achieve any other short-term, narrowly bounded goal.

All possible solutions to the world food problem can be grouped into three major categories:

– Produce more food. Both technological and social changes can bring more land into production and increase yields on land already cultivated. These policies aim to move the economic limit closer to the physical limit to food production. Future extension to non-land-based food production (such as single-cell protein and hydroponics) raises the physical limit itself by substituting other resources, particularly energy, for land. Most current policy efforts fall into this category. They have the advantage of relatively short-term payoffs and of emphasizing technological sophistication, the major asset industrialized countries have to offer. The costs of these policies tend to be economic and environmental, rather than social. They require little change in the way industrial societies are used to doing things, but they demand major revisions in the life styles of non-industrialized populations.

– Allocate food more efficiently. In this category fall efforts to control agricultural prices and trade flows, to change nutritional habits, to establish buffer stocks, to provide famine relief, to reduce luxury consumption, and to restructure economic systems. All these policies attempt to move the social limit and, by changing priorities, the economic limit closer to the physical limit. They would allow more people to be nourished, even if food output did not increase at all. These policies could reduce hunger very rapidly, once actually implemented. Their costs are almost entirely social; they require attitude changes and new institutions. Their effect on the environment would be minimal. They would require economic readjustment, but probably very little additional economic cost in terms of total investment or resources.

– Slow population growth. Current efforts here are dominated by family-planning programs. A few governments have experimented

with rewards or punishments for conforming or nonconforming family sizes.[41] Population-control policies are necessarily long term; they may not produce visible results for decades. Their costs are largely social; they would probably result in net economic and environmental benefits. The aim of population stabilization is to avoid all limits to food production, and therefore it offers the only permanent solution to the food problem.

Discussions about food and population policy sometimes degenerate into arguments about which of these three options to pursue exclusively. I believe it would be more fruitful to decide which mixture of all three would be best; how much time, research, thought, and investment to devote to each. When that decision has been made, the detailed administration of each option will require further implementation decisions. For example, under the category of producing more food, secondary policies turn upon questions such as the best way to market new grains or fertilizers, the most effective form of agricultural education, and the appropriate budget to be allocated to nitrogen-fixation research. Most decision-makers necessarily spend a majority of their time on such secondary, implementation questions, often with no opportunity to review the primary decision about the relative emphasis on major options. I will begin here with this primary question and move from there to questions of implementation.

Current policies in most countries seem to concentrate on producing more food, with some emphasis on food distribution, and only a few serious efforts at population control. The time horizon, model, and value set I have presented here would suggest that, although all three options must be pursued vigorously, the order of priorities should be reversed. Population control is the only ultimately effective solution and the one with lowest total costs; therefore it should receive the most effort. Since population control measures cannot be accomplished quickly, however, redistribution and more efficient food production will be needed to minimize

41. See, for example, Willard A. Hanna, *The Republic of Singapore: Population Review 1970*, American Universities Field Staff Reports, Vol. 19, No. 5 (1971) and *China's Experience in Population Control*, Committee on Foreign Affairs, U.S. House of Representatives, Washington, D.C., U.S. Government Printing Office, September 1974.

medium-term food shortages. Redistribution can produce almost immediate results with low ecological and economic costs, and it is also morally desirable, according to my values. Therefore it should receive emphasis second only to population stabilization. Food production, the third priority, should be labor-intensive in order to use the major resource of the most needy countries, and should be concerned with conservation of energy and natural ecosystems, as well as with increased output.

Setting the policy priorities in this order raises many secondary questions about how such measures could be implemented. Is redistribution consistent with market economies? How can governments influence birth rates? What ecologically sound food-production technologies are possible? What would a world based on the model and values presented here be like?

VII. IMPLEMENTATION CONSIDERATIONS

One reason that current policies emphasize technological adjustments rather than socioeconomic adjustments may be that governments have already at hand the mechanisms, institutions, and personnel necessary to implement technological changes. Western governments, in particular, are accustomed to guiding technical activities. When it comes to directing a deliberate change in values, life styles, or social arrangements, however, current governments have almost no experience and very little imagination. For example, many people can picture government involvement in population stabilization only in terms of direct dictation of individual family sizes, with punitive action for offenders who produce too many children. Visions arise of policemen in bedrooms and of forced sterilization. If Orwellian measures are the only imaginable way to implement population policy, it is not surprising that such policy is carefully avoided. Unfortunately, the very belief that no acceptable social-change policy exists cuts off all discussion of government involvement in social change, and therefore the innovative thinking that might produce acceptable policies is not encouraged.

I would like to discuss implementation considerations here in just enough detail to indicate what directions might be followed. My aim is to outline some possible programs, more to stimulate imagination and generate new ideas than to ascribe any completeness or uniqueness to the examples I have chosen. I assume that once a general direction is agreed upon, experimentation, observation, evaluation, and revision can be used to work out operating details.

These implementation recommendations have been derived from the Composite Model and the value set already presented. I believe they are consistent with that model and those values. The recommendations have been conceived as a whole and should be evaluated in that light. I would not advocate some of the individual recommendations unless they were combined with the others.

One last word of warning before the list of recommendations begins: food-population issues, perhaps above all others, are impossible to separate cleanly into foreign and domestic spheres of influence. Domestic food prices may be changed by new export arrangements or massive donations for famine relief. New agricultural technologies can alter the lives of American farmers as well as African ones. The annual increase in the United States population, because of its higher rate of per-capita consumption, increases the effective demand on the world food supply by nearly as much as the much higher annual increase in the population of India. Even if the United States were primarily interested in improving the food supply-demand balance in the Third World, our influence might be greatly enhanced by consistent population and food policies at home. As George F. Kennan stated in a speech on foreign policy in 1954:

> Now this problem of the adjustment of man to his natural re-
> sources, and the problem of how such things as industrialization
> and urbanization can be accepted without destroying the tradi-
> tional values of a civilization and corrupting the inner vitality
> of its life—these things are not only the problems of America;
> they are the problems of men everywhere. To the extent that
> we Americans become able to show that we are aware of these
> problems, and that we are approaching them with coherent and
> effective ideas of our own which we have the courage to put
> into effect in our own lives, to that extent a new dimension will
> come into our relations with the peoples beyond our borders.[42]

---

42. George F. Kennan, *Realities of American Foreign Policy* (Princeton,

1. Population Policy

In the spirit of the above quotation, I believe that the single most effective policy the United States could implement to promote population stabilization in the world is to announce and seek the goal of population stabilization at home. Population stabilization has already been recommended by the Commission on Population Growth and America's Future,[43] who took into consideration domestic needs alone. Stabilization of the United States population would also enhance population policy efforts abroad, by weakening suspicions of genocide and imperialism, and by providing us with practical experience in programs we are urging others to adopt. Although fertility in the United States is relatively low, our population is still growing. No deliberate governmental policies have been responsible for the recent decline in the birth rate, and none has yet appeared to prevent it from rising again. What sorts of policies could possibly do that?

The birth rate is the result of millions of individual decisions made by families and affected by the complex of rewards and constraints, economic and social, perceived at the family level. Better birth control methods help families achieve the number of children they desire more efficiently and at lower cost. But birth control cannot stabilize population unless families happen to desire, on the average, the number of children just required to balance the death rate of the population. Birth control programs are necessary, but not sufficient to ensure eventual population stabilization.

Governments continually influence the economic and social conditions felt by families, and thus governments are already involved in determining birth rates, implicitly and almost accidentally. Such accepted governmental powers as taxation, housing policy, public health administration, highway construction, education, and monetary policy all affect family incomes, expectations, costs, and location. Any of these factors could alter childbearing decisions. For example, birth rates are known to increase in times of economic

---

N.J., Princeton University Press, 1954), quoted in *The New Yorker* (April 21, 1975), p. 29.

43. Commission on Population Growth and the American Future, *Population and the American Future* (New York, Signet, 1972).

growth and to decrease in depressions;[44] and apartment size may have an influence on family size in several industrialized countries.[45]

Since there is no question that governmental policy will influence birth rates, we need ask only whether the influence will be accidental and unpredictable or deliberate and consistent with other social policies. Stabilization measures in the United States could begin with reexamination of current policies that are inadvertently pronatalist, including unequal income-tax rates for single persons and childless families, subsidization of middle-income housing facilities, and the remaining forms of discrimination against women. Positive steps could include demographic education both in schools and in the media, and free clinics for contraception, abortion, and sterilization. Probably most effective of all would be the public acceptance of a small family norm through as many channels of public information as possible, from presidential speeches to advertising campaigns.

With respect to population growth in other countries, I feel that the United States should support all locally originated policies to reduce birth rates. We should not attempt to impose any particular strategies or techniques, or to oppose measures acceptable to other cultures but not to ours. An American advisory service could provide aid in family planning, demographic record-keeping, and other population-related services, but only as requested by the recipient nation.

Although I very much favor national autonomy in dealing with population questions, I believe United States policy should be insistent upon one simple condition: measures to lower death rates should be linked directly with measures to lower birth rates. All forms of death control, from public health consultations to food donations, should be available on request of any nation, but only as a package that includes serious population stabilization programs, chosen by the recipient, as well. No nation need be pressured to accept this package, but under no condition should one part of it be available without the other. The choice of high birth and death

---

44. Richard A. Easterlin, "On the Relation of Economic Factors to Recent and Projected Fertility Changes," *Demography*, 3 (1966), 131.

45. Bernard Berelson, ed., *Population Policy in Developed Countries* (New York, McGraw Hill, 1974).

rates may be more acceptable to other cultures than it is to ours. The choice of low birth and death rates may take a long time to achieve, as it did in our own country, but we should help implement it upon request. The one unacceptable choice, from a global viewpoint, is high birth rate and low death rate. No ecosystem can support that choice for long, and our own policy should be to refuse any attempt to implement it. Clearly this policy should be followed only in combination with our own domestic population-stabilization efforts; we should not impose conditions on others that we are unwilling to impose on ourselves.

From a short-term viewpoint, this policy may appear coercive and antihumanitarian. It is coercive in that it dictates one major constraint to all nations—birth rates shall not be maintained higher than death rates. That constraint is derived from the physical laws of the planet, however, not from the selfish desires of any one group of people. The condition of population stabilization interferes with some freedoms, but it lets each government accomplish that interference as it sees fit. At the same time it creates other freedoms by reducing the threats to survival, welfare, and equity that overpopulation would bring.

As for humanitarianism, decreasing death rates in an otherwise unchanged society may appear beneficial for a few decades, but the resultant population growth rates will ultimately hinder efforts at further development. In the long run a short-term humanitarian impulse could produce a population driven to its physical limits with little hope of betterment. According to my value system, a nonindustrialized society might better postpone decreases in the death rate until social and economic conditions have evolved to permit concurrent decreases in the birth rate. Then both vital rates can move downward in phase, as they did in the demographic transitions of the West, and a *permanent* reduction in mortality and fertility can be achieved.

2. Distribution Policy

I believe that distribution policy, like population policy, should begin at home. The Bucharest and Rome Conferences demonstrated that a nation with 6 percent of the world's people consuming 30–40 percent of the world's resources can be viewed only with deep suspicion by the Third World. If the United States hopes to persuade other countries to follow long-term, globally oriented population and food policies, we must actively try to reduce our own consumption of food-related commodities, including fertilizer and energy. Measures to be considered include luxury taxes on grain-fed meat, tobacco, and highly processed foods; limitation of fertilizer use to agricultural purposes; control of pet populations; nutrition education; and numerous energy-conservation measures, from minimum fuel-efficiency standards for automobiles to deregulation of natural gas and petroleum prices. These measures would do more than increase the international credibility of the United States. They would also improve our domestic economic health by reducing our dependence on imports of vital resources, and by hastening the coming technological transition from nonrenewable to renewable resources.

Domestic conservation policies may increase the already large amount of food the United States has available for sale on the world market. Some of this surplus should be allocated to grain buffer stocks for countering weather-induced emergencies. I believe the remainder should be sold on the international market, not given away. Donated food provides short-term aid to poor countries, but at the same time it destroys local incentives, encourages corruption, and tends to lower death rates without providing an incentive for lowering birth rates.

Reduction in food aid does not imply reduction in other kinds of aid or disinterest in the plight of the poor. Quite the contrary, if food-importing countries are to benefit from United States surplus on the international market, they must have purchasing power derived from their own economic systems. At least in the medium term, the development of those economic systems could be hastened by foreign aid, but aid of a different kind than direct transfers of Western food, capital, or technology. This paper is not meant to be a disquisition on economic development. I would simply like to mention two directions of change in aid policy that might lead to a fair and permanent global redistribution of economic power.

First, a new attitude about the ability of the United States to develop other countries might be useful. Current examination of several past decades of foreign aid is resulting in a healthy skepticism about the general applicability of Western methods, resources, and organizational forms to non-Western societies. Out of this reassessment should come not discouragement and abandonment of effort, but a constructive humility and openness to other ways of doing things. If we could approach the problem of each country's development as a co-explorer with that country, willing to listen and learn as well as to teach, we might not only be more welcome, we might also make more progress. Further suggestions along this line are included in the following section on food production.

Second, a more systematic understanding of the distributional consequences of international trade is needed. The Third World countries have often complained that the international terms of trade discriminate against them. Recent studies confirm that the operations of multinational corporations[46] and of the world food market[47] both result in an effective subsidy to the rich nations from the poor. If the international economic system regularly undoes what aid programs are attempting to do, then a restructuring of trade as well as aid would certainly be in order.

One last factor to be considered under the topic of redistribution is the relationship between the free market and equity. I have already described some of the short-term regulatory advantages of the free market in my description of the Western Economic Model. A long-term problem of the market system, however, is that it creates and exacerbates inequality by rewarding the most competitive producers and consumers with the means to produce or consume even more competitively in the future.[48] Ultimately the system leads to its own destruction by producing oligopoly. If the advantages of the market system are to be preserved, this long-term tendency must

---

46. Richard Barnet and Ronald Muller, *Global Reach: The Power of Multinational Corporations* (New York, Simon and Schuster, 1974).

47. H. Linnemann, "Fourth Report to the Club of Rome" (Amsterdam, The Netherlands: in press).

48. For further discussion of this aspect of the market system, see Bertram G. Murray, Jr., "What the Ecologists Can Teach the Economists," *New York Times Magazine* (December 10, 1972), p. 38; Garrett Hardin, "The Cybernetics of Competition," *Perspectives in Biology and Medicine*, 7 (1963), 58, reprinted in Shepard and McKinley, *The Subversive Science* (Boston, Houghton Mifflin, 1967); and D. H. Meadows, "Equity, The Free Market, and the Sustainable State," paper, Proceedings of the First Biennial Assessment of Alternatives to Growth, The Woodlands, Texas, October 19–21, 1975.

be constantly opposed. Domestic policies to redress the distributional imbalances of the market could include, on the demand side,
a truly progressive income tax and a minimum income allowance,
and on the supply side, meaningful enforcement of antitrust legislation and a land reform that limits farm size, similar to land reforms
we often suggest to other countries. For reasons given in the next
section, I do not believe that a reduction in the size of producing
units would reduce total efficiency. Even if it did, I would value
the gains in freedom, equity, and stability of smaller units of production more highly than the slightly greater output from larger units.

3. Food Production Policy

Agricultural research and development is already well funded
in this country, and it has contributed greatly to increased production all over the world. I would add to the ongoing efforts only two
suggestions. First, we need a national policy to preserve our own
agricultural land and keep it in production. Second, food production
research should focus on the particular needs of nonindustrialized
areas, including tropical agriculture, and on intermediate-scale
technology.

Intermediate agricultural technology is an approach that emphasizes tools and inputs that are appropriate for villages and small
farms and that can be manufactured and repaired locally from
renewable materials. It also involves more human and less fossil fuel
energy. Examples of intermediate agricultural technologies include
digesters to produce fertilizers from household and urban organic
wastes, biological pest control, windmills for pumping water, solar
grain driers, small sturdy hand tractors, methane generators, and
many sorts of handtools. Some of these suggestions may sound like a
return to old-fashioned practices. But new designs, materials, and
knowledge are now being combined with traditional methods in
some ingenious attempts to capture the best of the new and the old.[49]

Intermediate technologies are ideally suited for nonindustrialized
countries with excess labor and a shortage of capital. They are

---

49. For examples see such publications as *Appropriate Technology* (quarterly from Intermediate Technology Publications, Ltd., 9 King Street, London
WC2E8HN) and *Coevolution Quarterly*, Box 428, Sausalito, Calif., 94965.

naturally conservative of commodities whose prices are now rising, such as petroleum and natural gas. Ecologically, intermediate technologies are much more acceptable than current Western farming methods. They can combat erosion and gradually improve soil fertility and they tend to introduce fewer foreign substances into ecosystems, since they are based on naturally occurring renewable materials.

The intermediate scale is fully compatible with redistribution goals that call for smaller farms. Neither intermediate-technology farming nor smaller units of production are likely to reduce output. In many countries smaller farms consistently outproduce large farms on a per-acre basis, although they do produce less output per man-hour.[50] In other words, they maximize returns to an increasingly scarce factor of production, land, rather than to an increasingly abundant one, labor. These production methods are therefore capable of producing both increased total output and increased rural employment.

The most promising aspect of small-scale, intermediate-technology may be its potential for promoting self-sufficient production and maintenance on the village level. This approach may be the key to the redistribution necessary to keep poor consumers in the market, and ultimately to the social changes that can bring about real, internally generated development and the demographic transition. As E. F. Schumacher says:

> Give a man a fish . . . and you are helping him a little bit for a very short while; teach him the art of fishing, and he can help himself all his life. On a higher level: supply him with fishing tackle; this will cost you a good deal of money, and the result remains doubtful; but even if fruitful the man's continuing livelihood will still be dependent upon you for replacements. But teach him to make his own fishing tackle and you have

---

50. For examples from developing countries see Keith Griffin, *The Political Economy of Agrarian Change* (Cambridge, Mass., Harvard University Press, 1974), pp. 38, 42, 59. For data from the United States, Japan, and India, see Kusum Nair, *The Lonely Furrow* (Ann Arbor, University of Michigan Press, 1969).

helped him to become not only self-supporting, but also self-reliant and independent.[51]

VIII. CONCLUSION

There may be no more important social problem in this century than the increasing imbalance between the human population and the resource base that sustains it. This problem is creeping, diffuse, and undramatic compared with others that command attention—nuclear proliferation, international monetary disturbances, oil prices, or the politics of the Middle East. Yet the food-population problem is related to all these problems, and to others now barely visible on the horizon. Although solving the food-population problem is unlikely to mitigate all world problems, many world problems and conflicts will certainly get worse if the food-population balance is not restored.

> As physical resources are everywhere limited, people satisfying their needs by means of a modest use of resources are obviously less likely to be at each other's throats than people depending upon a high rate of use. Equally, people who live in highly self-sufficient communities are less likely to get involved in large-scale violence than people whose existence depends on worldwide systems of trade. . . . As the world's resources of nonrenewable fuels—coal, oil, and natural gas—are exceedingly unevenly distributed over the globe, and undoubtedly limited in quantity, it is clear that their exploitation at an ever-increasing rate is an act of violence against nature which must almost inevitably lead to violence between men.[52]

The food-population situation will not be improved without a major global change in policies, priorities, and social institutions. No problem can be solved while preserving every aspect of the system that generated it. The system must change, but this is a statement that should be viewed not with despair but with hope. We surely

---

51. E. F. Schumacher, *Small is Beautiful*, p. 186.
52. Ibid., p. 57.

can imagine many worlds better than one in which a large fraction of the population is poor and hungry. Some of the necessary changes, such as lower birth rates, are already happening spontaneously, but slowly, and need only be accelerated. Other changes, such as redistribution, are desirable in their own right. New technologies based on conservation of resources and preservation of small-scale control will surely be welcomed in the petroleum-depleted long run by rich and poor countries alike.

Although many of the policies I have recommended may seem extreme from the well-fed and only slightly worried perspective of the American middle class, all are intrinsically possible, and most are clearly beneficial to current as well as future generations. My suggestions require a shift in viewpoint more than any real sacrifice. Millions of Americans are voluntarily moving toward satisfying, productive life styles based on small families, less consumption, and more concern for the unfortunate of the world.[53] My own family has moved in that direction, and the result is not a loss but a clear and substantial gain in the quality of our lives.

In this paper I have followed an idealistic process and come to idealistic conclusions. I do not believe that idealism is out of order in policy discussions. Social change can occur only when there is a perceived gap between the ideal and the real. Thus any society that is evolving, not stagnant, should welcome both criticism of the current state of the system and descriptions of possibilities that are yet unrealized. Politics, "the art of the possible," can make no progress without occasional reminders that more is possible than is currently being done.

---

53. For examples of "how-to" publications with circulations in the millions, see *Organic Gardening and Farming*, Organic Park, Emmaus, Penna. 18049, *Mother Earth News*, P.O. Box 70, Hendersonville, N.C. 28739, and Frances Moore Lappé, *Diet for a Small Planet* (New York, Ballantine, 1971).

EDITOR'S NOTE

In a recent article, John P. Lewis, a former AID official and now Professor of Economics and International Affairs at Princeton University, observed that "dominant Western opinion is not just disillusioned over development; it has almost stopped considering it." He went on to predict that "if this blindness persists, we are heading for disaster."* In the essay that follows, Professor Kasfir examines the American commitment, or lack of commitment, to promote development. The discussion focuses on Africa not because it is typical but rather because it is the hardest area in which to justify an American commitment to development. If one can demonstrate the desirability of such a commitment in Africa, he argues, it should be even easier to make a similar case regarding other areas.

Although the trend toward a diffusion of power in the international system has generally had the effect of increasing the relative importance of small nations, this is not uniformly true. In terms of development and, Kasfir reasons, the Cold War, rivalry of the bipolar world furnished one of the strongest incentives for the United States to aid in development in the Third World. This incentive has now been greatly weakened.

Although Kasfir's essay offers a rather pessimistic view of what role America can and will play in promoting development, one should remember that he is dealing with the extreme rather than the typical case.

* John P. Lewis, "Oil, Other Scarcities, and the Poor Countries," World Politics, 27 (October 1974), 64.

VII.

Interdependence and American Commitment to Promote Development in the Third World: Africa—the Hardest Case

Nelson Kasfir

What impact does the growing acceptance of global inter-dependence, as the basis of foreign policy, have on the American commitment to assist Third World development? Although the shift from reliance on anticommunism to reliance on interdependence has increased the influence of many countries on United States goals, the reverse may be true for the poorest and weakest states. Increasing attention to interdependence has the effect of *reducing* the importance of most of the world's poorest countries for American policy-makers. One important indication of this shift in foreign-policy priorities has been the erosion of the American aid budget for development.

The question for the next five years is whether America will continue to give foreign aid to poor countries. The trend over the last decade makes this a real question. To answer it requires asking whether it is in America's national interest to continue giving aid. As Baldwin's introductory essay in this study suggests, it is becoming more difficult to calculate the United States national interest, because resources have grown more scarce and priorities more obscure. The hardest case to make for a continued commitment to promote development over the next several years will be in subsaharan black African countries, because they have the most remote tie to furthering American national interests. But if a successful rationale can be found for American commitment to aiding African countries over the next five years, the case for support for development elsewhere in the Third World is likely to be stronger.

Giving development aid to poor countries will remain in the American national interest over the next five-year period. Several reasons are discussed in the last section of this chapter. Together they provide a defense of a minimalist position—a floor below which the aid budget is not likely to fall. To set these reasons fully in context requires understanding why this American commitment has become seriously eroded over the past decade.

Consequences of Basic Changes in the Conduct of United States Foreign Policy

The American commitment to development has weakened as emphasis on bipolar rivalry between the United States and the U.S.S.R. has diminished. The growing acceptance of a multipolar, multilevel, and multiunit conception of international activity has introduced a far more complex view of the world. In part this has been the product of increasing agreement that the United States cannot control outcomes in many situations, and further that in many other cases there is little to be gained even when it can heavily influence other national leaders.

By recognizing that many kinds of units have differing amounts of influence on various issues, United States foreign-policy makers have been reducing their estimates of potential American influence to more realistic aspirations. The Vietnam war probably provided their single most important lesson, though the political changes brought about by the concerted political and economic actions of the oil-producing countries may turn out to be more significant. There are many new actors in the world today—new states, new multinational corporations, and new international charitable or- ganizations—and these have played a growing role. As a result the complexity of calculations that foreign-policy makers must introduce has greatly increased. Goals to which American resources were regularly committed in the early 1960's are no longer felt to be worth the cost. The United States, in other words, was never as powerful as its policy-makers believed it to be. In addition it is probably somewhat less powerful today than it actually was ten or twenty years ago.

The consequence of this change in the conduct of foreign policy has amounted to a reassessment of American interest in poor countries located far from global centers of stress and conflict. In a bipolar world poor nations commanded attention no matter where they were located, because they were believed to be important prizes in the struggle for world supremacy. Today their demands are taken less seriously by the makers of United States foreign policy. Indeed, were the State Department to adopt officially a "pragmatic regional" approach (one of several options Baldwin mentions above), it would be likely to make more explicit the lack of influence poor nations have on American foreign policy. African countries generally have fewer linkages with other parts of the world than do other regions. Focusing on an "interdependent" approach reveals the paucity of African interdependencies with other areas.

For this reason, poverty—the basic reason for giving development aid—commands less concern in a complex multipolar situation than it did in the simpler bipolar world of the past decade. In short the present global conception of American foreign policy has contributed to a low profile in many poor states, which in turn has reduced American willingness to promote their development. Growing recognition of interdependence in many areas of the world has led to reduced emphasis on interdependence in others. Since official policy is one of the factors that can increase or reduce the level of interdependence between nations, the changes in United States priorities growing out of the multipolar model are contributing to a reduction in interdependence between America and the poor nations.

Erosion of the American Commitment to Promote Development

The attack on the American commitment to give aid for the development of Third World nations has come from many quarters in the past few years. Although there has always been domestic opposition to United States foreign aid from the right, criticism is now being voiced by former liberal proponents as well as radicals.

American interest in assisting other countries extends beyond the Third World and predates Point Four in President Truman's inaugural address of January 1949. The Marshall Plan provided economic assistance toward the recovery of Europe from the consequences of fighting World War II. Even earlier, however, United States policymakers had become interested in assisting the development of poor

nations.[1] Development was understood to mean economic growth—
an equation that has since come under attack. In the mid-1940's
financial assistance in the form of loans, grants, or technical personnel
was seen as a last resort. The more important tools to promote
economic growth were thought to be greater effort by the poor
countries themselves, higher investment of outside private capital,
and increased trade.

In the quarter century since Truman insisted that "we must
embark on a bold new program for making the benefits of our
scientific advances and industrial progress available for the improvement and growth of underdeveloped areas,"[2] much has been attempted. But experience does not seem to have been a good teacher.
The most easily identifiable, and the greatest, successes came first.
Western European countries used Marshall Plan aid to get back on
their feet. The effort to duplicate those achievements in the Third
World has led to frustration. Not only have many projects to promote development failed to achieve any noticeable progress, but a
school of thought now argues that what we have been calling "development" has actually made matters worse for the supposed
beneficiaries. Present criticisms extend not only to the issue of the
usefulness of promoting development, but to questioning whether
American efforts work against the very goals United States policy-
makers proclaim.

Changes in the level and the strategy of American developmental assistance to African countries since the early 1960's illustrate
the weakening of this commitment. Foreign aid to Africa reached a
level of $326 million in 1962 and fell to $163 million by 1973. The
American record looks better if P.L. 480 loans and Export-Import
Bank credit and loan guarantees are included, the total aid figure for
1962 being $471 million, with a drop to $397 million in 1972.[3]

---

1. David A. Baldwin, *Economic Development and American Foreign
Policy: 1943-62* (Chicago, University of Chicago Press, 1966), pp. 15, 16-24.
2. Inaugural Address, 20 January 1949.
3. Charles C. Diggs, Jr., U.S. Congress, House Committee on Foreign
Affairs, Subcommittee on Africa, Hearings, *The Crisis of Development and
Interdependence* (93d Cong., 1st and 2d Sess., 1974), p. 2 (cited below as
Hearings). This trend will soon result in the United States being replaced by
China as the most important non-European source of aid in Africa. Although
this is a dramatic illustration of growing multipolarity in the world, it should be

But aid per-capita figures have fallen more strikingly than total aid figures would suggest, because African populations have grown rapidly. Also, in 1962 many African countries had not yet received independence and were not candidates for aid. So aid per-potential recipient has dropped even more dramatically than the population explosion would imply. Aid expenditure figured as a percentage of American GNP has also declined more rapidly than the dollar figures alone would suggest. The degree of erosion of this concern is highlighted to some extent by the recent offer of $250 million of economic assistance to Egypt alone. This offer is one indication that neither inflation nor domestic concerns make it impossible for United States policy-makers to consider enlarging foreign assistance to Africa.

American aid to African development in the early 1960's evolved in response to the Cold War rivalry with the U.S.S.R., to a desire for a more vigorous assertion of America's role in the world, and most importantly to the notion of helping struggling new nations to find their feet. However, one domestic justification for increased assistance was the location of new markets for United States business directly through United States aid that could be tied to purchases from American firms, and indirectly through the growth of African economies that would later demand more goods that United States businesses might be in a position to sell. That aid justified on this basis might distort small economies was not then perceived to be a problem.

Another significant domestic justification for aid to Africa was the growth of the civil rights movement and the increasing political consciousness of American blacks. As part of the effort to recover their own ancestry, they took great interest in the independence struggles in Africa and sometimes borrowed techniques of African agitators to dramatize their own problems—such as the demand that the United Nations consider the American government's "denial" of national aspirations of the local black community. That African countries also might not tenderly protect the rights of minorities was not then perceived to be a problem.

The consequences of these justifications for expanding aid

---

remembered that most of China's African aid is invested in a single project—the Tanzam Railway.

during the Kennedy years was to spread aid broadly over the Continent even at the risk of doing so thinly. The standard United States response to the independence of an African country was to offer it a fancy new United States embassy, an aid program, and a contingent of Peace Corps volunteers. However, while the image was one of frenetic activity everywhere, American aid was actually heavily concentrated in approximately one third of Africa. In 1966 75 percent of African economic assistance went to eight countries.[4] In 1967, 600 of the over 700 direct AID employees in Africa worked in eleven of the more than thirty countries then assisted.[5]

Then came Vietnam and with it the first serious doubts about the efficacy and the morality of foreign intervention. Higher defense and aid expenditures in Southeast Asia raised questions about widespread aid elsewhere. The notion that the existence of a new state was a sufficient justification for the award of aid suddenly came under scrutiny. Congress passed an amendment to the Foreign Assistance Act that limited to ten the number of countries in the world that could receive AID Development Loans and to forty the number of countries that could receive Technical Assistance (with discretion given to the President to increase the totals if he felt it was in the national interest).

As these indications of Congressional restiveness were growing, President Johnson (in May 1966) asked Edward Korry, then Ambassador to Ethiopia, to review AID's Africa program to determine how it might contribute more effectively to development. The Korry committee of State Department and AID African experts let it be known that they were approaching this question " 'as if we had no previous policy.' "[6] AID continued this fiction after the Korry Report was accepted, by claiming that it "had adopted a new policy for Africa based largely on Ambassador Korry's recommendations."[7]

---

4. Stated in "Recommendation A" of the "Korry Report," reproduced in Hal Sheets and Roger Morris, *Disaster in the Desert* (Washington, Carnegie Endowment for International Peace, 1974), p. 71.

5. "Proposed Foreign Aid Program, FY 1968," Agency for International Development, p. 206.

6. *New York Times*, 5 July 1966.

7. U.S. Agency for International Development, *Proposed Foreign Aid Program, FY 1968*, p. 202.

AID's summary of its "change" of policy on the basis of the Korry report included five points:[8]

1. The reduction of "its regular assistance programs from the more than 30 countries now assisted to the 10 countries where development prospects are best or where there is a special U.S. interest or relationship."[9]
2. To assist these ten "in cooperation with other aid donors and under the leadership of an international organization."[10]
3. An exception would be made to aid Zaire (that is, it would be added to the list) to help solve its balance of payments problem and help its government build up its internal authority.
4. In all other African countries current capital and technical assistance programs would be completed, but no new ones started.
5. AID assistance would then be limited to support for regional institutions and multidonor projects plus a small "Self-Help" fund for each country.[11]

Basically, the Korry Report seems to have been an elaborate strategy to establish a rationale to protect the aid budget from further Congressional action, and thus was not a new approach to African development. The basic recommendation in the (then confidential) report asserted that "The United States should continue to concentrate its major economic assistance in those key African countries where the United States has major economic development or political and security interests."[12] Focusing on this bureaucratic rationalization of the existing deployment of aid assistance, one former foreign-policy maker said that since "every year was getting

---

8. Ibid., pp. 202–203.

9. These ten were styled "development emphasis countries." They included Nigeria, Tunisia, Ethiopia, Ghana, Liberia, Morocco, Sudan, Kenya, Tanzania, and Uganda.

10. The point of this wording was to avoid any commitment to channel aid funds to these countries through multilateral institutions, while appearing to be fully cooperative.

11. Regional projects involving the ten development emphasis countries were also candidates for this type of assistance.

12. "Recommendation A," Sheets and Morris, p. 71.

tougher on the Hill . . . the Korry Report made a virtue of necessity and kept our hand in where it mattered."[13]

As the continuing decline in the American aid budget to Africa makes clear, the Korry Report only slowed down the erosion in the American commitment to promote development. There were additional factors as well. One important general factor that diluted earlier justifications for aid to Africa was the break-up of the civil rights coalition of white liberals and middle-class leaders of the black community and the consequent loss of influence of the most significant domestic constituency for African development—aside from the specific interests of American firms doing business in particular African countries. As Radway points out in his chapter in this study, prices, jobs, and schools are likely to present more important issues to black politicians seeking election in the next five years than African concerns. Had the award of Ugandan citizenship to Roy Innis (director of CORE) occurred in 1965, it might have posed a dramatic though unlikely solution to the American blacks' dilemma of relating to the continent of their ancestors. But in 1972 it attracted only moderate attention from the black community.

A second factor was a growing United States domestic disillusion with development in Africa. Perhaps the inevitable consequence of a "revolution of rising expectations" that affected United States foreign-policy makers as strongly as it did African leaders in the early 1960's was the acceptance of unrealistically short time horizons for economic development and unjustifiable expectations that democratic practices would be maintained and expanded. The African landscape contains many half-completed projects financed by a variety of donors[14] as well as others which never got out of the

---

13. Ibid., p. 8.

14. Two Ugandan examples suggests different aspects of the problem. AID has put much effort into the assistance of the Ugandan cooperative movement (which has been one of the most promising in Africa). However, this effort was weakened by Ugandan insistence on overly rapid expansion of cooperatives for ideological reasons under the Obote regime, and by the multiple breakdowns of law and order, transport, and factory operations under the Amin regime. A second case is the UNDP project to increase cotton yields by transforming the irrigation system in the Mubuku scheme. In some five years (twice the anticipated time), and at staggering capital costs, twenty-one farmers had their incomes increased by up to a factor of ten. At that point the Ugandan government decided

planning offices. Many projects were completed but cost more than any contribution they can make to the economy, not to mention its development. At the same time there are many others which make perfect sense and are contributing to further aims of African governments. Some projects—particularly roads, schools, and administrative training institutes (a favorite with American development advisers)—are functioning but are hard to judge, since their contributions to political and economic goals are largely indirect and long range. The complexities involved in seeing a development project through have generally been greater than those anticipated. As often as not the problems in completing these projects are the consequence of American officials who do not (or cannot) spare a sufficient number of trained administrators to carry out the specific responsibilities they have accepted. The perceived time frame for development has grown longer and consequently (if illogically) carries less urgency.

Political changes in Africa have also made the task of defending an ambitious aid program to Congress and the public far more difficult. Over the past fifteen years the volume of participation in all spheres of political life has steadily declined virtually everywhere in Africa, with the limited exception of Tanzania. At the national level constitutional safeguards for political liberties and minorities were overturned: opposition parties were harassed and banned, dominant parties were turned out of office by military officers, elections were canceled or rigged, and parliaments were restricted or abolished. At the local level district and provincial councils were dissolved and the autonomy of farmers' cooperatives and workers' trade unions eliminated. Much of what passes for participation now is either symbolic or unstructured (for example, the individual and collective political activities of soldiers in the Ugandan Army over the past three years). The willingness or, indeed, the ability to assist the development of African countries without the continuous political support of their governments introduces new doubts about aid that were not present (or were brushed aside) fifteen years ago.

The sharpest attack on the continuation of American assistance for development, however, is the conceptual one. After a multitude of conferences devoted to discovering what development means,

---

to turn the scheme into a prison farm and evicted the farmers. See S. A. Gitelson, "The Mubuku Irrigation Scheme," *East African Journal*, 9 (May 1971), 5.

there is more confusion than ever. It is necessary to discuss some of the difficulties found in the term, because the conceptual dispute itself goes to the core of the question whether it is *possible* for the United States to promote development in the Third World.

The debate over development has become polarized into two ideologically opposed camps—liberals on the one hand and radicals on the other. Up to now United States aid policy has been dominated by the liberal point of view, but the two camps have produced paradigms of the development process based on mutually exclusive fundamental assumptions.

In essence, those who accept the liberal paradigm assert that Third World natons, in order to develop, must go through a process similar to that followed by the West over the past several centuries. With the advantage of new technologies and assistance from the West, however, mistakes can be avoided and the process can be accelerated. The problem is to overcome existing obstacles. Holders of the radical paradigm, on the other hand, insist that the liberal formulation itself is the obstacle to overcome. Western capitalism is still growing, and Western states are searching for new ways to incorporate Third World countries into their own economic structures. The problem is to overcome dependency on the West.

The differences between liberals and radicals can be broken down into their opposition on four fundamental considerations in development: the importance of indigenous traditions, the arena in which important economic change must occur, the best strategy for achieving the production of wealth, and the value of growing interdependence in the world. Positions taken on each of these considerations tend to overlap those taken on the others. That is, a high degree of internal coherence exists within each paradigm.

Beyond these four differences, liberals and radicals also disagree on the desirability of different forms of social order—the appropriate mix of socialist and capitalist patterns of organization. For liberals, indigenous traditions (the first consideration) provide the central obstacle to development. The liberal view of development generally grows out of the notion that economic take-off requires a rapid increase in the rate of savings, which in turn requires the destruction of traditional obstacles to savings and creation of attractive opportunities for domestic investment. Since the Western countries have accomplished "take-off," their methods for "overcoming tradition" are regarded as worthy of imitation. This simplistic perspective has been criticized and modified by a number of liberal writers over the past decade. The notions that there can be only one path to modernity, that modernity means becoming more like the West, and that traditional practices must necessarily be entirely replaced by new practices in order to modernize have all been sharply criticized.

For radicals these criticisms are beside the point. As often as not, in their view, what Westerners have described as traditional obstacles to development are only a smoke screen to hide a struggle by outsiders to gain control over Third World economies. Colonialism is seen as having given Europeans the opportunity to undercut promising indigenous industries and local entrepreneurs and to substitute new patterns of production and commerce that feed directly into the industrial structures of Western Europe and the United States. Thus the mining enclaves and plantation economies as well as the assembly plants of multinational corporations create and then exacerbate a situation in which inhabitants of the Third World country become more "traditional" *because* more sophisticated patterns of technology are imported into their homeland.

Second, liberals see the question of the arena of development as basically concerned with the domestic economy. Through an appropriately organized planning unit, national political leaders can design an economic structure that will achieve important goals for their citizens. Radicals argue that this effort is doomed to failure and can only blind these leaders to their actual conditions, or, in fact, enmesh them further. (Most African planning offices were staffed by European expatriates during the 1960's, for example.) Basic control, the radicals argue, lies in the international arena, because the richer countries have sufficient resources to impose economic decisions on the poor.

Third, the economic strategy that liberals prefer requires heavy emphasis upon comparative advantage in order to generate as much income as possible, and ultimately to achieve self-sustaining growth. It is important to encourage foreign investment and tolerate increased local inequalities in income in order to do this. Radicals point out that this results in a "perverted pattern of development" tending to emphasize a single crop or mineral and making the Third World country increasingly dependent on the continued acceptance of that product in the world market. Instead, the poor country must

sacrifice some immediate economic growth (which tends to benefit the few and the foreigner anyway) in favor of laying the basis
for a more self-sufficient economy. An integrated economy, not
wealth, is the more immediate goal of development. Furthermore,
foreign investment often means accepting sophisticated capital-
intensive foreign technology in which the poor country's economy becomes dependent on a rich country for spare parts and
must at the same time tolerate unnecessarily high rates of unemployment.

Fourth, liberals argue the beneficial qualities of the growth
of interdependence. Aid from richer countries helps to increase
trade and provides increased cultural exchange. Closer contacts
are created between people in different countries. The risk of war
is reduced. Radicals respond by asserting that aid has strings which
often lead to a capital drain from the poor countries to the rich
ones. Cultural exchange usually turns out to mean accepting Western
norms to the detriment of local values. Closer personal contacts
mean that members of the elite in the Third World country establish
advantageous economic links for themselves at the expense of
the interests of the rest of the population. The risk of war is reduced,
because the poor countries have no choice but to accept the terms
offered them by the rich. An interdependent world is a rich men's
club.

In spite of these irreconcilable differences, there are areas of
agreement between holders of both paradigms. Greater production of
wealth and creation of new economic activities are values accepted
by both, though the emphases are different. Both accept technological solutions to local problems, though differing on the values by
which competing technologies should be judged. Both see the ultimate goal as the increase in the range of opportunities open to the
individual.

In addition, both heavily emphasize the importance of expanded participation in the development process. Involvement of
the masses is a self-evident proposition to the radicals. Recently,
the liberals have come to share it. Title IX was added to the United
States Foreign Assistance Act in 1966 to ensure that projects are
selected which maximize the "participation in the task of economic
development on the part of the people of the developing countries, through the encouragement of democratic private and local

governmental institutions."[15] Several liberal scholars have constructed elaborate rationales in which mass participation is made
one of the defining characteristics of development.[16]

Acceptance of the radical paradigm of development does not
leave much room for American assistance to Africa. Aid justified
on the basis of helping American business or the integration of
African economies into world trade, and aid which requires the
recipients to "buy American," perpetuate a condition of under-
development that distorts African economies. Multilateral aid is not
much better, since multilateral institutions tend to be controlled
by the rich countries.[17] If the United States adopted a policy of aid
without strings, as the Norwegians have,[18] it might be directed
toward what radicals sometimes call "authentic development"—
stressing autonomy and a more balanced economy.

Current Economic Factors Retarding the Development
Process

If all of these reasons for the difficulties of justifying aid were
not enough, two new factors have demonstrated sufficient impact on

---

15. Section 281. The systematic removal by African governments of
opportunities to participate in private and local democratic institutions frustrates
the possibility of giving aid under this section.

16. See Norman T. Uphoff and Warren F. Ilchman, "Development in the
Perspective of Political Economy," in Uphoff and Ilchman, *The Political Economy
of Development* (Berkeley, University of California Press, 1972), pp. 75-122; and
Edgar Owens and Robert Shaw, *Development Reconsidered: Bridging the Gap
between Government and People* (Lexington, Mass., Lexington Books, 1972).

17. The differential use of the new Special Drawing Rights intended to
protect foreign currency reserves has heavily favored the United States and the
United Kingdom, which together have received more benefits from the SDR system than all 89 of the poor countries. Table B-7 in Robert E. Hunter, "The
United States and the Developing World: Agenda for Action 1973" (Washington,
The Overseas Development Council), reproduced in *Hearings*, p. 179. It is worth
noting, however, that SDR's make it possible for developed countries to give aid
without worrying about their reserves, and thus might incline them to give more
untied aid: Paul Streeten, *Aid to Africa: A Policy Outline for the 1970's* (New
York, Praeger, 1972), pp. 135-136. This hypothetical opportunity does not
seem to have unduly influenced American decisions concerning aid expenditures,
however.

18. Zdenek Cervenka, "Scandinavia: A Friend Indeed for Africa?" *Africa
Report*, 20 (May-June 1974), 40.

economic activities throughout the world to make any response to development issues (among others) over the next five years qualitatively different from responses in the 1960's. These are inflation and the rapid increase in oil prices.[19] They are, of course, interrelated. Their consequences are not easy to discern. No matter what definition of development is accepted, however, they make the task of development far more difficult for all LDC's except the oil producers, and weaken any justification for assistance from industrialized nations.

Where development means the installation of new or expanded factories, communications networks, or mechanized distribution systems, it means increased use of oil. But the price of oil has gone up by approximately 400 percent. This means that if developing African countries *cut back* their consumption of oil to the level used in 1971, it will cost them (as a whole) about $1 billion more than it did then.[20] This is approximately six times the current United States aid figure (presuming that African countries were suddenly able to use this aid as they alone chose). The problem varies in importance from one part of Africa to another. Nigeria, currently the eighth largest producer of oil, is clearly in no difficulty from this quarter. Chad, on the other hand, spent 75 percent of its earnings from exports on oil in 1972 *before* the price went up fourfold![21] And there are the secondary effects on critical goods made with oil and imported into Africa. Rising prices of petrochemicals and fertilizers make any agricultural strategy of development precarious.

Inflation also has a differential impact on African countries. Inflation has benefited the price of a number of commodities produced in Africa—cotton and phosphates, for example. Other countries have not been so lucky. On the other hand, the terms of trade for all African countries with industrialized states have steadily worsened for the past fifteen years. Experts in UNCTAD have

---

19. The ability of OPEC to force the industrialized nations to quadruple the price they pay for oil suggests that the assertion of dependency in the radical paradigm of development must be qualified.

20. Testimony of George R. Kenney (Director, Economic Policy Staff, Bureau of African Affairs, Department of State), *Hearings*, p. 150.

21. Ibid. Central African Republic, Niger, Upper Volta, Burundi, and, to some extent, Mali share the same plight.

estimated that the average annual loss from advance changes in the terms of trade have been approximately equivalent to 40 percent of total aid to poor countries.[22]

The cumulative impact of the basic changes now emerging from the oil price increases and inflation more generally is to raise squarely the question whether African countries currently are developing or going into reverse. That has been a difficult question to raise in the past, partly because it is unpalatable to Africans sensitive to suggestions about inferiority and partly because widely held conceptions of development did not allow it. Development might progress slowly or rapidly, but it was always seen to go forward.

Two Contributions of the Radical Paradigm

As it happens, one of the two important contributions that the radical paradigm of development offers is the notion that what is now being called development may be positively harmful to the nation that is experiencing it. Without necessarily suggesting that there is only one path of development, it is possible to say that nations may decay as well as develop.[23] Of course, decay can be either the consequence of what is mistakenly regarded as development or simply a matter of neglect for reasons of sudden disaster, continuing poverty, or lack of concern by leaders. The process of stopping or even retarding decay in itself promotes development. The great task of African assistance over the next five years may well be the retardation of decay.

The other important lesson that the radical paradigm suggests is that the concerns of development must focus directly upon the problems of the poor nations and not upon the concerns of the rich. The statement seems obvious, but the strings attached to aid often require compromises that have worked against the interests of a poor nation. A trivial but graphic example is the Tororo Girls School in

---

22. Cited in testimony by Sean Gervasi, *Hearings*, p. 13.
23. The notion of political decay has been worked out to complement the meaning of political development: Samuel P. Huntington, *Political Order in Changing Societies* (New Haven, Yale University Press, 1968). But so far as I know, the concept of decay has not been analyzed for development more generally.

Uganda, a secondary school financed as a showcase by American aid in the mid-1960's. A visit soon after completion revealed that many of the lights lacked bulbs, because the lamps had the American-style screw mounts instead of the bayonet variety common in Uganda. The telephone switchboard in the school also had closed down for lack of American spare parts.

Closely related to this problem is the danger of providing developing nations with technology that has been developed to meet the present problems of industrialized countries. Many of the assumptions that support the cost-benefit advantages of sophisticated machinery do not exist in Africa. Such machines are designed for situations in which labor not capital is the critical constraint. For their operation and maintenance, they presume not only literacy but high levels of education. Several African countries have imported Western tractors only to discover that they lost money every minute each was in operation. What they often need is a 1920's tractor adapted to African conditions; but these are no longer available in the West (nor is the knowledge and machinery to make them). An aid program that assisted African countries in the development of their own problem-specific technology would contribute greatly.[24]

Whether the liberal or radical paradigm is accepted, there is advantage in adopting a relativistic definition of development. Here it means fundamental improvement in the capacity to solve or cope with the problems facing a particular society. The question should be whether a poor nation is becoming more capable of producing the basic necessities that sustain life in the first instance, and then whether it is improving on these capabilities. In this approach both the reversal of development (that is, decay) and the problem of ethnocentrism can be handled satisfactorily. Decay, rather than being ignored, can be seen as an increasing incapacity to handle the essential problems of that society. Development, on the other hand,

---

24. A project to equip and train Sudanese to build concrete boats for use in the Nile and Southern Sudan is an excellent example of what can be done when a project is thought through from the point of view of the recipient. See Frederick Lees and Charles Tett, "Report of an IORD Mission to the Southern Region of the Democratic Republic of the Sudan to investigate the possibility of mounting a Rural Development Project" (London, International Organization for Rural Development, 1973). (Stenciled.)

need no longer be equated with the values and technology designed by industrialized nations. Effective control in an African country may require techniques different from the latest engineering advances found in the West.[25] This approach poses the next set of serious questions to raise about each society examined: *whose* control is being enhanced over *which* problems? One might also ask whose problems are made worse by solving someone else's difficulties. Political issues—never far from the basic questions of development—necessarily become central here.

The implication of this approach for American assistance is that aid without specification of use is more likely to promote development than aid with strings. Making the acceptance of an American foreign policy aim or the purchase of American products or the agreement to American designed solutions to local problems the premise for aid may produce decay rather than development. Except in those cases where tied aid fortuitously coincides or significantly overlaps with local developmental priorities as seen from the point of view of the poor nation, no aid may be preferable to aid with strings.

The possibility of designing a rationale for maintaining current levels of expenditure for aid, let alone increasing them, is not likely to be made more politically viable by insisting that development priorities ought to be based solely on the problems of African countries instead of private and public benefits for Americans (as Radway emphasizes in his discussion of "domestic constraints"). Perhaps

---

25. An example of the change in attitudes on the part of policy-makers that this approach requires is suggested by an offhand reference in a discussion of the proportion of classrooms in Africa constructed through AID funds. The author notes that "(a) few poles and a thatched roof, mud huts, makeshift space, and the like, frequently serve as classrooms. Such facilities are not comparable to the type of classroom that is provided through AID assistance." "Classrooms in Africa," AID Statement, *Hearings*, p. 42. The real question is whether schools constructed of cement (which is not readily available in most African villages) are actually more appropriate than mud huts. The latter are far cheaper, can be put up by villagers, are cooler, and are just as functional as cement rooms. They also avoid the implicit assumption that going to school means escaping from rural society—an assumption that is reinforced by classrooms that connote greater wealth and status than do the homes of the parents of those students.

Third World nations will have to be satisfied with what they get, and arguably it is up to them to reject aid that does not clearly benefit them.

The Future of the American Commitment to Third World Development

As suggested above, the United States has responded with a low profile toward Africa in part because of the growing complexity of a multipolar world. But a low profile does not mean no profile. The United States maintains its relations with African countries and is even prepared to expand them.[26] In a few cases the United States is strongly concerned to maintain good relations (though primarily with countries with somewhat lower needs for development assistance), while in others it has reduced its development commitment. In a multipolar world the United States will not often treat the continent as a monolithic unit. In the next five years a minimal aid budget seems likely to continue to be seen as supporting the national interest, and for the following reasons.

The primary rationale for continued American aid over the next five years is probably United States willingness to abide by international expectations. The obligation of rich countries to aid poor ones has become one of these expectations, and one that is unlikely to disappear during the present decade. It is integral to definitions of appropriate international conduct. Just as poor countries are expected to have development plans (even if they are merely ornamental), rich states are expected to have assistance programs (even if they are slightly threadbare). Americans, as Baldwin argues in the Introduction to this volume, are unlikely to proclaim their unwillingness to help others. The United States is unlikely to cancel its aid program, and thus policy-makers are free to consider making it more relevant to African development problems—even though they may have to pay the cost of further reductions in levels of expenditure.

---

26. For example, the United States government announced its willingness to reestablish diplomatic relations with the Republic of the Congo without regard to the latter's acceptance of "scientific socialism." *United States Foreign Policy 1972: A Report of the Secretary of State* (Washington, Government Printing Office, 1973), pp. 449, 464.

Secondly, the United States has an interest in maintaining a global system in which it continues to play a dominant role. Although the proponents of a radical paradigm of development may wish this were not so, national policy-makers undoubtedly feel that the ability to continue to play this role will remain an important United States interest during the next five years. But in a multipolar world, direct intervention to maintain the position of the United States and its conception of a global system becomes increasingly less justifiable. Development assistance even without strings, on the other hand, helps to continue an active American role in the world. Because it is a positive sanction, development aid escapes some of the criticism leveled at more coercive forms of involvement in international affairs. Development projects may produce changes in Third World countries which will fundamentally alter (or more precisely accelerate the alteration of) this global system. But it seems unlikely that most developmental changes in Third World countries (besides the oil producers) will not have this sort of impact on international politics during the next five years.

Thus the United States can afford to offer aid that focuses on the recipient's perception of its development problems, and presume that the diffuse good will it receives will support the current pattern of world politics. A relatively small expenditure may provide major returns toward this limited goal.

Thirdly, where the United States has a direct economic interest in trade or raw materials, it will be likely to treat development problems as more worthy of attention. The most important example during the next five years will be the importation of critical supplies, in the case of Africa predominantly oil. United States oil imports from Africa increased from 3.7 percent of total oil imports in 1970 (and 0.8 percent of total United States supplies) to 14.1 percent of imports (and 4.9 percent of total United States supplies) in the ten months of 1973 *preceding* the outbreak of the Arab-Israeli war.[27] Oil has replaced coffee as the most valuable United States import from

---

27. Testimony of Sheldon P. Wimpfen, *Hearings*, p. 151. United States oil imports from Nigeria rose from 47,900 barrels a day in 1970 to 441,000 barrels per day in the first ten months of 1973. By March 1974 the figure was near one million barrels a day. "May we all say a little prayer of gratefulness on that cooperation," added Mr. Wimpfen.

Africa. The growth of oil imports is the most important reason why they United States balance of trade with African countries changed from a surplus to a deficit in 1972.[28] There are certain other products in which African countries provide critical supplies to the United States. Where development assistance helps the United States preserve access for future use of such products, there is no difficulty in justifying it. Maintenance of a good climate in the areas of Africa where there are high levels of United States private investment also supports development assistance. About 75 percent of the $4.1 billion of United States private investment in Africa is in the developing countries. Much of this investment is in oil production. Again, however, this justification is of limited value, because the priorities are reversed—countries most likely to receive development assistance according to this criterion are those which are rapidly becoming able to finance it themselves.

The last reason why the American commitment to a development aid program will continue into the 1980's is the humanitarian rationale that Americans will continue to give aid because they believe they should. Even here one can argue that certain kinds of aid are serving the interest of the United States as well as meeting moral obligations. Basically, the argument is a prudential one. Development assistance that prevents disasters may be cheaper than disaster relief. Building roads in the Sahel might have been cheaper than maintaining an airlift for several months and paying for scarce rail capacity. Rural development projects might have reduced other costs of famine relief. These are not panaceas, however. The projects to rechannel the rivers of the Sahel, for example, would cost far more than famine relief. A further prudential consideration within the humanitarian rationale is that the United States may share a global interest in the expansion of the international reserves of grain and other foods. Where development assistance helps achieve this goal, the United States indirectly benefits from its assistance.

Beyond these considerations, it is reasonable to argue that the United States has an interest, though a noneconomic one, in altruistic action that goes beyond whatever international obligation its policy-makers may regard as supporting a development aid budget.

---

28. Figures for the years 1966 through 1972 are presented in the statement of Guy F. Erb, *Hearings*, p. 97.

Americans have consciences and, more than citizens of most countries, expect their government to promote goodness, sometimes even at the expense of state interests. Restoring national self-respect after Vietnam will not be accomplished by canceling foreign aid. It seems reasonable to assume that even if the sole justification available were the humanitarian rationale, it would be politically unwise for policy-makers to attempt to eliminate the aid budget entirely during the next five years.

How much weight are these rationales likely to have, particularly given the wide range of attacks on the promotion of development assistance? It is impossible to predict how the rationales will be balanced against attacks on aid, but it seems unlikely that the proponents of increasing assistance for development will be in a strong position. For the most part, policy-makers will have to fight to maintain the levels of the limited budgets they now disburse. The rationales presented suggest, however, that there is a floor below which development assistance will not fall during the 1970's. Consequently, there is a strong case for reconsidering the nature of development and uses to which aid should be put. Acceptance of this position means that one task for United States policy-makers over the next five years will be to find ways to remove the strings to aid so that it serves more fully the antonomous development of Third World countries.

EDITOR'S NOTE

India has occupied a unique place in American foreign relations since World War II. It has served as the laboratory in which the United States learned to deal with the emerging nations of the world. Although some of the "experiments" conducted in this laboratory did not work out, such failures helped United States policy-makers to understand such nations better.

The sensitivities and aspirations of new nations, the population-food problem, and the complications of cold war politics have been important elements in United States relations with India. Recently, India joined the ranks of the nuclear powers and thereby added a new dimension to the situation. Still, India and the United States are both interested in promoting stability in South Asia, and Erdman argues that this fact should be the basis for American policy. The "heart of United States policy," he says, "should be a shift from a military tilt toward Pakistan to a political tilt toward India, accepting India's preeminent position in the region." Regardless of whether one accepts or rejects the policy recommendations of this paper, it is obvious that simple calculations of cold war advantages can no longer serve as adequate guides to formulating American policy toward India and Pakistan.

VIII.
The United States, India, and India's Neighbors

Howard L. Erdman

Introduction

With the arrival (March 1975) of William Saxbe as ambassador to India, the United States was again reminded of its history of troubled relations with the states of South Asia. The timing, at least, could not have been less auspicious. Saxbe was scheduled to arrive in New Delhi at the same time the United States removed its ban on arms sales/shipments to South Asia, viz., the United States would be willing to rearm Pakistan.[1] Saxbe delayed his arrival and hovered in Bangkok until the announcement was made. He reached India when anti-United States sentiment was intense and increasing. On more than one occasion thereafter the notoriously blunt Saxbe said that the United States and India—despite all of the rhetoric about the world's two most populous democracies—would never be close friends. Grudging mutual respect was the best for which one could hope, but even that would be difficult to achieve.[2] Saxbe remarked somberly, "it could happen that we'll take our place just like any other embassy here, represent the people of our country, the declining few, and not participate in any manner in anything else."[3] Pakistan appeared happy not only with the decision to permit the flow of arms but also with the new evidence of strained relations between the United States and India, a major beneficiary of United States economic aid, including

---

1. See the *New York Times* (henceforth *NYT*), February 24, 1975.
2. *NYT*, April 25, 1975.
3. Ibid.

the supply of enriched uranium to fuel some of India's nuclear reactors.[4]

Does the decision to help rearm Pakistan reflect a United States interest that goes beyond considerations of earning foreign exchange and of supporting United States arms manufacturers? If so, what is that interest and how is it understood in view of the knowledge that India would take a dim view—to put it mildly—of further military support to Pakistan? Does continued United States economic aid to India reflect a United States interest that goes beyond considerations of maintaining a relatively benign, humanitarian image?[5] If so, what is that interest and how is it understood in view of the knowledge that India is not going to dance to any tune emanating from Washington? Is it plausible to suggest, as Saxbe did, that the United States has so little at stake in this region that it could maintain a modest mission in India and "not participate in any manner in anything else," viz., to terminate United States aid? How the United States has perceived its interests in this region, how fruitful its policies have been, what the next decade holds in store for South Asia and how the United States might be affected by and might itself affect the conditions in South Asia—these are the broad issues with which this chapter is concerned.

South Asia,[6] comprising a very sizable segment of the world's population and having abundant, if relatively undeveloped, natural resources, has not been one of the main focal points of United States foreign policy, but it has attracted considerable attention. Some of this attention has been generated by the behavior of others, as in United States efforts to secure treaty allies in the region during the years of the cold war, and perhaps even now, in a period of detente. Some attention is more remote from global power if not ideological

---

4. For a short time after the May 1974 detonation of a "nuclear device" by India, there were reports that the United States would discontinue the supply of enriched uranium, but this did not come to pass.

5. Cf. Kasfir's chapter for further discussion of the issue of aid and the United States image abroad.

6. Included here are India, Pakistan, Bangladesh, Sri Lanka, and the Himalayan states of Nepal and Bhutan. Afghanistan, sometimes subsumed under this heading, is not extensively considered here; and Sikkim, about which more below, is not separately listed because of its dependent legal position vis-à-vis India.

struggles, as India, for example, claimed some attention as the world's most populous democracy, and one of few such regimes among the less developed countries (LDC's). In some quarters, India and the Peoples' Republic of China (P.R.C.) have been and are still viewed as alternate development models, although interest in this sort of issue does not appear to be as great now as it was in past decades.

In general, South Asia is known as one of the most populous and poverty-stricken regions of the world. More specifically, Bangladesh has now widely been accorded the dubious distinction of being the world's prime "basket case." India, in many eyes, has an image as an eternal mendicant—a major recipient of United States foreign economic aid—who has the indecency to bite the hand that occasionally feeds her.[7] Pakistan has long appeared to be the United States favorite in the region, as a recipient of more United States economic aid per capita than India, and as a partner in the Central Treaty Organization (CENTO) and the Southeast Asia Treaty Organization (SEATO), which entailed substantial military aid as well. United States-Pakistan ties are reflected in Gary Powers' ill-starred, Peshawar-based U-2 flight over the U.S.S.R.; in Henry Kissinger's apparently more auspicious, Rawalpindi-based flight to Peking; and in the (in)famous "tilt" toward Pakistan, symbolized by the peregrinations of the *Enterprise* in the Bay of Bengal in the grim days of the Bangladesh independence struggle in 1971.[8] The February 1975 decision to make arms available to Pakistan again is widely viewed, especially, in India, as a continuation of this tilt.

About Sri Lanka (formerly Ceylon) little is known and no one seems much to care, although if naval competition in the Indian Ocean increases, this could change. Afghanistan, remote and exotic, has been the scene of low-key United States-U.S.S.R. competition. The Himalayan region resonates mainly among those who (hope to) visit Katmandu (Nepal) for another facet of the exotic (or for drugs),

---

7. Exceptions include (a) those who see India as the land of spiritual enlightenment and (b) the preponderance of Indian scholars who generally seem determined to be India's ambassadors to the United States. See Harold Isaacs, *Images of Asia: American Views of China and India* (New York, Harper and Row, 1972).

8. For all Bangladesh references see Jack Anderson, with George Clifford, *The Anderson Papers* (New York, Random House, 1973).

and for the handful who remember that Hope Cooke, a United States socialite, married the now-deposed (1975) ruler of Sikkim. Bhutan? It is practically impossible for anyone to get there from anywhere, which is of little consequence given the fact that few people even know it exists.

Frivolity aside, many if not most states in the region will be involved in United States foreign-policy calculations, even if the latter are primarily responses to the initiatives of others both inside and outside the region. To understand where this region stands and where it seems headed would require considerable knowledge of both the internal conditions of and relations among all of its states. Space does not permit anything but a cursory review of these matters, but there are sources available which provide basic background information.[9] Nevertheless, certain facts of life about the region can be identified as the backdrop for, if not the determinants of, United States foreign policy toward the region.

Retrospect

Before proceeding with the analysis it may be useful to consider briefly what our foreign policy toward South Asia has been, particularly during the Nixon-Ford administrations—which form the immediate backdrop for present orientations and options. It is clear that whatever claim to international statesmanship may have been advanced by, or in support of, Nixon (or Kissinger), corroborating evidence would have to be sought elsewhere than in South Asia. In this region United States policy has been inept and culminated in the crudest reversion to gun-boat diplomacy with the dispatch of the *Enterprise*-led task force into the Bay of Bengal during the Bangladesh war.

Well before this misguided venture, however—notably in the Eisenhower-Dulles years, less so under Johnson, and even less so

---

9. E.g., W. Norman Brown, *The United States and India, Pakistan, Bangladesh* (Cambridge, Harvard University Press, 1972). Although dated, Norman Palmer, *South Asia and United States Policy* (Boston, Houghton Mifflin, 1966), remains useful. See also Michael Brecher, *New States of Asia* (London, Oxford University Press, 1964). The general question of defining "regions" is extensively covered by Brecher and supplements Baldwin's discussion in Chap. 1, above.

under Kennedy—United States policy in this area reflected the bipolar, big-power approach to the international arena. Order, balance, stability or "the structure of peace" rested on the initiatives and will of the great powers; lesser powers and their interests and aspirations counted for little. Calculations were made in terms of cold-war assumptions— whoever is not with us is against us (the Indian view of the Eisenhower-Dulles position), or whoever is not against us is at least potentially with us (the Indian view of the Kennedy position).

The aims and consequences of this approach are well known: minimize communist influence in the region and maintain as many friendly or neutral states as possible. In fact, this led to the decided "tilt" toward Pakistan, which resulted in massive shipments of military hardware, presumably to help contain communism. But to what ends were these arms to Pakistan put? The military power thus supplied encouraged Pakistan's military establishment to believe that it could contain any domestic unrest, even if it was unrelated to communist influence in the country; it was used to initiate wars against India, accompanied by the United States refusal without careful inquiry and on-site inspection to accept the fact that United States arms were used for nonspecified purposes (and here the Johnson administration was *nearly* as culpable as those of Eisenhower and Nixon, during the 1965 wars and with the "short tether" policy in connection with United States food and other aid to India during the mid-1960's); and, ultimately, to suppress systematically the legitimate interests and aspirations of Pakistan's eastern wing, some of whose leaders stated publicly that military aid to Pakistan meant first and foremost West Pakistan's ability to control and exploit the East. The result of this manifestation of "realpolitik" was the United States-countenanced and supported genocidal policy of the West Pakistan regime toward Sheikh Mujibur Rehman and his followers, and the dispatch of the *Enterprise* to the Bay of Bengal. It must be remembered that military aid in the pipeline (and some not yet in it) was allowed to go to Pakistan; that "non-lethal" spare parts were sent; and that United States aircraft and perhaps other supplies were made available to Pakistan by, *inter alia*, Jordan and Iran.[10]

---

10. The Shah, in proposing broader regional cooperation, assured India that Iran would not supply Pakistan with weapons. A very good review of United States policy, which generally parallels the analysis presented here, can

And what do we see? A policy which needlessly alienated India and, ultimately, Bangladesh, in both cases with heightened U.S.S.R. influence; a truncated and humiliated Pakistan, which has turned increasingly toward the P.R.C. for rearmament; and, sadly, a country, Bangladesh, which is the world's prime basket case and target for those who would fish in troubled waters. The policy secured *none* of the stated United States objectives. A combination of dire needs which no single country can alleviate; a determination not to be anyone's pawn; and an openness toward the United States which has not often been reciprocated—all combine to provide the opportunity to retrieve *some* standing among the countries of the region. But to do so will require more attention to political than to military strength; a recognition that military hardware is not only expensive in dollars and cents but also rarely enlists the willing support of those it rules; and, most relevant here, a recognition that by opting for political rather than military strength, the United States can retrieve some standing at relatively low cost in India. The United States must develop (or regain?) the capacity to relate to other nations, including the LDC's, in ways that recognize their interests and their aspirations and strengthen their political rather than their military power. If this cannot be managed, then let the United States follow a policy of "benign neglect" rather than "more of the same," because past policy has been unsuccessful.

Why Bother?

There are, however, several lines of analysis which culminate either in the question "Why bother?" or in the conclusion "write South Asia off." These issues must be confronted, even though such a confrontation is no easy task.[11]

One line of analysis holds that South Asia has been and may safely continue to be relatively neglected in United States foreign

---

be found in Baldev Raj Nayar, "Treat India Seriously," *Foreign Policy*, 18 (Spring 1975), 133-154.

11. Humanitarian considerations might dictate some attention under any circumstances, but even here there is considerable ambivalence. Cf. Kasfir's chapter and its discussion of a minimum level of United States aid in terms of the United States image—both self-image and that (or those) held by others.

policy because the region lacks great strategic significance when viewed from a military-oriented, super- or major-power perspective.[12] This is sound insofar as the military capability of the states in the region *directly* to harm the United States is concerned. However, capabilities such as India's potential for nuclear weapons development and for diffusion of nuclear technology, coupled with the region's geopolitical importance, warrant attention by the United States. Further, the likelihood that intrastate and interstate tensions in South Asia will continue to disturb the region and may invite outside intervention detrimental to United States interests underscores the need for attention, even if the basic disposition of the United States is to adopt a "hands off" policy.

A second line of analysis holds that détente permits and/or requires that the United States follow a hands off policy. On the one hand it has been contended that with détente the major powers[13] are less likely avidly to seek client states in the region. There is ample evidence to suggest, however, that even as major states outside of the region move toward détente and as bipolar, cold war assumptions and activities recede (not an irreversible process in any event), the states in the region will continue to bulk large in the calculations of many outsiders. Thus the U.S.S.R. seems anxious to have sympathetic regimes in the region, in part to avoid the hegemony of the P.R.C.; conversely, the P.R.C. is anxious to avoid being confronted by a ring of hostile regimes on its southern borders. It may be that jockeying for position will be more salient for the U.S.S.R. and the P.R.C. than for the United States, but the position of the United States will in some measure be affected by the results of this jockeying. For example, will the sea lanes be open for the free movement of petroleum from West Asia to Japan (which country also has a major interest in India's vast coal and iron reserves)?[14] It may be that the United States base at the British-owned island of Diego Garcia—about which more later—would suffice to protect the vital interests of the

12. Cf., however, the earlier rationale for Pakistan's inclusion in CENTO and SEATO.

13. The United States in 1974 bestowed the title "major power" on India, but as the phrase is used here it does not include India.

14. Some relevant analysis will be found in W. A. C. Adie, *Oil, Politics, and Seapower: The Indian Ocean Vortex* (New York, Crane, Russak, 1975).

United States and its allies and friends; but some positive standing in one or more of the major states in the region would certainly help. Further, in view of her own nuclear capabilities and in view of the fact that she has not only uranium deposits but also the largest known reserves of thorium, India must certainly be reckoned with in calculations concerning sources of nuclear energy.

Another détente-related view holds that détente with the P.R.C. *requires* the United States to maintain a very substantial distance from South Asian states. This is open to very serious question: no persuasive argument has yet been set forth to show that détente with the P.R.C. requires the granting to the latter of virtual *carte blanche* in South Asia. No doubt the P.R.C. would have reason to oppose the emergence of a potent, hostile force in the subcontinent. But for this to happen, either very substantial foreign military bases in one or more of the region's states would be required or India would have to make enormous strides (with or without external assistance) in the realm of nuclear weapons and delivery systems. Neither should be deemed a credible threat to the P.R.C.'s security in the period under consideration here. But even if a low profile were favored for reasons of détente, it is extraordinarily unlikely that, for example, détente with the P.R.C. *required* the marked pro-Pakistan tilt in 1971, culminating in the presence of the *Enterprise*-led task force in the Bay of Bengal. Similarly, it is very doubtful that détente now requires extraordinary deference at all levels and in all respects to the P.R.C.[15] One might even argue that a significant United States presence (with Diego Garcia deemed sufficient) would help relations with the P.R.C., insofar as the latter is greatly worried about the U.S.S.R. The main point, however, is that the United States should be able to maintain a presence of the type set forth below, without jeopardizing détente and the P.R.C.'s position in the broader Asian context.[16] Here again the United States must be sensitive to India's interests: the tilt toward Pakistan in 1971 was widely viewed in India as evidence of a threat from the United States, the P.R.C., and Pakistan, and renewed arms shipments to Pakistan have intensified such suspicions.[17]

---

15. This relates to the levels of analysis and multiple issue areas, as above, in Chap. 1.

16. See above, Chap. 1.

17. Adie, pp. 44–47, touches on some of these points.

A third line of analysis holds that the United States cannot alleviate meaningfully the enormous problems of the region. Certainly the United States as the world's breadbasket, a key element in United States–India relations, is less formidably endowed than it was a few years ago. In addition, among certain neo-Malthusians there is a firm conviction that the United States *should not do much even if it could*, because major states in the region, notably India, allow their populations to grow at alarming rates. According to this view, to save a few starving millions now is no blessing, as it will only mean many, many more starving millions—well beyond anyone's capacity to help—a few decades hence. Needless to say, these themes are attractive to and are echoed by those who ask what all of our aid to India has achieved or "got us"; by those resentful of foreign policy lectures by many of India's prominent public figures, notably the late V. K. Krishna Menon but also by Prime Ministers Nehru and Indira Gandhi; and by those who find that India, instead of being supinely grateful (to the point of being a docile "client" regime) for aid provided, perversely insists on biting the hand that feeds her.[18] Once again India has borne the brunt of these attacks and it is therefore all the more imperative to see much of the rhetoric for what it is and to seek the much-vaunted more mature relationship between the United States and India.

There is no doubt that the problems of the region are enormous, and there is no doubt that for their alleviation the states of the region must themselves bear the major responsibility. Some are obviously better able to do this than others, with Bangladesh bringing up the rear for the foreseeable future. Of the remaining states—merchants of gloom notwithstanding—India does have considerable potential to manage her own problems tolerably well, given a few breaks from mother nature, a bit more internal discipline, and some timely, periodic aid to help cushion the impact of the energy-food-population crunch. India *can* improve her food situation enormously, with some assistance, and she also has substantial infrastructure in the industrial realm, which provides the basis for more sustained self-reliant, diversified growth—essential to earn foreign exchange—with traditional foreign exchange earners

---

18. An anti-India scholar once remarked to me that the United States should countenance nuclear tests in the atmosphere—over India. At least he had the virtue of being honest.

facing a declining market. Not all will share this relatively optimistic assessment, but this brief study will seek to respond even to the merchants of gloom and the advocates of *triage*. There is an element of truth but also much exaggeration in the assertion that "in a world of interdependence, India cannot, as some have suggested, be allowed to sink—for we would all go down together."[19] The fact is that we would *not* all go down together, just as it is not true that if in the long run we are all dead, we all die simultaneously and in the same fashion. But the same author also cited a statement by Tagore, used by India's Prime Minister, Indira Gandhi, in a foreign-policy address, which is relevant: "Power has to be made secure not only against power, but against weakness; for there lies the peril of its losing balance. The weak are as great a danger for the strong as quicksand for an elephant."[20] This will not set well with those whose calculations are limited to divisions, nukes, and delivery systems. Also, it may very well be interpreted to mean that the United States should simply *avoid* the South Asian quicksand, hoping perhaps that the U.S.S.R. and the P.R.C. will run afoul of it. All is not quicksand in South Asia, however; and those who are desperate will not have the decency to die without a struggle that will impinge upon the interests of the United States. Consequently, it is in the United States's own interests to recognize the character of the quicksand and, while avoiding some of its manifest hazards, attempt to solidify the South Asian terrain by helping to substitute terra firma for at least some of that quicksand.

There is a final preliminary point to be made. Even if it be granted that the United States should not ignore South Asia, need there be any sense of urgency in developing a new South Asia policy? If it be argued (as I have done) that *past* United States policy toward the region has been inept but that the United States may retrieve the situation in some measure, why should a reorientation be undertaken now? Why not muddle through for a few more years or perhaps have another tilt toward Pakistan? There is no entirely compelling

---

19. Robert L. Hardgrave, Jr., *India: Government and Politics in a Developing Nation*, 2nd ed. (New York, Harcourt, Brace, Jovanovich, 1975), p. 230.

20. Ibid. Cf. Thucidydes: "since you know as well as we do that right, as the world goes, is only in question between equals in power, while the strong do what they can and the weak suffer what they must."

answer to this kind of query, but some persuasive arguments can be advanced. Certainly, the United States can learn *something* from the effects of its past policy toward South Asia, even if the region and the world seem to be in a fluid state. While the latter might caution against precipitous action where considerable ambiguity prevails, all is not fluidity (or quicksand), and there are some facts of life and discernible tendencies that can provide a basis for a viable policy. Properly perceived and cautiously addressed, there are opportunities for the United States to deal constructively with *some* of the problems of the region.[21] This situation may be a form of insurance policy: a modest expenditure now may protect against far greater expenses later.

As a minimum, the United States has an interest in the stability of the region, if only to deter the intervention of others and to avoid spill-over effects that would seem to require a United States response. For example, the P.R.C.'s possible involvement in Bangladesh (especially if that unhappy state deteriorates even further) and/or the P.R.C.'s introduction of substantial military hardware into Pakistan would both be deemed by India prejudicial to her interests and would doubtless elicit compensatory responses that might be further destabilizing. However, even in the absence of *outside* intervention in South Asia, continued famine conditions and other problems in Bangladesh will encourage the flow, already evident, of Bangladesh people into adjacent Indian territory. As in 1971, such an influx will not only strain India's economy but also complicate a very delicate multicultural situation in India's own northeastern states. India could not view this with equanimity. These are only a few examples of the developments that would invite outside attention; others will be examined below. But it is worth emphasizing for those oriented toward global, major-power perspectives that a major source of great-power tension is *regional* instability and tension. Global security and order cannot be divorced from regional balances and bilateral relations on the one hand, and the great nonstrategic problems—population, food, resource scarcity and exhaustion, energy, and inflation—on the other.

One basic fact, implicit in the title for this paper, is that for

---

21. A broader statement of the problem of timing with respect to certain regions and issue areas is found above, in Chap. 1.

the next several years India will be the dominant actor in the South Asian political subsystem. Corollaries are that although other states in the region may intrude into the thinking of United States foreign-policy makers, (a) some will do so because of India's activities—real or imagined—toward them; (b) no viable policy toward the other states in the region can ignore India's interests; and (c) the stability of the region, in which the United States has an interest, is almost inconceivable without India's own stability. Put another way, even if the United States should decide to pursue a policy of tilting toward Pakistan, it should do so with an awareness that India is the dominant regional actor[22] and is not likely to be an impotent by-stander while the United States engages in its regional application of the principles of *realpolitik*.

If regional stability and a positive United States presence are desirable, how best may these be achieved? There can be no simple formula, but given the record of United States policy toward the region, the nature of the broader international environment, and the "facts of life" in South Asia, *the heart of United States policy should be a shift from a military tilt toward Pakistan to a political tilt toward India, accepting India's preeminent position in the region.* The task now is to examine the evidence that supports the implicit assumptions and corollaries of this central proposition, viz.:

1. Intra- and inter-state conditions will be characterized by at least intermittent instabilities, which will in turn encourage outsiders to fish in troubled waters.

2. India's domestic regime, committed to some form of social-ism, is likely to endure for several years with its present proclivities, socialist in principle, quite pragmatic in practice; and it is about the best regime that one could expect, from the vantage point of United States interests.

3. India's foreign policy poses no significant threat to United States interests either directly or indirectly, with the possible excep-

---

22. The notion of a South Asian "region" or "subsystem" is by no means an unambiguous one, although the states involved have shared certain historical experiences in gross terms—namely, exposure, in varying measure, to British rule and considerable postindependence interaction, cordial or otherwise. Again, see Chap. 1 above, and Brecher, *New States of Asia*, for an examination of some of the problems of "regions" in analyzing internal developments.

tion of nuclear proliferation, where India will still have to go a long way to catch up with the world's preeminent diffuser of nuclear technology, the United States.

4. The United States can help modestly in the task of maintaining stability in the region, the soundest course focusing on India's preeminence and stability.

A basic premise is that the United States, alone or in concert with other great powers, cannot now (if it were ever possible) control fully the shape of the world in which we live. What follows is an analysis of likely lines of development in South Asia and of productive policy responses thereto. Those words were chosen with care: "responses" because it is impossible for the strong to impose fully their will or image of the world on the lesser powers or nonpowers. Put differently, it seems appropriate to accept as givens many situations that were considered amenable to engineering solutions in the not-too-distant past.[23]

South Asia: Intra- and Inter-State Tensions

Past, present, and projected conditions—intrastate and interstate—indicate that there will be considerable tension and the strong possibility of sustained instability in South Asia.

A. The multicultural character and developmental pains of states in the region provide the basis for much of the intrastate tension in the region. The demise of the "old" Pakistan is the most notable example, but within the two "new" states there are strains along cultural lines—for example, the agitation for secession or at least greater autonomy on the part of Pathans in Pakistan; the tension between Bengalis and non-Bengalis in Bangladesh. Sri Lanka has long struggled with the problem of relations between people of Tamil (South Indian) origin and the Sinhalese majority. India also has significant problems along these lines, including some overtly secessionist movements (e.g., among some of the Sikhs in the Northwest; the Naga tribesmen in the Northeast; earlier by the Dravidian movement in South India); some strong parochializing tendencies (e.g., the Shiv Sena—Shivaji's Army—movement in Bombay which vehemently attacks those who are not "sons of the soil" of the

---

23. Cf. Chap. 1 for more general consideration of this point.

State of Maharashtra, with weaker counterparts elsewhere); the periodic unrest generated by questions concerning the official language of the Indian Union—that is, between proponents of Hindi and of English; and strains related to inflation and the vicious circle of energy-food–population–foreign exchange, some of which problems are shared by other states in the region. Although they vary in terms of intensity over time and space, these problems will certainly continue to trouble the states in the region for the foreseeable future.

B. In terms of interstate tensions, the residual friction between India and Pakistan bulks largest, with efforts at normalization of relations inhibited by recurrent disputes over the status of Kashmir; the United States decision (1975) to remove the ban on arms aid to Pakistan; the Pakistani allegation that India and Afghanistan are fomenting unrest among some segments of the Pathans; among other less striking causes. In addition, there has been growing disillusionment with India in Bangladesh; and Bangladesh's dire position has led to the movement of some of her nationals into adjacent Indian territory, adding to India's economic burden and to the burden of dealing with an already difficult multicultural situation in India's northeast states. This has been intensified because of P.R.C. assistance to some dissidents. India – Sri Lanka relations are relatively cordial at the time of writing, but if the problem of residents of Indian origin in Sri Lanka flares up, as it has from time to time, one should expect at least low-level tension, though probably no major crisis. There will be continued jockeying for position in the Himalayan region, with India having a far more important security interest than the P.R.C. in maintaining sympathetic regimes in Bhutan and Nepal. Here the steady movement toward absorption of Sikkim into the Indian Union, which culminated in the April 1975 Sikkim vote to become a regular State within India, has provided ammunition for those (including Pakistan and the P.R.C.) who charge India with expansionist tendencies, whatever the legal niceties of the situation may have been. And the P.R.C. has regularly charged India with harboring a Dalai Lama government in exile. As in the case of intrastate tensions there will be ebb and flow, with no prospect on the horizon of region-wide normalization on a stable, long-term basis.

Even if there were to be relative stability within and among all states of the region, states outside the region would engage in some jockeying for position, but opportunities would seem enhanced by the tensions noted. As mentioned earlier, this may well be more salient for the U.S.S.R. and the P.R.C.; but the United States must also be affected in some measure by the results of such maneuvering, probably more so than the military-oriented analysts are prepared to acknowledge. The effects on India of a massively rearmed Pakistan may be easy to anticipate—namely, some renewal of an arms race. Less obvious but of perhaps greater consequence will be effects of deterioration of conditions in Bangladesh, where India would almost certainly be obliged to adopt a forward position to minimize the flow of Bangladesh nationals into India. It is inconceivable that the region could be stable if India herself were not stable; but India's stability and its contribution to regional stability depend in significant measure on what happens in Pakistan and Bangladesh, with or without outside intervention.

India: Broad Outlines of Domestic and Foreign Policies

The broad path that India has chosen to follow in domestic and foreign affairs does not threaten United States interests in any major way, despite a stated preference for some form of socialism at home and a tilt toward the U.S.S.R. (in part, a reaction to United States policy) abroad.

A. At this juncture, with efforts at détente, it does not require an elaborate justification to live with India's version of a socialist regime: if the United States can try to get on with the U.S.S.R. and the P.R.C., it should be able to make the same effort with India. What is worth noting is that despite charges of CIA dirty tricks and other attacks on the United States presence in India, the latter's economic program has permitted extensive United States participation; it has not involved capricious nationalization of foreign-dominated concerns; and though industrial policy in India has been and will remain far from clear and consistent, it cannot be argued that overseas investors have been duped or manhandled. India's mixed economy may not be a playground for United States investors, including multinational corporations, and some opportunities may be shrinking; but in general India's economic development policy is more pragmatic than much of the rhetoric and her close relations with the

U.S.S.R. would suggest.[24] It should also be noted that with a very large hard-currency debt, India has been scrupulous about her payments, however much she may work toward rescheduling of that debt. From the vantage point of United States and allied economic interest, then, India has "behaved" tolerably well.

B. Barring presently unforeseen calamities, India's existing political system should remain more or less intact for the period with which we are concerned, and should be able to cope with a wide array of domestic and foreign problems.

1. Despite ominous noises from merchants of gloom at home and abroad, India has been able to maintain a parliamentary, constitutional regime, dominated by the Congress Party at the center and in most of the states in the federal system.[25] A competent, if often sluggish and overtaxed civil service is an additional source of stability.

2. Despite considerable factionalism and dissension with Mrs. Gandhi's Congress Party (conditions which have existed in one form or another since the party's inception), this party is likely to maintain its hegemony domestically. The criticism that the ruling party lacks discipline, dedication, etc. in the face of India's dire needs and of her aspirations is both at home and abroad often exaggerated and misguided: much of this flabbiness is inevitable in so heterogeneous a country with a democratic political system.

---

24. India's approval of a United States Steel / Birla fertilizer venture, her reasonable handling of the ESSO takeover, and many other examples could be cited in support of this proposition. Recent agreements with United States firms for offshore oil exploration are also fairly generous.

25. There are many problems of which Indians themselves are well aware. Some of the multicultural tensions have been dealt with—reasonably well thus far—through adjustments in the federal system, as, e.g., in granting greater autonomy to certain dissident groups or regions, including the troubled Northeast, where Bangladesh's fate is a major factor. Also, there has been considerable parochialization in the economic realm, where states vie for new industries, try to regulate the number of outsiders who may set up new industries or who may be employed in the labor force, and so on. The declaration of a state of emergency on June 26, 1975, and actions taken pursuant thereto, cast doubt on the validity of this proposition as of December 1975. See, however, the argument below, p. 261, where the mechanisms of departure from open parliamentarianism are correctly identified. Mrs. Gandhi has insisted that the emergency will be lifted at some unspecified date.

3. Popular agitation, presently centered on food, inflation, and that perennial whipping boy corruption, will continue to be troublesome; and even generous assistance from abroad will not dissipate popular protest, which in some states has taken ominous turns. However, there is no likelihood of the formation of a viable, coherent, nation-wide alternative party which could replace the Congress, although there have been repeated efforts to form one.

4. Even if Mrs. Gandhi's party should start to come apart at the seams, or should it confront seemingly intractable protest, the most likely change in India's political life will be increasing reliance on a number of constitutionally available but somewhat authoritarian procedures, such as: president's rule, whereby the center can take control of a state if the latter cannot manage its own affairs; detention and other actions under the Maintenance of Internal Security Act; and actions under a formal declaration of a state of emergency. Mrs. Gandhi, much to the distress of many of her own party colleagues, as well as political opponents outside her party, dealt harshly with a 1974 railway strike, using some of the aforementioned measures; and in some cases the Central Reserve Police and units of the army were deployed to restore or to maintain order, enforce curfews, and the like, in riot-affected states.

5. The army has thus far remained true to its tradition of nonintervention in politics, save when required by the civilian political leadership. There is some apprehension, however, that if the military is repeatedly requested to intervene to maintain law and order, it might start thinking about running the whole show itself. Some of those who advance such a thesis argue that India's nuclear detonation was *in part* a gesture to the military, to show it that the civilian government was capable of doing things potentially useful to the military—a view I do *not* share.

6. Whatever changes might take place in domestic political life, including military intervention, the population will not be easily depoliticized. This is not to say that the bulk of the population would rise up in defense of parliamentary democracy in the event of its apparent erosion. What it does mean is that any effort to diminish substantially popular inputs (including demonstrations, strikes, riots, guerilla-type activity) will be less successful than in many less politicized countries. This should discourage any temptation for the United States to let India flounder or to assist in its

floundering in order to facilitate the installation of a presumably more sympathetic (military) regime in New Delhi, for any such regime would encounter serious problems of its own. Given the travels of the *Enterprise* and assorted escapades of the CIA, however, it is understandable that even generally moderate Indian public figures express suspicion of United States motives. In this respect Ambassador Moynihan's contention is precisely on target: Prime Minister Gandhi, among many others in India, wants evidence that the United States accepts the present regime and is not engaged in dirty tricks, as in Chile.[26] Such evidence is not easily produced (how does one prove that one is not doing something?), and such suspicions will not be easily allayed. The problem will almost certainly become unmanageable if the United States engages in, or countenances, the substantial rearmament of Pakistan, which again emerges as a crucial factor in United States policy toward the region.

C. In the realm of foreign policy India has incurred the wrath of more than a few Americans as a result of lectures on international morality, the cold war, United States involvement in Indo-China, etc. Many Indians are themselves disturbed by the propensity of their government to use a double standard in judging the United States and the U.S.S.R. and by the propensity to say "we told you so" when matters turn out unfavorably for the United States (as in Indo-China). Less moralizing and abrasiveness on both sides would help maintain more cordial relations.

However, even if one looks only at India's "affronts" it would be difficult to conclude that India's international activites have been prejudicial to the interests of the United States. To be sure, in the days of the cold war India's neutralism was viewed adversely vis-à-vis Pakistan's willingness to join CENTO and SEATO; but there is considerable evidence to indicate that the interests of the United States were better served by the former than the latter. Moreover, India has done much to secure a more stable international environment through UN peacekeeping and related activities. And despite

---

26. This, of course, indicates the interrelationship of United States policy in various parts of the world. Even if the United States were not involved in subversion in India, the fact that it was involved elsewhere would very much impair United States credibility.

charges[27] against her in 1971 that she was responsible for escalating the Bangladesh conflict, India behaved with great restraint throughout and after the struggle. On balance it would appear that much if not most of the stated displeasure of the United States stemmed from India's proclivity to bite the hand that intermittently feeds her rather than from acts demonstrably contrary to United States interests.

1. Viewed in terms of South Asia, India's position is now one of clear preeminence. Is this preeminence a substantial threat to her neighbors? The evidence suggests strongly that it is not. As the dominant power, with enough problems of her own domestically, India is not likely to be aggressive with her neighbors—subject to the caveats noted earlier.[28] Her present position satisfies all but a small number of fringe elements whose influence in the government is meager and whose influence in any readily conceivable alternative would also be virtually nil. India is more likely to behave toward her neighbors as does the United States toward Canada and Mexico (acknowledging that the position of "big brother" is not free from criticism in North America).

What is the evidence? In terms of the period of the Bangladesh war India, contrary to United States assertions, fought a limited holding operation in the western sector; she withdrew speedily from Bangladesh and disengaged on the western front; she played a major part in the return of some 80,000 Pakistani POW's without war crimes trials. India has generally sought to normalize relations with her neighbors, both before and after the Bangladesh war. Agreements were signed with Sri Lanka concerning the status of residents of Indian origin in that country and concerning the international boundaries and the status of some small islands in and around the Palk Straits which separate India and Sri Lanka. India, very sensitive to possible charges of expansionism, has reacted by maintaining a low profile in Bangladesh while trying to settle some difficulties concerning smuggling and more open forms of economic relations. The status of some small areas in limbo since partition in 1947 has been clarified, and the access to waters from the eastern rivers

---

27. See Anderson and Clifford.

28. Rearmament of Pakistan and spillover effects of deterioration in Bangladesh.

(feeding both India and Bangladesh) has been the subject of extensive but generally low-key negotiations.

A central element is, of course, relations with Pakistan. Here, too, India has sought to normalize relations, incrementally, by dealing with such matters as postal and other connections between the two countries first, leaving more problematical issues, such as boundaries (including in Kashmir), for later consideration. Considerable progress has been made, but as at earlier junctures one should not expect smooth and continuous improvement in bilateral relations between the two countries. India's nuclear detonation has been cited as a clear and present danger to Pakistan; Pakistan's efforts to rearm are viewed with concern in India, even with respect to non-nuclear arms; India absorption of Sikkim into the Indian Union has been assailed by Pakistan (along with the P.R.C.) as evidence of India's expansionist tendencies; and the Kashmir case continues to crop up as a troublesome legacy of the 1947 partition.

India's policies have thus been conciliatory, but efforts at normalization will not uniformly convince neighbors of India's benevolent intent. Again, rearmament of Pakistan and deterioration of conditions in Bangladesh are likely to generate responses from India which will be considered aggressive; and for stability in the region one must look not only to India's stability but also to settled conditions in neighboring countries.

2. At the same time, India will surely seek to use her technology, including her nuclear know-how, to effect better relations with a variety of states outside of the region. Many factors are involved here; among them are a sincere desire to assist other LDC's; an interest in retrieving a more prominent position as a leader of the LDC's; and an interest in securing a reliable supply of desperately needed crude on favorable terms. Negotiations and/or agreements concerning nuclear cooperation with Argentina, Brazil, Iran, and other countries suggest the range of India's efforts to obtain advantages of a psychic and material character.[29] Despite oil agreements with the United Arab Emirates and Iraq, India is not likely to inter-

---

29. President Julius Nyerere of Tanzania at a conference encouraged LDC's to "buy Indian," on the grounds that India's technology was sufficiently advanced to enable the LDC's to become less reliant on the more advanced industrial countries.

ject her nuclear know-how into the Western Asian arena: in energy terms she has too much to lose if there is another Arab-Israeli war, and India's involvement in West Asia will be either not so great or of a different character if Pakistan is not rearmed.

3. Establishment of a United States base at Diego Garcia is firmly opposed by India and other states as far afield as Indonesia, Australia, and New Zealand; and India is continuing efforts to bring pressure to bear for a reconsideration by the United States. On the face of it, Diego Garcia appears to be a continuation of the cold war orientation and superpower competition for influence in the Indian Ocean area. Alternatively, it may be seen as a base from which the United States might move against oil-producing states in West Asia—that is, with gunboat diplomacy. Either way, India will be critical and in one respect at least legitimately so: Diego Garcia will be a United States base despite titular sovereignty of the United Kingdom, while the U.S.S.R.'s present facilities around the Indian Ocean depend more substantially on the good will of "host" countries. Whatever the U.S.S.R. presently has in Somalia, Madagascar, or Bangladesh by way of facilities and/or berthing-visiting rights is not on a par with the facilities contemplated for Diego Garcia (cf. President Ford's contentions to the contrary, where, fortunately, he did not include in his list, as others had, the Indian port of Vizaghapatnam as one of the U.S.S.R.'s "bases"). Diego Garcia will certainly generate undesired pressures by the U.S.S.R. on other states in the region, including India, to obtain comparable facilities in the Indian Ocean. India, declaring her desire to have the Indian Ocean as a "zone of peace," has recently announced that she will not allow the U.S.S.R. to establish a base comparable to Diego Garcia in the Andaman Islands,[30] but she will certainly be subjected to continuing pressure by the U.S.S.R. in the event the United States proceeds with its plans.

4. Despite cordial relations with the U.S.S.R. and the Eastern European countries, India, in the course of evolving her domestic and foreign policies, does not want to become overwhelmingly

---

30. In response to an inquiry by Indonesia. In the event that a naval build-up in the Indian Ocean should appear inevitable, India would doubtless use the law-of-the-sea conferences to attempt to minimize its impact by opting for a 200-mile limit to include naval craft.

dependent upon or beholden to any single patron or bloc. India's orientation toward the U.S.S.R. is understandable—given its geographical proximity (and the state of India-U.S.S.R.-P.R.C. relations), certain ideological affinities (anticolonialism internationally, some form of socialism at home), and the relatively low-key, astute foreign policy of the U.S.S.R. The United States will have to accept these givens,[31] but they should not preclude amicable relations between the two countries, especially if one looks beyond India's often abrasive rhetoric to her actual policies. It would appear that the most volatile component in this mix is the price of the United States–P.R.C. détente, the full dimensions of which lie beyond the scope of this paper. As noted above, however, there has been no persuasive argument that that price is complete deference by the United States to the P.R.C. in South Asia.

Though all of this (and more) suggests that India is not likely to achieve a high degree of discipline and determination in dealing with her problems, it is clear that with the present level of political organization India can achieve a great deal domestically and internationally. Instead of being tempted to watch India decay, the United States would be well advised to support the incumbent regime and the broad domestic and international path it has chosen to follow. In no significant particular, with the remote possibility of nuclear proliferation, is this leadership and this path inimical to the interests of the United States. That assertion is, of course, linked to the argument advanced earlier—that we are better advised to look to political strength and stability, rather than military might, to promote and/or maintain conditions conducive to United States welfare and security.

---

31. Obviously, modifications are possible: the U.S.S.R. has withdrawn somewhat from its full support of India on the Kashmir question and has given limited military aid to Pakistan. In addition, many Indians recognize that the U.S.S.R. is a very tough bargainer in the economic realm and that it is not a clearcut battle between the "good guys" and the "bad guys" in terms of "strings" or terms with respect to foreign aid and trade. For some useful material see Vadilal Dagli, ed., *Indo-Soviet Economic Relations* (Bombay, Vora, 1971). The U.S.S.R. was also sharply critical of India's nuclear detonation, although cordial relations were maintained. In the spring of 1975 the U.S.S.R. sent an Indian research satellite into orbit and will evidently continue to assist India in this sphere.

United States Opportunities

In view of the above propositions, the United States could adopt policies that are *responsive* to India's needs, with due regard also to the interests of India's neighbors. Not everyone can be satisfied with the following policy recommendations, but they constitute relatively low-cost policy for the United States in furthering its own interests:

A. Recognition of India's preeminence in South Asia (which is not incompatible with a recognition of the positions of the P.R.C. and Japan in the broader international environment), to be demonstrated in large part by the explicit refusal of the United States to rearm or to countenance the rearming of Pakistan to a level that would cause India to escalate. For maximum credibility in the light of legitimate Indian suspicions, no arms for Pakistan at all, directly or through intermediaries.

B. Reconsideration of Diego Garcia as a possibly unnecessary legacy of cold war assumptions, with the understanding that if the United States proceeds with this idea, it is all the more important to refrain from arming Pakistan—that is, compounding the felony in India's eyes.

C. Bilateral and multilateral efforts to keep Bangladesh afloat, in part to minimize spillover effects and the attendant temptation for India to intervene.

D. Debt rescheduling and as much short-term assistance in food and fertilizers as possible, in order to ease the impact of the world energy crisis and as recommended by the World Bank—through multilateral efforts as far as possible—for example, by a world "food bank."

E. Longer-term efforts to secure more stable commodity prices and trade preferences to help India in the area of foreign exchange and to contribute otherwise to her development by assistance in exploration for oil and other energy sources; continued supply of enriched uranium for India's atomic energy program; increased capacity for fertilizer production in India and elsewhere; improved grain storage facilities (preferably through multilateral channels or through the United States Cooperative League); assistance in improving and streamlining the power and transportation systems. In many of these areas India would prefer multilateral approaches but will of necessity accept bilateral agreements.[32]

F. Explicit emphasis on United States support for *cooperative* development ventures among the states in the region. This would enable the United States to render aid to many, perhaps all, states in the region, while helping India and contributing to the progressive normalization of relations among South Asian states.

G. Consideration given to sponsoring India for a permanent seat on the Security Council. In light of United States and Indian doubts about the UN, this may not seem to be such a boon; but it would be one way in which the United States could indicate to India that India's own efforts at development and her maintenance of democracy are appreciated. If India could continue to support the P.R.C.'s admission after the 1962 war, the United States should not find it difficult to contemplate this possibility, which in any event will not produce any dramatic anti-United States votes (or vetoes) beyond those already available.

Peroration

United States–India relations will in the future, as in the past, involve differences of opinion and often abrasive rhetoric. In democracies, where divergent views are not, and should not be, suppressed, strident objections to any policy will be heard. What is important is to minimize the abrasiveness and to focus on actual policies rather than rhetorical flourishes. Many of the recommendations made or implied above will elicit ample criticism in the United

---

32. In many areas India has made clear her own preference for multilateral channels. For example, after her nuclear detonation, she noted with approval the World Bank's position on continued aid (as in the case of Sweden, which condemned the detonation but maintained her aid) as a declaraction of independence from the United States, but also expressed concern that the World Bank's new approach would lead to meddling in India's domestic affairs. Also, it should be noted that the WHO was accused of "covering" United States experimentation in biological warfare in India—a sign of the suspicion of United States motives, even through some multilateral channels. Furthermore, as long as there is tension between India and Pakistan, India will doubtless prefer to deal bilaterally with Muslim states in West Asia and North Africa, in order to detach these possible allies from Pakistan.

States, and for a variety of reasons even benign activities of the United States may be greeted with criticism and hostility in India. A more mature relationship between the world's two most populous democracies will and must accept these facts of life.

From the United States side, however, it would seem important to avoid unnecessary provocation by reciting the familiar litany—with one major addition: India's population growth must be reduced; India should pursue an agriculture-first policy instead of giving priority to a broad, heavy-industry base; India should use labor-intensive rather than capital-intensive techniques, given her un- and under-employment; and now (the major addition) India should not squander precious resources on such luxuries as nuclear research and development. Many Indians share these criticisms of the government of India's policies, and the government of India knows better than most how difficult it is to juggle with very limited resources and with competing demands inevitable in a democratic country. The facts are that India *will* continue as best she can to alleviate her food/population/energy problem; that she will not be significantly deterred from her desire to build a strong and diversified heavy industrial base (in part to deal with that same problem), including a nuclear component; and that she *must* do many of these things to function effectively in an international market where India's traditional export earners have experienced a downward turn, with little or no relief in sight. Moreover, in this process India has become a modest aid-giver herself and has helped many LDC's to diversify their economies, to mutual advantage—a process that should be applauded rather than censured.

Segments of United States opinion (along with segments of Indian opinion) will criticize the GOI's policies, and vice versa. This should occasion no surprise, and foreign-policy makers should need no reminders along these lines, either in the United States or in India. United States foreign-policy makers do not have carte blanche to do what they will, and Indians know full well that almost everything that the United States does will have some strings attached, in the sense that the United States will want to protect her own interests. But a key link here is the perception or redefinition of what United States interests are in this region: having played and lost much at the game of guns and generals, the United States might be well advised (for her own self-interest) to consider political stability and parliamentary democracy as the alternatives in this pivotal world region.

The fundamental issue is simple, although it is often overlooked: India is determined to achieve first-class citizenship in the international community.[33] She will try as best she can to develop an industrial economy and to achieve maximum self-reliance in all respects. She will want to keep as many options as possible open, including the nuclear one;[34] and she will resist being browbeaten by any power if she can help it. Criticisms that emphasize neglect of agriculture, squandering of money on nuclear detonations, and orbiting satellites add up to this: others are trying to tell India to refrain from activities which alone will change her from "object" to "subject" status in international affairs.

In addition, what is important to understand is that India is no more willing to allow the U.S.S.R. to dictate what is permissible than to allow the United States to do so, despite India's proximity to the U.S.S.R. A corollary is that India is not likely to view the other LDC's as a group of equals, whose majority votes in the UN or elsewhere will be binding on her. She is in the longer run no more likely than is the United States to feel bound by majorities made up of states like Trinidad-Tobago and Chad. For the moment there may be a congruence of interests among many LDC's, and India may appear (as she doubtless hopes to appear) just one among many; but there is little doubt that she means to be much more than that. A case in point arose in connection with a UN vote on human rights violations by the Chilean junta that overthrew Allende. Herself charged with human rights violations by some international groups, India abstained on the UN vote to send an investigatory team to Chile. This was widely taken in India and elsewhere to reflect India's determination to avoid setting a precedent that could work to her disadvantage.

The Nixon-Kissinger bestowal of the title "major power" on India may have reflected an awareness of her self-image and aspirations. But obviously this by itself will accomplish little if, at every

---

33. Many of the points set forth here are covered in greater detail in Raj Nayar.

34. India, e.g., has refused to sign the nuclear nonproliferation treaty, but she supports general nuclear disarmament.

turn, or even just at a few crucial ones, the foreign policies of the super- and other major powers seem to relegate India to second-class international citizenship. A permanent seat on the UN Security Council would further respond to India's aspirations. More important, however, will be the actions and reactions of others as India seeks her place in the sun—an effort that will not be lessened by the label "major power" or the opportunity to veto certain proposals in the UN. The United States must indeed "treat India seriously."[35] Refusal to do so will necessarily lead to continued strains in United States–India relations—strains that would be diminished, if not eliminated, by policies that respect the legitimate aspirations of this very important less-developed nation.

---

35. The title of Raj Nayar's article.

REFERENCES

Adie, W. A. C., *Oil, Politics, and Seapower: The Indian Ocean Vortex* (New York, Crane, Russak, 1975).

Anderson, Jack, with George Clifford, *The Anderson Papers* (New York, Random House, 1973).

Brecher, Michael, *New States of Asia* (London, Oxford University Press, 1964).

Brown, W. Norman, *The United States and India, Pakistan, Bangladesh* (Cambridge, Harvard University Press, 1972).

Chakravarty, B. N., *India Speaks to America* (New York, John Day, 1966).

Dagli, Vadilal, ed., *Indo-Soviet Economic Relations* (Bombay, Vora, 1971).

Galbraith, John K., *Ambassador's Journal* (Boston, Houghton, Mifflin, 1969).

Hardgrave, Robert, Jr., *India: Government and Politics in a Developing Nation*, 2nd ed. (New York, Harcourt, Brace, Jovanovich, 1975).

Isaacs, Harold, *Images of Asia: American Views of China and India* (New York, Harper and Row, 1972).

Jain, A. P., ed., *India and the World* (Delhi, D. K. Publishing House, 1972).

————, *Shadow of the Bear: The Indo-Soviet Treaty* (New Delhi, P. K. Deo, 1971).

Palmer, Norman, *South Asia and United States Policy* (Boston, Houghton, Mifflin, 1966).

Power, Paul, ed., *India's Nonalignment Policy* (Boston, D. C. Heath, 1967).

Raj Nayar, Baldev, "Treat India Seriously," *Foreign Policy*, 18 (Spring 1975), 133–154.

Shah, A. B., ed., *India's Defense and Foreign Policies* (Bombay, P. C. Manaktala and Sons, 1966).

Stein, Arthur, *India and the Soviet Union: The Nehru Era* (Chicago, University of Chicago Press, 1969).

EDITOR'S NOTE

Only three of the essays in this book focus explicitly on geographic areas. Kasfir's essay uses Africa as a test case in examining the American commitment to development. Erdman concentrates on India as the dominant actor in South Asia. And Silvert discusses Latin America, a region with which the United States has always had—or claimed to have—a "special relationship." Professor Silvert tries to sort out myth from reality, examining the "special relationship" while identifying several ways in which Latin America is likely to command the attention of American foreign-policy makers during the next five to ten years.

IX.
The Changing Dynamics of Hemispheric Politics

Kalman H. Silvert

The increasingly rapid strengthening of many Latin American states is contributing to the growth of two apparently contradictory, but in reality self-reinforcing, tendencies: the nations are growing apart and into more self-contained diversity; but they are also becoming more able to pool particular strength into growingly effective international units for the purposes of global collective bargaining. This interaction of the national and the multi- and international aspects of the Latin American situation depends, in the first instance, on the evolving social organizations of the Latin American countries—their primary ability to create and use power. It is this aspect of the matter which I propose to examine. The reason is that the issues of crisis and violence, food and resources, and the building and uses of instruments of world order involve the intertwining of power, values, and will. These elements come together and have historical continuity within what is broadly called social organization. The core of international studies is not how one government affects another, or one army another, but rather how one total social order affects others. Relations among formal states are the day-to-day symptoms of the underlying question of how societies play on each other internally and, in so doing, how the latent, longer-term effects of such interactions work themselves out.

This approach is of particular importance to the nations of the Western Hemisphere. Although the notions of "America," the

---

* Portions of this article appeared in *The Americas in a Changing World* (New York: Quadrangle, 1975). Reprinted here with permission.

"Western hemisphere idea," or "special relationship" have about them a somewhat unreal romanticism, they describe what many generations of persons in both North and Latin America have taken to be true. And, romance or not, the immense cultural as well as political and economic presence of the United States is felt throughout Latin America. Less recognized but probably similarly potent is the subtle and pervasive influence of Latin America on the United States, an effect that may well be growing. The presence of strong and growing Latin communities throughout the United States is but one obvious piece of evidence. Also, we often forget that the one demonstrated instance of the possibility of a United States–Soviet nuclear exchange concerned a Caribbean country. Our reiterated armed interventions in the Caribbean and our repeated diplomatic and intelligence interventions in the politics of Latin American states throughout the hemisphere have affected our own views and practices of international law and relations as they have affected the concerned Latin states themselves. These obvious interactive effects are by no means the only ones, and they may not even be the most important influences flowing from south to north. Within the next five to ten years, I strongly suspect that we shall have to grapple with the following international stimuli coming from Latin America, serving up proof anew that if the Latins are the least developed of the European cultural offshoots, they are also the most developed of the underdeveloped. To wit:

Theoretical and normative issues. Until the 1950's, Latin America was not an important exporter of high culture and ideas. But since that time, two important sets of social science and ideological ideas have come from that region. One is an emphasis on the structural elements in economics, pushed especially by the U.N. Economic Commission for Latin America; and the other is a current vogue, "dependence concepts"—a neo-Marxist interpretation of international relations. Even though Latin American scholars did not succeed in conceptually taming their ideas about structural economic affairs and thus becoming effectively competitive with monetarists, say, in inflation control plans, the ideas behind structuralism remain strong. Present drives in the United States toward institutional economics bear a strong relation to these prior Latin American innovations. Dependence ideas have been much more influential, however, in affecting social science work throughout Western Europe.

Now that approach is being adopted widely in Africa and in such Asian countries as India. Such other ideas as "social marginality" and "right-wing populism" have also arisen out of the Latin experience, and are influencing thinkers internationally. Some social *phenomena* being underscored by current Latin American events, and already being used as exemplary material abroad, are as follows:

a. Nationalism as an idea and as a way of organizing communities will not die, not least because it remains a force of moment in the industrialized as well as the developing worlds. Because the more mature Latin American nations are having to face up to a choice between societies of total participation (of complete national community) or of classbound partial participation, the issue of nation is arising once again in its classical, even original, form. Explicitly, the concept of *citoyen*, the "universally belonging" citizen, coming to us from French revolutionary days, refers to a person who is totally at home in all national organizations *despite class*. More modern usage has given nationalism bad names—supernationalism, xenophobia, and the like being corrupted usages covering the basic egalitarian notion lying behind early ideas of national community.

b. Collectivism, too, is being seen as having meanings independent of political organization. The Latin American experience in economics reveals the presence of little true capitalism, defined as an economic system revolving about a freely competitive market. Instead, the evolution has been from state monopoly to private monopolies, and now either to a full return to state monopoly (Cuba), to mixed state and private monopolies (Peru), or to private monopoly (Chile). In any case, collectivism is the name of this economic order—whether private and planned or public and planned collectivism. The effects of these economic practices on international relations will certainly increase in the immediate future as common market organizations (particularly the Andean group) attempt to regulate multinational corporations through international political combinations, and government-private company negotiations are carried on.

c. The idea of corporatism is also being exported from Mediterranean cultures to the United States and Western Europe. The present academic fashion of studying corporatism has led to a new interest in Latin American practice, where corporate organization is designed to create patterns of representation by interest and occupational groups. The effect of an occupationally based hier-archical society is to permit institutional differentiation within an unchanging class context. Specifically, the purpose of corporatism is to permit industrialization and complexity to grow without permitting the egalitarian effects of national participation to be felt. Within the past fifteen months three international conferences on corporatism have been held, with the Latin case being predomi-nant in discussion. The vulgarization of the concept in such a book as Reich's *The Greening of America* is further evidence of the seepage of this concept.

Structural changes. In addition to normative and ideological issues posed for us from Latin America, we shall also have to grapple with structural changes in the way Latin American states conduct their international relations. The recent diplomacy of Mexico, in abandonment of over forty years of virtual isolationism, is designed to accomplish the following ends:

a. To convert the regular American foreign ministers' meetings into a formal, international political organization as a diplomatic analogue of the Economic Commission for Latin America.

b. To downgrade the importance of the Organization of Ameri-can States, effectively removing it from any major international political role and leaving to it only international administrative functions.

c. To force the recognition of Cuba as an indication of inde-pendence from the foreign policy wishes of the United States.

d. To create a means for collective Latin American bargaining with European and Asian powers, as well as with the United States.

The Mexicans presume that despite the political disparity among Latin states, a new political organization can find certain grounds for a common approach, particularly in regard to multi-national corporations, international commodity agreements, access to the United States market for finished goods, and claims of nationalism and sovereignty, especially as they are related to non-interventionism. Such commonality is, of course, easier posited than achieved. In any event, the United States must expect an attempt at new hemispheric organization and practice.

The Emergence of Latin American global actors. It is now evident that, for diverse reasons, certain Latin American countries already have assumed world significance. As is suggested by the first two points above, the reasons have to do not only with economic and even (as in the case of Brazil) imminent atomic-military possibilities, but also with ideological significance. Thus Cuba and Chile have claimed global attention and have had effects little understood by many North Americans. The Chilean experience, for example, is widely debated in France and Italy as having some relation to the evolution of their own political coalitions. The proposed merger between Chile's Communists and Christian Democrats—mooted during the entire Allende administration and once again proposed—buttressed notions of an "opening to the left" among certain of Italy's Christian Democrats. Similarly, in France the emergent "popular front" strategy of Western Communist Parties was recently given a trial run with the candidacy of Mitterand. Again, the Chilean case was an element in the debate. For an even longer time the same has been true of Cuba, and its use by leftists as well as rightists to underscore the difficulties not of socialist revolution but of administering into being a society pretending both to socialist planning and to freedom.

As Cuba and Chile have assumed importance on the political left, Brazil and Peru have significance on the right. Brazil is often used as an example of how to work an economic miracle under military auspices; Peru is as often employed as an American "Nasserist" experiment in changing social class structures under military tutelage. Francoism, militarism, *nasserismo, Opus Dei* and its policies, and many other ideologies of the right have their Latin testing grounds, as do approaches from the left. The significance of both is widespread.

A unilateral emergence onto the world scene is taking place also in more standard terms of trade and diplomacy. Brazil, for example, has an active Africanist policy and is entering the Latin American commercial scene by competing for industrial sales with Western Europe and the United States. Promising to become a nuclear power in the near future and widely seen as the dominant power in Latin America's near future, Brazil is increasingly adopting a foreign policy akin to that of many pre-World War II European countries.

In so doing, Brazil is but following the example of Mexico, which for many years has eschewed multilateral foreign entanglements in seeking to become individually involved with Europe and

Asia as well as with Latin America and the United States. Mexico now has the longest unbroken history of relations with Asian and Eastern European countries of any Latin American state.

The usual way to make this point about growing Latin globalism is to refer to its increasingly complex trade relations with Western and Eastern Europe and Japan. But the developments are much more complex and need to be seen in their full political, cultural, and ideological light as well as in commercial aspects. The future relations of North Americans and of North American institutions with Latin America will have to be taken in concert and in competition with the many other persons, agencies, and currents now actively at work in that area.

Human rights. A fourth area in which domestic Latin affairs will influence American reactions has to do with civil and human rights. This subject is of a different order from the first three mentioned; it taps attitudes lying behind partisan politics and transcends diplomacy. Important segments of the American public, organized and unorganized, react strongly to violations of human rights abroad and at home. No matter other facets of international affairs, this aspect of domestic doings always triggers response. The widespread reactions in Congress, as well as among the citizenry, to recent Chilean outrages is a case in point. The persistent willingness of the administration in Washington to blink at human rights violations from the right and to condemn them from the left is an important element in weakening consensus about American foreign policy. For reasons we shall return to at the end of this paper, human rights questions in Latin America usually provoke more than ordinary reactions in the United States. Note the cases of Cuba, Brazil, Argentina, and Chile, among others, and contrast them with reactions to recent happenings in Rhodesia and Uganda. The "Western hemisphere idea" may well be playing a strong part in the distinctions clearly being drawn.

In matters, then, of norms, structures, global outreach, and fundamental values, Latin American events will certainly cause domestic North American reactions within the near future. These attitudes will necessarily be conditioned by changed understandings of Latin America, as those nations continue their rapid development on intellectual and cultural as well as material fronts. I have chosen to emphasize these four sets of changes as the frame within which crisis, specific problem-solving, and accommodations to world-order problems will take place. But now another frame needs to be built, to indicate which Latin American countries are likely to be dynamic and effective and which in the near future are likely to change but little as the result of domestic occurrences. As has already been suggested, Latin America as a whole cannot be meaningfully discussed without categorizing its sets of countries, situations, occurrences, and experiences. Perhaps we can speak with sense about Latin America's generic characteristics: language, ethos, religion, world position, or historical experiences. But any similarly broad political statements are absurdities. Left with the categorical task as an imperative, an ethical question arises. There is no opportunity here to indicate fully the theory lying behind the selection of categories, and equally no chance to expound the tastes and passions lying behind the theory. Consequently, I will hew as closely as possible to conventional wisdom, in the expectation that such an approach will appear to the reader less coercive than would the presentation of a more idiosyncratic set of conclusions from a hidden array of normative and hypothetical premises. In addition, this section will be cast in the form of a line of argument in order to highlight the links in the reasoning.

Assumed is that one of the basic elements playing in politics, whether domestic or international, is power taken pure. Power can be viewed as the ability to force others to do what one wishes them to, despite their opposition. It can also be taken to mean the simple ability to take effective action even in the absence of an antagonist. For instance, power can be seen as placing fluoride in water systems despite opposing pressure groups, as well as having the knowledge to know what fluoride can do, and, indeed, having certain kinds of water-supply systems amenable to fluoridation. Power will be taken in both senses in this analysis.

Power—as coercive ability, knowledge, and available instrumentalities—is always in its applications mingled with preferences. "Pure" power and "pure" ideologies, preferences, and tastes come together to make up politically effective desires, the political analogue of what economists call "effective demand." But the subject is infinitely more complex for political than economic thinking. There is rarely a clean test of the quanta of power which "actors" bring to political drama, or melodrama. Political victory is only sometimes unequivocal for individuals, and almost never so for states. And, more importantly, the origins of power have to do with social organization, classes, races, idea-systems, and profound cultural values as they all filter through consensus, legitimacy, institutions, and policy. Uncomfortably difficult as these themes may be, they are the subject matter of international politics. The term "international politics" will be understood as the power-infused relations among formal states in pursuit of varied doctrines of the national interest, concerning all subjects that become consciously attended, from war to cultural exchange. This definition does not cover all relations among nations, of course—merely those which fall into the overtly political sphere. What we want to know about the way in which domestic factors fit into this statement follows:

— We want to know something about the *kinds* of power that can be brought to bear at any given moment by governments.

— We want to know something about the kinds of power that can be brought to bear *for certain purposes* by governments.

— We want to know the range of alternatives that can be seen by governments, interest groups, intellectuals, parties, and other interested and organized groups in a society.

— We want to know something about tendencies in the above three respects.

The first categories in which we should be interested, then, concern the patterns through which societies create and structure public power. In Latin America, generally speaking, they are:

Patrimonial states. A small ruling group uses a large group of non-nationally organized persons for economic purposes of a low order of complexity. Only a very small number of persons can be recruited for tasks at the national level, for there is hardly a "nation" in other than formalistic senses. If the upper groups are cohesive, such governments can make firm pronouncements for their own limited purposes. These political structures are fragile and weak in the face of external threat, but they can be persistent if internal division is avoided and social change at lower levels is not promoted. Haiti, Nicaragua, and Honduras are classical examples of this kind of governance.

Partially "organic," corporate states. As was said earlier, the purpose of corporatism at grand social levels is to permit the growth of institutional differentiation and specialization in the accomplishment of tasks, but without scrambling the class order. Hierarchy is stably incorporated within and across the corporate pillars—classically, the clergy, the landowners, the industrialists, the military, the bureaucracy, the merchants, and the trade unionists. The concept of citizenship exists in such situations, but it is strained. No Latin American country is an organic corporatism, although some show more than a few signs of such organization. Mexico's political party structure is corporate in form; the thinking of Chile's incumbent government is overtly corporatist, and it is pursuing policies to bring such a state into existence; Peronism and the present Brazilian government both show strong traces of this persuasion.

Literal partial nation-states. Again, as was said earlier, the nation-state seeks to integrate the universal *citoyen*, who can overcome the class-based accidents of birth and assume equality of condition before the state. No nation-state anywhere has succeeded fully in achieving the goal of complete equality of condition in political matters. But some, obviously, have come closer than others. Clearly, the political goal of Allende's administration in Chile was to mitigate, if not erase, class-rooted impediments to complete citizenship. Substantive equality before the laws and structures of the state was much more true than false for most members of the Argentine and Uruguayan upper and middle groups throughout all of this century, until very recent years. It was the loss of this class-related equality that caused great distress in Brazil after the coming to power of the military in 1964. The attempt to build the social nation characterizes the present Venezuelan polity. The class-inhibited partial nation-state is the political form that has been most characteristic of Latin American ideals (not practice) during the past fifty years. Attacks upon it in the attempt to substitute corporatism provide the fundamental pattern of domestic political strife in the more complex societies.

The emergence of the nation-state as ideal form has given rise to two fundamental areas of political clash in Latin America, as well as in the Western world generally; to wit:

The clash between nation and class. The idea of the secular nation-state is to provide arenas, or "marketplaces," in which equality of condition can play itself out in a rationalistic interchange which, it used to be supposed, would allow ever-growing efficiency within a self-correcting and thus self-sustaining mechanism. Further, a secularized natural law provided equality before the formal religion of one's choosing, without effect on other social roles. To be within a pertinent jurisdiction was the requirement for triggering equality before the laws. Citizenship carried with it equality before the ballot box, the ultimate definer of policy legitimacy. Capital or skill brought to the economic marketplace were not to be reinforced by monopoly, nepotism, political influence, or any other extraeconomic factor that could muddy the exercise of reason and talent in the search for advantage. Finally, public education was to assure an equalization of skills, despite the facts of class origin. These were more or less the ideals, and however imperfectly they were realized, in many nations they promoted mass mobilization of populations to new economic tasks, the emergence of popular (and populist) nation-states that could count on the willingness of masses of citizenry to die in defense of the polity, and they contributed to strengthening middle classes and to changing the nature of upper classes. However, nowhere has the construction of national communities of universal membership come to completion. In every case, including the United States, national movements have created vast new social and political powers, and they have also created a class order that can effectively resist completion of the incorporation of all persons within the community on conditions of essential structural equality.

The second crisis has to do with the form of the state suitable either for the pursuit of national ends or for the attempt to restrict the further expansion of national community. Although written in a somewhat different context, the following paragraphs from a recent book review illustrate the point most adequately:

> Popular sovereignty is an awesome idea precisely because it means nothing less than the existential freedom of a people to be responsible for its own fate, without recourse to any "father." The regicides created this terrible and magnificent freedom, the only one commensurate with the fullness of human potential. With the execution of Louis, they could solemnly declare to the nation: "From this moment, one will no longer write the history of France, but rather the history of the French."

> Yet the rule of one man with his entourage can reemerge

whenever a people, for whatever reasons, renounces the practice of its sovereign judgment, abandoning itself to that slow erosion of responsibility which turns citizens into subjects. Similarly, the "abiding pretensions of monarchy" are also the ones of all those who assert the power to rule alone . . .[1]

This problem is not appropriate to those relatively few Latin American countries that have hardly begun to grapple with the question of national community—Haiti, Nicaragua, Honduras, as mentioned before, and to a limited extent El Salvador and Ecuador. In all countries, of course, there are major segments of the population totally outside the "national question": the Indians of Mexico, Guatemala, Peru, and Bolivia; seminomadic populations in Brazil and Paraguay; and persons living on society's margins in both rural and urban areas. These concerns, however, shape national politics in all the other Latin American countries and affect elites everywhere.

As I see it, then, the three grand families of Latin American politics are those of patrimonialism, antinational sacralism, and pronational secularism. Note that so far we have been speaking of authoritarianisms, totalitarianisms, and democracies only by implication. The reason is clear: national community is a precondition for both the secular republicanism of democracy and the sacred paternalism of totalitarianism. Political situations in non-national societies are in a class by themselves, falling into types of authoritarian regimes far short either of the voluntarism of the perfectly integrated society or of the coercive control of totalitarianism. Our first set of categories had to do with social organization as inferential of power creation. The second set had to do with the quintessential problem of all national states. And the third, the usual display of kinds of political systems, deals with the formal structures for day-to-day governance, and for problem-recognition and solution. It is clear, however, that some rough relation must exist between the degree and nature of national social organization and the kinds of political systems possible in relation to them. Thus, on a rough set of guesses

---

1. Review by Richard Mowery Andrews of Michael Walzer, ed., *Regicide and Revolution: Speeches at the Trial of Louis XVI* (New York, Cambridge University Press, 1974), in *The New York Times Book Review* (June 9, 1974), p. 3.

concerning degrees of national integration, cohesion, and citizenship derived from economic statistics, urbanization, literacy, mobility patterns, cultural and racial homogeneity, extent and complexity and completeness of social services, and hunches concerning citizenry loyalty and anticipatory obedience to law, let us range the Latin countries on an approximate scale of national community.

The most complete social nations:

Cuba

Chile

Uruguay

Argentina

Harsh class divisions, but strengthening traditions of participation and social access of national institutions:

Costa Rica

Venezuela

Harsh class and regional divisions, racially reinforced stratification, but with growing access to national institutions, with the general exception of effective and continuous political participation:

Mexico

Brazil

Peru

Colombia

Panama

El Salvador

Harsh class divisions, very sharp urban-rural differences, sometimes racially reinforced stratification, and little growth in access to national institutions including the political:

Guatemala

Paraguay

Ecuador

Dominican Republic

Bolivia

Nicaragua

Honduras

Haiti

Formerly British Caribbean republics are omitted from this list, for by tradition and circumstance they comprise a special problem.

It should now be obvious that, given the bases of this argument, the countries that can effectively choose quasidemocratic or quasi-totalitarian forms of governance must come from the top half of the list. This exercise is not an idle one. If it had been gone through at the time of the Bay of Pigs, the planners of that operation might have been less ready to apply a technique learned from Guatemala, one of the most fragmented of Latin American countries, to Cuba, a country socially ready for nationhood. Similarly, it was silly for an Assistant Secretary of Inter-American Affairs to warn a conference several years ago that the United States "is on a collision course with Haiti," implying that if we did not treat "Papa Doc" well, he would opt for a *fidelista* course. Nonsense. But it was *not* nonsense to have viewed the urban guerrillaism of the early 1960's in Venezuela as bearing a functional relation to the choices then recently made in Cuba. The two countries share many characteristics, and their potentialities are still not radically different. In short, this array of cases suggests to us the limits of choices effectively open to the societies concerned. It also suggests that as one goes down the list, leadership can express widely varying opinions—being unconstrained by any complexity of followership—but that the ability of leaders to *act* on attempts at far-reaching and profound change is limited. Thus the governments of Arévalo and Arbenz in Guatemala could call for revolutionary change, but they could not manage to bring it about with a population that was over half Indian, three quarters illiterate, and about nine tenths rural.

The latency suggested by this categorization helps in prediction; but it also assists us to understand some of the reasons for the present array of types of governmental crises. Let us go down the list again, applying easy (and necessarily somewhat slovenly) labels to the types of governments involved. Thus:

In full crisis of nation vs. class

Cuba — a socialist authoritarianism, totalitarian in national political affairs, participant and democratic in many local affairs.

Chile — totalitarian military corporate state in the making at both national and local levels. Not yet fully settled down.

Uruguay — totalitarian corporate state under military tutelage.

Argentina — quasidemocratic state, unstable, undergoing attempt to establish a traditional liberal democracy with a populist cast.

Building nation, not yet upon the nation-class confrontation

Costa Rica — traditional liberal partial democracy.

Venezuela — traditional liberal partial democracy.

Totally mixed situations, politically and structurally

Mexico — mixed situation, with some elements of corporatism, some of liberal partial democracy, and remaining strong vestiges of patrimonialism, especially in rural and Indian areas.

Brazil — mixed situation under military control, with some elements of corporatism (strong), some of liberal partial democracy (weak), and remaining strong vestiges of patrimonialism in lower groups in both city and country.

Nationalizing elites, lagging populations

Peru — developmental military rule attempting to move from patrimonialism to some of the choices open in the Mexican and Brazilian scenes.

Colombia — civilian rule, using the forms of partial liberal democracy within the social structure and social habits of patrimonialism.

Panama — essentially patrimonial with some of the trimmings and promise of traditional liberal democracy.

El Salvador — the same.

Prenational

Guatemala — classbound military patrimonial rule, traditional in a slowly modernizing social setting.

Paraguay — the same.

Ecuador — the same.
Dominican Republic — the same, but with civilian oligarchical government.

Patrimonial   Bolivia — the same politically, with little social modernization.
Nicaragua — the same.
Honduras — the same.
Haiti — the same.

This ordering permits me to hear better when someone says, "Latin America is beginning to come on the world scene in an autonomous way, and we should start thinking of the region as we do of Europe." I immediately screen out all but the five or six first countries on the list. Or, when others say that Latin America will be comprised of client-states for many generations to come, I nod, thinking about the bottom half of the list. Also, it should be noted that all five of the lowest ranking countries—as well as some others— have in the past been the objects of direct military intervention by the United States. Non-national states close by a major power are always inviting targets for the impatience of military intervention; simply put, they are pushovers. At the other end of the list, covert activities have an inviting chance of succeeding when countries find themselves in the ultimate crises of national being, and thus are beset by empowered groups of citizens willing to seek assistance from abroad to confront their profound crises at home. It is this kind of opportunity which the United States is accused of having taken in Brazil, Chile, and other such countries.

To this point the discussion has centered about macropolitics. Before concluding, I wish to return to the specific problem-areas of concern to the Dartmouth College study group.[2] These themes are obvious, and they affect all nations of the world in varying degrees:

---

2. I have used the word "problem-areas" instead of "problems," for some Latin American countries do not recognize some of the points I shall name as being problematic. That is, they do not see certain relations either as existing or, if they exist, as being undesirable and therefore a problem. In other words, all "problems" are ideological statements in that they directly posit a disliked relationship.

ecological matters, population dynamics, urban-rural relations, education and citizenship, education and employment, patterns of industrialization, and communications, among many others. If the stakes are global, they are also particular to each nation and to every person. Thus these themes are obviously testing grounds for styles and types of international relations and organization. They permit us to mingle multilateralism with bilateralism in reconciling the universal with the particular aspects of these matters. Indeed, one of the better ways of testing the utility of the earlier typologies is to learn to what extent a nation either recognizes or has any interest in any of these subjects. For example, countries at the top and bottom of the array of states tend to have little problem with undue population expansion. The least developed countries "benefit" from high death rates, as in Haiti; the most developed have self-governing populations, as in Argentina. The in-betweens have rapidly expanding populations, as in Brazil, Mexico, and Costa Rica. The least developed have few ecological problems, as in Honduras. The most developed have populations that worry about the environment, as in Argentina. Again, the intermediates emphasize the quantitative over the qualitative, as in Mexico, Peru, and Brazil.

But matters affecting the nature of populations, especially evidenced in education and communications, are of a different order. They are unavoidably ideological. In the last century education was seen as preparing persons of broad culture who would build their economies, polities, and societies. In this century education serves to supply manpower; labor is seen as a commodity, becoming but another factor of production. Communications, to take another example, can be taken as instrumental for sales, or for "preparing" persons for occupational roles. Or they can be promoted as a good, per se—as enrichment of human experience and understanding valuable in itself. The transfer of international experience and knowledge in these fields is a first-order task with profound long-term political implications.

The task of policy prescription should not be confused with the equally difficult job of operationalizing policy, of adjusting pre-established structures of thought to the facts of given cases. Policy is not a simplistic statement of preferences, nor is it a set of *ad hoc* adjustments to exigencies. Rather, policy is an explicit preference system that includes guides for application and a statement of appropriate styles and instruments of application. In this view, policy is akin to the common law, and opposed to civil law pretensions to anticipate all possible human behavior.

Because policy contains statements of goals, I began this paper with an apology for an inability to reveal all the normative premises lying behind it. In closing this argument, however, there is at least one assumption that should be admitted and clarified. I have deduced this paper from Latin American cases, but I have also suggested prescriptions that may well have much wider application. Are those prescriptions, nevertheless, in any way intimately and particularly linked to the countries of the Americas? I do see such a connection, and presume the existence of a "special relationship." These policy suggestions possibly have more pointed and meaningful application to United States–Latin American relations than, say, to United States–Central African relations, or to United States–South Asian affairs. I cannot prove my point with hard data, or make more than a reasonable case for it. But I do not rest it merely on old-fashioned Monroeism, pan-Americanism, or similar romanticisms. Instead, I see the particularity in Western hemisphere affairs as having something to do with the following elements:

— Republicanism is a long-standing common ideal of governmental structure in the Americas.

— The ideal of egalitarian democracy has, until very recent years in some countries, comprised a key element in the ideological constructions of all reigning groups.

— Capitalism, as a market economy of private participants, has also until recent years been a dominant ideological commitment, if decreasingly an actual practice.

— Until very recently, all states as they have grown competent have moved toward an extension of educational systems and other aspects of public welfare.

— The existence of class and racial barriers has been generally seen as undesirable, even while the privileges they confer have been enjoyed and defended.

— The crises of republicanism and of class and nation have become the common property of all the more developed societies, including the United States.

One could extend this list, concomitantly introducing

elements that more clearly distinguish American from Western European experience. But I wish only to suggest that it is reasonable to assume that indeed there has been a "Western Hemisphere idea." If structures and practices have partially belied the idea, the fact of a widespread common commitment is a subtle and profound potential instrument for collaborative and controlled change.

Editor's Note

The study of foreign policy problems often ignores the domestic political context in which foreign policy-makers must operate. Professor Radway's essay reminds us that political decision-makers must consider what is possible *as well as what is* desirable *in formulating foreign policy.*

Two potential developments identified by Radway appear especially ominous in the light of the other essays in this volume. On the one hand the American public may ignore the trends toward interdependence and opt for an ostrich-like nonresponse to the emerging foreign policy problems. On the other hand, Americans may become more aware of increased interdependence, become resentful of it, and lash out at its perceived causes in an untimely way. There is no guarantee that increased awareness of the world outside will lead the American public to support wise and responsible foreign policies.

Radway also suggests that it will be harder to maintain centralized coordination of United States foreign policy in an increasingly interdependent world. The prospects for achieving the increase in centralized control that Ringbakk recommends do not look bright.

X.
Domestic Attitudes as Constraints on American Foreign Policy Leaders

Laurence I. Radway

This essay attempts to forecast domestic attitudes that are likely to constrain American foreign-policy leaders in the next five years. "Leaders" are defined somewhat arbitrarily to include only the President, the Secretary of State, and their senior White House and State Department aides. The purpose of so narrow a definition is not to suggest that "leaders" form a monolithic group;[1] still less is it to deny the importance of other Federal agencies or of the Congress. On the contrary, it serves to bring into bolder relief the distinctive interests and influence of other executive and legislative agents. For the same reason, "constraints" are defined as attitudes pressed upon "leaders" not only by private citizens but by critics within the government. Prevailing public opinion is not regarded as a constraint to the extent that it is held by "leaders," as indeed it usually is, especially in the case of the President. The analysis of constraints properly begins with a search for attitudinal differences between leaders and followers or within the ranks of each.

Because such differences are relatively sharp during debates over *military* intervention and disengagement, it is useful to start by examining such debates in recent American history. This will also provide a background for subsequent discussion

---

1. Routine bureaucratic competition between White House and State Department staffs is limited by the personal loyalty that ties many White House personnel to the President and by the relative weakness of State's domestic constituency. Organizational interests it has aplenty, and these bring it into conflict with external agencies, but in these encounters it is rarely aided by anything like the farm organizations that support the Department of Agriculture in similar relationships.

of constraints in the different issue area of foreign *economic* policy.

Interveners and Disengagers

American governments oscillate between periods of active diplomatic and military intervention in world affairs and periods of disengagement when priority is given to tasks at home and foreign relations are left largely to business, religious, educational, and other nongovernmental enterprises. Historians may differ about precise turning points, but certainly the number of interveners increased during 1916-17, 1940-41, 1948-50, and 1963-65, while the years 1920-37, 1945-46, and 1969-75 included periods in which the number of disengagers grew.

Individuals are more difficult to characterize than epochs, since the dispositions to intervene and to disengage are complex phenomena grounded in a variety of motives, interests, or impulses. In the following discussion both interveners and disengagers are subdivided into two groups, so that a four-part typology emerges. For some individuals, of course, none of these four categories is relevant. There are others, like Lyndon Johnson, who cannot be pigeonholed neatly. But the categories do permit the classification of a significant number of Americans. They appear to be related to important status differences in our society. And a good deal can be learned about constraints on leaders by examining why and when the number of citizens in each category changes, and in what directions people move.

1. Collective Security Interveners. Opposed to changes in the status quo by force, they support treaty commitments, mutual aid programs, and multilateral enterprises, together with national preparedness, to defeat or deter aggression. Examples include Wilson, Stimson, Franklin Roosevelt, Truman, Eisenhower, Acheson, Rusk. Some (e.g. Stimson) place more stress on national power than others (e.g. Wilson). But all perceive America to be responding defensively to a threatening international environment and support collaborative measures to cope with it.

2. Eagle Screamers. Nationalist and imperialist war hawks prepared to take the initiative in deploying force unilaterally (i.e. "to throw America's weight around in the world") because they perceive opportunities to enhance national prestige, pride, territory, or trade, or to "civilize inferior races." Examples include Alfred Mahan, Albert Beveridge, Theodore Roosevelt, the senior Henry Cabot Lodge, Douglas MacArthur, Curtis LeMay, and the *Manchester Union Leader's* William Loeb.

3. *Domestic Priority Doves.* Like nineteenth-century "Little Englanders" (e.g. John Bright and Richard Cobden), they welcome international economic and cultural exchange, but have grave reservations about the development and use of force, unilaterally or multilaterally, because they place an exceedingly high priority on peace, because they fear that intervention will end in the enslavement or exploitation of weaker peoples, and especially because they believe that an "imperial" policy will undercut democratic liberties and delay social reforms at home. Spokesmen include Carl Shurz, the later William Jennings Bryan, Congressman Charles Lindberg, Sr., Oswald Garrison Villard, Norman Cousins, and George McGovern.

4. *America First Disengagers.* Classical xenophobic isolationists, opposed to foreign involvements of all kinds, whose attitude is summed up in the phrases, "Let 'em stew in their own juice," or "It's not worth the life of one red-blooded American." Pessimistic about the cost-effectiveness of military action, their antipathy to foreigners leads to withdrawal rather than intervention. But they are capable of transformation into Eagle Screamers if the nation is attacked or humiliated or if intervention is undertaken to end foreign ties rather than to preserve them. Like Eagle Screamers they tend to be economic nationalists. Spokesmen include William Borah, the *Chicago Tribune's* William R. McCormick, General Robert E. Wood, and perhaps George Wallace.

Socio-Economic Status

It is hardly surprising that *spokesmen* for each of these positions are individuals of high socioeconomic status with relatively coherent sets of intellectual convictions. But *garden variety adherents* have tended to be drawn from several social strata. Affluent and highly educated citizens loom relatively large in the ranks of Collective Security Interveners and Domestic Priority Doves. In the last decade citizens with incomes over $20,000 and with college, especially graduate, degrees have been more likely to identify themselves as internationalists. In the last two or three years they have also been more likely to support cuts in the defense budget. On the other hand, citizens earning, say, less than $10,000, and with considerably less schooling, or schooling at less prestigious institutions, loom relatively large in the ranks of Eagle Screamers and America First Disengagers. These are characteristically tough positions not based on trust or tolerance for what is alien or different. Faced with the proposition "We must maintain our dominant position in the world at all costs," strongest support still comes from individuals who have no more than a grade-school education and whose incomes are under $3,000.[2]

But the matter is a bit more complicated because there is a second effect of status which sometimes reinforces and sometimes dilutes the first. Americans of medium and high status usually consider themselves to be part of the political system. Because they are involved, they are also aware, and unless they have a specific reason for not doing so, they tend to rally around duly constituted authority whenever it is acting on behalf of the system as a whole. As "good citizens" they are usually prepared to support the foreign policy of their President whatever that policy may be (e.g. even if he abets an invasion of Cuba or mines Haiphong Harbor). At lower

---

2. Here, as elsewhere, quantitative statements about public opinion are drawn from established polling sources (e.g. *Gallup Opinion Index* and *The Harris Survey*). See also John E. Reilly, ed., *American Public Opinion and U.S. Foreign Policy: 1975* (Chicago, Council on Foreign Relations, 1975); Bruce Russett, "The Americans' Retreat from World Power," *Political Science Quarterly, 40* (Spring 1975), 1–21; William Schneider, "Public Opinion: The Beginning of Ideology," *Foreign Policy*, No. 17 (Winter 1974), pp. 88–120; Donald R. Lesh, ed., *A Nation Observed: Perspectives on America's World Role* (Washington, D.C., Potomac Associates, 1974); William Watts and Lloyd A. Free, *State of the Nation 1974* (New York, Basic Books, 1974); John E. Mueller, *War, Presidents and Public Opinion* (New York, John Wiley and Sons, 1973); Albert Cantril and Charles W. Roll, Jr., *Hopes and Fears of the American People* (New York, Universe Books, 1971); Lloyd A. Free and Hadley Cantril, *The Political Beliefs of Americans* (New Brunswick, Rutgers University Press, 1967). See also Milton J. Rosenberg et al., *Vietnam and the Silent Majority* (New York, Harper and Row, 1970), and Herbert McCloskey, "Personality and Attitudinal Correlates of Foreign Policy Orientation," in James N. Rosenau, ed., *Domestic Sources of Foreign Policy* (Glencoe, Illinois, The Free Press, 1967).

rungs of the social ladder, however, this phenomenon of followership is diluted by apathy, an inability to perceive any personal relationship to remote affairs, and a general sense of helplessness.

Opinion Changes

In 1940–41, 1948–50, and again in the early 1960's, the number of Collective Security Interveners grew as individuals of high status became apprehensive about changes in the international environment. The initiative in pushing the United States into a posture of confrontation was taken by "the best and the brightest" in government, finance, law, the universities, and the prestige media. Their names may be found in the rosters of members of the Committee to Defend America by Saving the Allies, the Committee on the Present Danger, and the Council on Foreign Relations. Subsequently these sentinels were joined by followers and by Eagle Screamers.

Individuals of very low status, on the other hand, tended to drag their heels during each of these periods because they were so little involved in the political system that they were unaware of, or apathetic about, leadership cues. This explains why opinion pollsters found high school dropouts to be less supportive of the Vietnam war than, for example, middle-class graduates of small sectarian colleges.

During the process of disengagement from Vietnam, the initiative was again taken by individuals of relatively high status, in this case mostly in the private sector. They were essentially Domestic Priority Doves, many of whom had been Collective Security Interveners in the first years of the Cold War. Middle Americans, deferring to the views of the President and often resentful of high-status war protestors, were more likely to stand fast. Lower-status individuals, many of them originally Eagle Screamers, shifted to the opposition relatively late, as casualties and draft calls continued to rise and as it became clear that the government had no plan to break the military stalemate. Their attitude was perfectly epitomized in the phrase "win or get out." The delay in their shift into the opposition, together with the tendency of middle American followers to support the President, explains why Baptists and Catholics came to oppose the war later than members of some smaller and higher-status denominations (e.g. Presbyterians or Congregationalists). It also helps to explain why opposition developed later in the House of Representatives than in the Senate: House members tend to be more sensitively tuned to the mass electorate they encounter so often.

Although the argument has been controversial to this point, it is more important to note that practicing politicians act as if it were valid. In the years immediately before and after World War II, each time the White House sought support for collective security, for the United Nations, or for international economic cooperation, it undertook to mobilize private elites. And in 1969 and 1970, as the Nixon Administration confronted Domestic Priority Doves, it went over the head of the private elites to appeal directly to the silent majority.

Emerging Moods

Both kinds of disengagers—America Firsters as well as Domestic Priority Doves—are more numerous today than in the flood tide of the Cold War. Both kinds of interveners are correspondingly less numerous, and they are likely to remain so unless there is a dramatic revival of anxiety about external threats to vital American interests. The percentage of people who can be identified as isolationsists, while still a minority, has doubled in the last two or three years, the increase being greatest among people with only a grade-school education and with incomes under $10,000. The percentage of United Nations enthusiasts is only half what it was a decade ago. Americans are today inclined to think they should concentrate more on domestic problems, less on coping with the international environment. If there is a slogan for the times, it is "fight less, do less, pay less."

Though other factors play a part (e.g. the revival of Japan and West Europe and the divisions in the communist world), the major factor in this shift has clearly been Vietnam—its cost, its inconclusiveness, and its capacity to generate painful domestic turmoil. But Vietnam itself must be understood in the light of our whole history as a nation. For three centuries Americans took it for granted that they were uniquely moral. For a much shorter but still significant period they took it for granted tht they were uniquely powerful.

Vietnam, by challenging both assumptions, provoked a swing toward disengagement fully as powerful as the swing toward intervention provoked thirty years earlier by the experience of Munich. Today large numbers of Americans fear that their country is sliding backward both in moral stature and in raw power. Dispirited, afflicted by self-doubt and self-pity, they worry about inflation, oil, and crime while the Japanese flood their markets with very good automobiles, the U.S.S.R. builds larger missiles, and Taiwanese kids run off with the Little League World Series. All of this nourishes contemporary support for disengagement.

To the extent that it can be done, however, it is helpful to distinguish the relative strength of the two kinds of disengagers, Domestic Priority Doves and America Firsters. If the earlier analysis is valid, relative strength will be influenced significantly by the size of attentive private audiences, which in turn will vary with different kinds of foreign-policy issues. A small audience will often include a larger proportion of high-status individuals than a mass audience. Although prepared to serve somewhat unobtrusively as good citizens of the world, such high-status individuals, in the contemporary world environment, will be skeptical of military instruments of policy and insistent on improving the quality of American life. A mass audience is likely to be less benevolent about foreigners and more interested in insulating the United States against shocks that may be inflicted on it in this era of increasing interdependence.

How large an audience should be expected? Two hypotheses are plausible. One is that the audience will be *small* because the United States is moving "from an era of confrontation to an era of negotiation"; because it will be hard to generate much drama or much sense of urgency about the complex and shifting multilateral relationships that will characterize this new era; and because, even when the stakes are large, the process of disposing of them will often appear technical, protracted, and tedious. The other hypothesis is that the audience will be *large* because in the emerging era of interdependence the material well being of every citizen will be affected profoundly by events beyond his borders. If this is so, foreign-policy issues should generate the kind of citizen concern heretofore directed to taxes, drug abuse, medical insurance, and high prices.

The view taken here is that both outcomes are likely, each for a different subset of foreign-policy issues. Domestic Priority Doves will probably be relatively influential in a smaller public concerned with such questions as force redeployment and military aid. America Firsters will be relatively influential in the larger public that is coming to be concerned with import and export policy.

Intervention

The present view of foreign-policy leaders, expressed in the somewhat murky Nixon Doctrine, is that the United States should preserve its considerable influence in the world but at less risk and less cost, especially in lives. While some Congressional and private critics prefer the somewhat tougher formulations of Senator Jackson, a larger number of critics of the Administration are Domestic Priority Doves, prepared to cut cost and risk still further even if American power is reduced in the process.

The attitudes of Domestic Priority Doves are more likely to constrain decisions about force deployments, defense budgets, or military aid than decisions about armed intervention; for there appears to be a national consensus that the threshold for intervention, especially by ground forces, should be raised—to a level where it can be crossed only in the event of graver threats to national security than those which prompted most of our military actions in Asia and the Caribbean since 1950. Moreover, the danger today seems less, not more, obvious. Even senior officers at the war colleges are now more likely to think that nationalism, not Communism, is the source of revolutionary ferment in the third world, and the number of them believing that the threat of Communism to the United States has decreased during the past decade is double the number thinking it has increased.

Large majorities of Americans supported the commitment of troops to the Dominican Republic in 1965, just as they had been ready to support the use of force, if necessary, to defend Berlin a few years earlier. But by the fall of 1967, most Americans opposed sending troops "if a situation like Vietnam should arise again elsewhere." A particularly sharp drop in support for intervention took place between 1970 and 1973, with the result that current polls reveal a growing reluctance of Americans to commit themselves in advance to send ground combat troops to defend Thailand, Japan,

Israel, Berlin, or even West Europe. Significantly, this reluctance is marked both among the young elite (Domestic Priority Doves) who are most likely to hold leadership positions tomorrow, and among older and less educated citizens (America Firsters). By 1973, for example, 53 percent of those who had only an eighth-grade education (and over 60 percent of those who actually had an opinion on the subject) were opposed to fighting to defend West Europe. In the same year Congress took the unusual step of voting to force a halt in the bombing of Cambodia. By early 1975 nearly eight out of ten Americans opposed military aid to Indochina because of fear of reinvolvement.

On the other hand, the sudden fall of South Vietnam and Cambodia obviously bothered moderate doves enough to arrest pressure for drastic cutbacks in American force levels overseas. Support for the defense of Western Europe has remained especially strong, particularly among the well educated elderly. And many less well educated Americans are still suspicious about détente and wary of Soviet intentions. Moreover, the example of Chile shows that covert intervention remains an instrument of policy; that multinational corporations sometimes seek its use;[3] and that while a majority disagreed with the way it was apparently used in this case, a plurality continues to support more restrained covert measures on the ground that "if others do it, we must too."

Finally, most Americans are still likely to rally around the flag, at least for a while, if the President commits it to battle, or for that matter if he simply puts on a show of force. But the more important point is that during the next five years presidents are likely either to share the caution of ordinary people about getting "sucked into another Vietnam," or to fear an eventual voter backlash if they do so, or both.

Pro-Israel sentiment, to be sure, continues to be strong, especially among older Democrats. If anything, it appears to have been increased as a result of Arab oil policy, and it is possible, though not probable, that it could spark military intervention in the event

---

3. Availability of covert intervention, like the availability of government-supported insurance against expropriation, may well have discouraged multinational corporations from developing more sophisticated techniques to protect their stakes.

of another oil embargo.[4] But over the long run—probably longer than five years—support for the defense of Israel per se is likely to weaken not only among the general public but within the American Jewish community, where fewer will remember Nazi atrocities, and where even now some of the articulate young are becoming critical of what they regard as Israeli militarism and its ties with the affluent West.

In principle, American blacks could develop a comparable support for the aspirations of blacks in Southern Africa if racial violence grows there. Although this support would probably not bring blacks into the arena of large-scale campaign donors, it could have a substantial impact on the presidential politics of a number of states with large electoral votes. But for at least ten years blacks have consistently been more opposed than any other sector of the population to military action abroad. They are farther in time and space from Africa than are most other American ethnic groups from their ancestral homelands. No black politician has yet won an election by dramatizing his opposition to repression in Durban or Salisbury. And in the next five years, prices, jobs, and schools will probably continue to be more important to the black community than the struggle of some remote people for self-determination.

To summarize, there is little prospect that foreign policy leaders will be pushed into fights which they are reluctant to start, or that they will be more eager to start fights than the public at large. They will almost certainly be more apprehensive than the general public about any fresh effort to enact war powers legislation. But this is the principal respect in which leaders are likely to feel constrained by private opinion in the issue area of intervention.

Force Deployment and Military Aid

On the other hand, leaders will probably feel constrained by pressure, primarily from Domestic Priority Doves, for more rapid withdrawal of American forces from Germany, Korea, Thailand, the Philippines, and other overseas bases. As suggested earlier, the immediate effect of the fall of Saigon and Pnom Penh was to inspire

---

4. Defenders of an American base at Diego Garcia now point to its potential utility in the event of another war in the Middle East.

caution about cutbacks in the American defense posture, lest other nations—or Americans themselves—get the impression that the United States need no longer be taken seriously as a dominant power. But the assumption here is that pressure for such cutbacks will revive. Capitalizing on détente and on the shift of attention from military to economic aspects of foreign policy, critics of existing forward deployments will continue to emphasize local opposition to the American presence along with familiar complaints about balance of payments and defense budget cuts. And they are likely to find an increasingly sympathetic ear among Pentagon planners disturbed about the low morale of offshore troops or concerned about the marginal utility of manpower skills sorely needed by units based at home.

Withdrawal of forces from overseas *could* be matched by compensatory military aid—supplies, facilities, training—designed to strengthen host country forces. And such programs will continue to be supported by residual "collective security interventionists" within the foreign-policy leadership. But they are likely to be opposed by America Firsters as well as by Domestic Priority Doves. The former will feel that too many past beneficiaries of military assistance have proved to be ungrateful[5] and unreliable allies unprepared to sacrifice in their own defense. The latter will argue that prospective beneficiaries are not all that vulnerable to communist subversion or aggression; that some have oppressive regimes that we should not wish to sustain; that others use our weapons in local wars against neighbors whose good will is also important to us; and than an unacceptable risk of involvement by American troops will remain as long as foreigners plan to fight with American supplies.

In the short run, public pressure to continue military aid will be strongest in the case of Israel, and such pressure will continue to influence a significant number of elected officials. This is not merely because there are important concentrations of Jewish people in a few states with large electoral votes, but because Jews are distinctively generous campaign contributors, especially when many candidates must otherwise depend on their own resources.

---

5. Some, for example, were unwilling to give landing rights to American planes flying military supplies to Israel.

Defense Budget

Defense budget issues must be viewed in the broader perspective of what have come to be called national priorities. Since the mid-1960's the fraction of Americans who feel that their government should concentrate more on domestic than on international problems has risen from about one half to three quarters of the total. War and peace issues, at the top of the citizen's mind for perhaps thirty years, are now deemed less important than high prices and tax reform. This shift has been accompanied by a decline in support for defense spending. Fifteen years ago most people supported the then current rate of defense spending, and a few more wanted to raise it than to lower it. Today far more (over 50 percent) would cut it than raise it (15 percent). While Domestic Priority Doves are the most heavily committed to defense cuts, support for them is so great that it probably extends to America Firsters, who are old-time fiscal conservatives.

To be sure, there are counterforces. The prospect of no longer being Number 1 unsettles most Americans, even if they want the United States to be less involved in the world.[6] America Firsters are likely to be more critical of total dollar figures than of the specific force levels or weapons programs on which they are built; Trident and the B-1 bomber program have survived all challenges to date. Ordinary citizens are likely to be especially worried about technological advances or strategic arms agreements that appear to give the U.S.S.R. parity or better in offensive nuclear capabilities. Older war veterans and conservative labor leaders can still be aroused by anticommunist messages. Decisions to close military bases continue to draw howls from local communities. If a severe recession generates massive unemployment, there is likely to be heavy pressure to expand the defense establishment as a relief measure.

But few things are more certain than powerful opposition to the larger defense budgets that the Pentagon will feel compelled to request simply to maintain existing force levels at a time of rising manpower and materiel costs. Inflation-ridden consumers will resist higher taxes, especially if they are imposed for such intrinsically

---

6. Before World War II the American Legion, although opposed to intervention, strongly supported "preparedness" or rearmament.

unheroic values as "bargaining chips" or "parity" between civilian and military pay. Liberal-left forces in Congress, now gaining in seniority as well as sheer numbers, will press ever more forcefully the competing claims of pollution, health, education, and mass-transit programs.

Economic Aid

In foreign economic policy, differences will arise between a leadership disposed to take a moderately cooperative stance toward an interdependent world, and a populace with a low tolerance for economic deprivation attributable to foreigners. This is an issue area in which less-educated America Firsters are likely to be particularly vocal. The odds are that they will supply the strongest opposition to economic aid and the greatest support for tough trade and investment restraints to cope with unemployment, commodity shortages, high prices, or excessive foreign control over the American economy.[7] The intent of these measures will be to insulate the United States against what are felt to be some of the shocks of interdependence.

The unpopularity of economic aid is obvious to any practicing politician. In the last few years this has become one of the Federal expenditures least loved by the man in the street. First-generation American women making $2.40 an hour in the stitching room of a shoe factory regard aid beneficiaries as akin to "welfare chiselers." The fact that some former beneficiaries are now held responsible for higher gasoline and fuel oil prices makes matters worse. Foreign-policy leaders may want to help Bangladesh for humanitarian reasons, or to sustain American prestige, or to prevent an unfavorable tilt in some regional balance of power. But working people couldn't care less. To generate even weak support for economic aid, foreign-policy leaders will have to concentrate it on projects that bring relatively obvious and immediate returns to American taxpayers. Agricultural productivity programs may qualify. The development of foreign universities probably won't.

---

7. Schneider, "Public Opinion."

Job Protection

One aspect of interdependence is the tendency of American firms, including large multinational corporations, to close domestic plants or to threaten to close them or to choose not to build or expand them, because they have the option of operating through foreign subsidiaries. In some cases they do so to avoid antitrust laws or higher taxes. But what worries some American labor leaders is that such developments may also reflect a readiness to sacrifice American jobs in order to avoid higher wages, costlier fringe benefits, or restrictions on hiring practices. Some also fear that the export of American technology will increase the productivity of foreign workers at the expense of their own members. Especially if unemployment rises dramatically, powerful sectors of organized labor are likely to press for (a) restrictions on the right of American corporations to locate abroad, (b) tax disincentives, and (c) lay-off allowances to cushion the shock for displaced employees.

At the same time they will continue to fight for higher tariffs on labor-intensive commodities (e.g. shoes, women's apparel) that compete with American products. Frequently, the workers threatened by such imports are poor whites or foreign-born individuals with but a limited command of English. Typically, such individuals develop extraordinary loyalty to leaders who can voice their aspirations, and those leaders, accordingly, acquire considerable political clout. It must also be understood that in 1974, while Watergate made wealthy donors reluctant to contribute to political campaigns, labor unions were more generous. Democratic candidates for the Senate and House got more money from labor than from any other single source. In the case of the merchant marine unions, it was clear that the chief end in view was protectionist legislation. Moreover, survey data indicate that interest in tariff protection, at least as a temporary measure, is by no means confined to union members. The argument that American jobs must be safeguarded is supported by the general public by a margin of 5 to 3. Such sentiment must obviously serve as a constraint on low-tariff advocates within the foreign-policy leadership.

Price Protection

But labor protectionists are going to face opposition from a variety of forces—classical free-traders, large food exporters, multinational purveyors of technologically sophisticated products, power realists within the Administration who hope to strengthen détente by making Russia and America more dependent on each other for markets and supplies, and, last but not least, an increasingly self-conscious consumer movement that will draw support from all social strata, including liberal labor leaders critical of George Meany's leadership.[8]

In the past, consumer advocates have been more interested in removing restrictions on oil and food imports than on the importation of manufactured goods. And in the past they have not shown much political clout. Indeed, if the history of consumer protection in America proves anything, it is that its champions have difficulty forming themselves into a durably organized political force. But the present experience with inflation is also unprecedented. Rising prices have already created an exceptionally large audience for critics of the restrictive practices of regulatory agencies. The odds are that in the next five years consumer advocates will offset some of the pressures for protectionism, at least in the case of household goods. Moreover, concern about inflation may produce a demand that the government support the pooling of purchases from abroad, or go into the market itself, in order to get more favorable terms for the ultimate consumer at home.

Consumer anxiety will also generate unprecedented demands to curb the export of goods whenever surging foreign demand leads to extraordinary price increases at home. Debates over export control will pit America Firsters and perhaps some high-status conservationists against internationalists within the foreign-policy leadership. Most American workers know about the Soviet wheat deal, and most condemn it. Without being able to trace the relationship between feed grains (corn, soybeans, wheat) on the one hand,

---

8. For example, leaders of unions of automobile workers, communications workers, machinists, and state, county, and municipal employees.

and meat and dairy products on the other, they also know that the increase in wheat prices was followed quickly by a general increase in food prices. They will respond warmly to politicians who preach American food for American families. And they will be joined by major commercial and industrial users—bakers in the case of wheat, builders in the case of lumber, electric utilities in the case of coal.

Foreign-policy leaders, supported by private citizens of high status, will point out that food exports must be increased for humanitarian reasons or to provide foreign exchange to buy oil. But the recent Arab embargo has facilitated widespread popular acceptance of the idea of export controls as a retaliatory device. Canada's still more recent decision to limit the export of crude oil to the United States ("If anybody's lights are going to have to be turned out," Ottawa reasoned, "why should it be ours?") furnishes another precedent that may prove contagious. And if the supply of still other commodities can be manipulated successfully by foreign cartels in order to squeeze higher prices out of the American consumer, the demand to strike back with food restrictions of our own will intensify. But even in the absence of what are perceived by Americans as extortionate demands (and by foreigners as long overdue adjustments in the terms of trade), the demand for American food will rise faster than the supply, and this will strengthen demands for export controls.

The argument that Americans already consume more than their share of scarce resources, so compelling to high-status advocates of redistribution, will hardly persuade the public at large. Of all industrial countries in the years right after World War II, the United States was surely the least vulnerable to communist subversion or aggression. Yet it was probably the most apprehensive and vehement in its anticommunism. Today, although Americans are the least needy people in the world, they are also the least deferential and the least fatalistic. Consequently, they are the least likely to accept with equanimity any abrupt reversal of their fortunes. Especially in the case of working-class citizens the possibility exists that a warm response will be struck by a Wallace-style leadership if it attempts to exploit popular readiness to accept economic protectionism.

Foreign Investment in the United States

If it is unusual for Americans to worry about shortages in time of peace, it is even more unusual for them to be concerned about foreign "imperialism." But familiar firms like Bantam Books, Bond Clothing, Texas Gulf, F. A. O. Schwarz, Grand Union, and Gimbel's are now passing into foreign hands. The Japanese are acquiring American hotels and foreign lands. Arabs with enormous holdings of petrodollars stand ready to acquire raw land, office buildings, and shopping centers or to buy into our depressed stock market. The potential for xenophobic backlash is great. To avert it, foreign interests already take pains to keep a low investment profile (e.g. by avoiding more sensitive industries and limiting themselves to acquiring only minority interests). Nevertheless, domestic concern has already provoked executive and legislative pressures for advance notification and full disclosure, and there are likely to be continuing pressures to prohibit foreign investment in nuclear or hydroelectric power, aviation, railroads, newspapers, radio, or television. The demand for such limits will be experienced as a constraint by foreign-policy leaders to the extent that they wish to avoid the appearance of adopting a double standard as they continue their traditional support of overseas investment by American firms.

Economic Nationalism and State-White House Relations

Increasing public support for import, export, and investment controls could produce strains within the foreign-policy leadership in the next few years. Other things being equal, such a surge of economic nationalism is likely to be reflected in a political figure like the President before it is reflected in a career Foreign Service. The latter is not only one layer removed from domestic electoral forces but also more directly and continuously exposed to foreign pressure for access to American markets and supplies. It would take time for a relatively internationalist diplomatic corps to adjust to a President or a Secretary of State with the protectionist reflexes displayed, for example, by former Treasury Secretary Connolly.

Governmental Constraints

One meaning of interdependence is that more countries will influence the United States more profoundly. An important side effect is that within the United States foreign-policy powers will be less highly centralized than in the era of great power confrontation. Other things being equal, a political system is more likely to be controlled tightly from the center if its members agree on a single overarching goal, if that goal is success in any adversary relationship with another system similarly controlled, and if it must be pursued in an environment that puts a premium on secrecy, surprise, and rapid maneuver. To be sure, the personality or style of political leaders makes a difference. But even if the next president is a consummate autocrat, the transformation of the international environment will make it hard for either the White House or the State Department, or both together, to dominate the policy process.

Two distinctive networks will link the new international environment to a new domestic pluralism. First, the cost of commodity imports will generate foreign exchange requirements that must in turn increase the influence of several old-line agencies (e.g. Treasury, Commerce, and, especially, Agriculture) which have a stake in pushing American exports. Second, great-power détente will increase the influence of newer agencies (e.g. HEW, Energy, HUD, Transportation, Environmental Protection) which speak on behalf of urgent domestic needs. Because all such agencies have strong supporters in Congress, legislative uneasiness about competing foreign-policy priorities is likely to increase, particularly on the House of Representatives side.

Powerful domestic forces also work in the direction of pluralism. One is the changing composition of Congress, again especially evident on the House side. It is not widely appreciated that almost 50 percent of the membership of the House has entered since 1970. Major changes effected by the 1974 elections reduced the average age of members to below 50 for the first time in this century. Although the newcomers' liberalism can be exaggerated, the odds are that growing numbers will join Domestic Priority Doves in the Senate in challenging foreign-policy leaders on national security issues. A second domestic force is the evident popularity of bridles on the war-making power. Most citizens prefer that no troops be deployed abroad without the consent of Congress. Many back a far more drastic formula that would in effect revive the Ludlow Amendment of the 1930's. In November 1973 pollsters asked, "Should Congress be required to obtain the approval of the people by means of a national vote before declaring war?" An affirmative answer was given by 43 percent of all respondents who had completed only grade school and by 53 percent of all respondents between the ages of 18 and 24! A third domestic force is the pressure of Establishment intellectuals, reacting to Watergate as well as Vietnam, to cut the presidency down to size. Columnists, professors, foundation officials and clergymen have rediscovered the joys of Whiggery along with the virtues of disengagement. Thirty years ago their clarion call, expressed in the famous words of the report of the President's Committee on Administrative Management, was "The President needs help." Today their anguish over "the arrogance of power" celebrates and legitimizes demands for the fragmentation of power.

Summary

In an effort to predict attitudinal constraints on foreign policy leaders, this paper has identified three major variables: (a) an evolving international environment, (b) accordion-like changes in the size of foreign-affairs publics, and (c) corresponding changes in the composition of these publics. It has been argued that détente reduces the size of the audience for the politicomilitary aspects of foreign policy, leaving it more nearly the preserve of citizens of relatively advanced education and high status, while interdependence increases, perhaps permanently, the size of the audience for economic aspects of foreign policy, enhancing the relative influence of citizens with less education and lower social status. Poll data are utilized to relate education and status to attitudes on specific issues. Conclusions are that little general support will exist for armed intervention abroad; that continuing demands are to be expected for cuts in aggregate defense budgets; that still greater pressure will exist for cutbacks in foreign aid; that various forms of economic protectionism are likely to appeal to a large number of Americans; and that decision-making processes in foreign affairs will be less highly centralized than they were in the flood tide of the cold war.

EDITOR'S NOTE

Multilateral diplomacy has played an ambivalent role in United States foreign policy. Both the League of Nations and the United Nations grew out of United States policy initiatives, but America never joined the former and is threatening to withdraw from the latter. In a sense the existence and the location of the United Nations symbolize both American recognition that the world is interdependent and foreign recognition of the need for American involvement in world affairs.

Life in an increasingly interdependent world is going to involve many frustrations and irritations that are likely to be hard for Americans to accept. In many ways American ability to adjust to the "new United Nations" will serve as an indicator of American ability to adapt to life in the emerging global village.

In this essay Professor McNemar examines the sources of United States disenchantment with the United Nations, depicts several plausible scenarios of the future evolution of the United Nations, and evaluates a number of policy options available to United States foreign-policy makers.

XI.
The United States and the United Nations

Donald W. McNemar

The role of the United Nations in American foreign policy has come under increasing examination as the nature of the Organization and American interests have shifted in the period following the cold war. The rise of a majority of Third World nations within the United Nations has prompted United States policy-makers to question the value of the institution as an instrument of American policy. The decline of American influence in the Organization coincides, however, with an increasing awareness that many contemporary issues are interconnected on a global scale. United States officials are faced with formulating a strategy for participating in a United Nations which the United States cannot dominate as it did in the past, but which may be necessary for the cooperative solution of international problems in an age of interdependence. This reassessment of the U.S./U.N. relationship began in the 1970's, and the task of effectively using the United Nations as an instrument of foreign policy will constitute an important midterm policy problem for the remainder of the decade.

The desirability of reevaluating United States participation in the U.N. was signaled publicly by John Scali, then United States Permanent Representative to the U.N., in his "Tyranny of the Majority" speech to the General Assembly in December 1974. The Ambassador summarized American dissatisfaction with recent events in the U.N. organs and argued:

> The function of all parliaments is to provide expression to the majority will. Yet, when the rule of the majority becomes the tyranny of the majority, the minority will cease to respect or obey it, and the parliament will cease to function. Every majority

must recognize that its authority does not extend beyond the point where the minority becomes so outraged that it is no longer willing to maintain the convenant which binds them.[1]

The Scali proclamation presented both a warning to the rest of the world that the United States had become disillusioned with the Organization and a challenge to the new majority to make the institution workable. American dissatisfaction with the U.N., as evidenced in the opinion polls, showed that the percentage of Americans who believed that the U.N. was doing a good job of solving the problems it has had to face dropped from a high of 87 percent in 1959 to a low of 33 percent in November of 1975.[2] A United Nations Association poll in early 1975 of the newly elected members of the 94th Congress found that only 26 percent felt that actions of the U.N. in the last year had been helpful to improved relations. At the same time, 51 percent felt that the U.N. was becoming less important as far as United States foreign policy was concerned.[3] Similarly, in a Harris poll in December 1974, 28 percent of the public included the U.N. in the category of agencies "playing a very important role" in determining United States foreign policy, while only 3 percent of United States leaders did so.[4] Skepticism about the value of the U.N. was widespread and even more intense among American leaders than citizens.

While American support for the Organization had been eroding throughout the Nixon and Ford years, a series of specific actions during the 1974 General Assembly furthered the disillusionment and prompted the Scali speech. The controversial actions began with the Assembly's decision to invite participation of the Palestine Liberation Organization, the first time a delegation not representing a member state was accorded such treatment. The exclusion of

---

1. John Scali, Text of Address to the General Assembly, *New York Times* (December 7, 1974), p. 15.

2. Figures from Gallup polls reported in Richard N. Gardner, *The United States and the United Nations: Can We Do Better?* (New York, The American Assembly, 1972), pp. 8-9, and "U.N. Performance Rating Declines to New Low Point," *Gallup Opinion Index* (January 1976), pp. 27-29.

3. "The New Congress and the U.N.," *The Inter Dependent*, II (February 1975), 2.

4. John E. Rielly, ed., *American Public Opinion and U.S. Foreign Policy 1975* (Chicago, Chicago Council on Foreign Relations, 1975), p. 28.

South Africa from participation in the General Assembly and the restriction on Israel's right to speak in the debate on Palestine furthered the impression that the Third World nations were resorting to extralegal measures. The adoption of the Charter of Economic Rights and Duties of States without guarantees for adequate compensation for nationalized property and with encouragement for raw material cartels was opposed by the United States as violating existing international legal standards. Finally, the decision of the UNESCO General Conference to cut off support for the agency's regional program in Israel on the grounds that Israel had ignored the U.N. resolutions against altering the cultural character of Jerusalem prompted quick Congressional legislation to withhold voluntary contributions to UNESCO.

These specific actions by the U.N. organs in 1974 led many Americans to question the relationship of the United States to the U.N. and prompted Scali to call upon the new majority to restrain extralegal and unenforceable acts, so that the U.N. could be reformed into an instrument for building consensus. In early 1975 the initial steps in a reassessment of United States policy toward the U.N. were launched with Congressional hearings in both the House and Senate, the appointment of Daniel P. Moynihan as the new Permanent Representative to the U.N., and major speeches analyzing the United Nations by Secretary of State Henry Kissinger.[5] This process of readjusting relations between the United States and the United Nations will continue to be an important policy problem over the next decade.

I. The Nature of U.S./U.N. Relations

At the core of United States relations with the U.N. is the fact that American attitudes and interests increasingly differ from the

---

5. U.S. Congress, House Subcommittee on International Organizations of the Committee on Foreign Affairs, *Review of the 1974 General Assembly and the United States Position in the United Nations.* 94th Cong., 1st sess., 1975; U.S. Congress, Senate Committee on Foreign Relations, *The United States and the United Nations.* 94th Cong., 1st sess., 1975; and Henry Kissinger, text of address to Milwaukee Institute of World Affairs, *New York Times* (July 15, 1975), p. 4.

vast majority of nations in the world. The U.N. reflects the realities of international politics, and in the present setting the United States is frequently in the minority. In all of the United States defeats in the U.N. during 1974, the actual voting margins were overwhelmingly against the United States position.[6] The problem is not merely one of shifting a few votes in the general Assembly to reestablish the ascendency of American views; rather the stands of the United States on many questions of social justice and economic development are viewed as reactionary and status-quo oriented by the majority of nations who control votes in the U.N. bodies.

Richard Gardner summarizes this problem: "The fact is that the basic cause of our problem at the U.N. is not the U.N. itself. It is the increasing divergence between the United States and the majority of mankind on fundamental issues."[7] Congressman Donald Fraser made the same point even more sharply at the hearings of the House Subcommittee on International Relations. Fraser noted that the current attacks on the U.N. are a bit like the practice "of chopping the head off the messenger who brings the bad news. The U.N. forum provides the place in which we get the bad news that some of our policies don't seen to be well thought of in the world community and therefore we attack not this problem but the organization which produces the opportunity for those views to be made public."[8]

The significance of this divergence between the United States and the majority of states is increased when recent shifts in military

---

6. The vote to invite the PLO to participate in the plenary meetings on Palestine was 105 in favor, 4 against including the U.S., and 20 abstentions. When the President's ruling to exclude South Africa was challenged, it was upheld by a vote of 91 in favor, 22 against (U.S.), and 19 abstentions. The Charter on Economic Rights and Duties was passed by a vote of 120 in favor, 6 against (U.S.), with 10 abstentions. The vote in UNESCO to withhold funds from Israel was 59 in favor, 34 against (U.S.), with 24 abstentions. Although the U.S. was in opposition to all these highly publicized votes, Joseph M. Segel testified in the Senate hearings that the U.S. "joined in adopting 125 resolutions (90 by consensus), while voting against only 17 resolutions and abstaining on 32 others." Testimony in Senate hearings, *The United States and the United Nations*, p. 97.

7. Richard N. Gardner, "Mirror, Mirror," *The Inter Dependent*, II (February 1975), 1.

8. Fraser statement at hearings on *Review of the 1974 General Assembly and the United States Position in the United Nations*, pp. 62–63.

and economic power are assessed. What began after World War II as a normal erosion of the inordinate military and economic capabilities that the United States possessed relative to other participants was hastened by the loss of American prestige in Indochina and now seems destined to result in a collapse of the traditional liberal international economic order. The success of OPEC threatens the entire monetary system with drastic inflation. Policy adjustments may help to stabilize the economic order, but the prospect of returning to the earlier system of dominance of the dollar and unlimited access to raw materials seems unlikely.

Likewise in the military field the spread of terrorism and the proliferation of nuclear weapons to India and other Third World nations represents a potential for violent disruption which must be considered by the superpowers. The United States remains a dominant actor in terms of military and economic power. However, the SALT agreements incorporate an acceptance of a parity status between the superpowers, and the success of the OPEC strategy illustrates the vulnerability of the old economic order. The current context represents a shift away from American dominance in terms not only of the rhetoric of the General Assembly, but also of the economic and military power of the new states. American views diverge from the new majority at a time when the Third World's capacity for disruption with nuclear terror or energy embargoes has increased.

Although the United States is in a minority position within the United Nations, the option of simple withdrawal is not feasible. The increasing awareness of the interdependent nature of many foreign-policy issues suggests the need for cooperative efforts undertaken by international organizations. Many of the vital global problems, such as those involving the oceans and the environment, simply cannot be solved by national approaches alone; they require transnational involvement.[9] Closely related to the need for cooperation on a horizontal plane across national boundaries is the fact that many of these problems require a lengthened time perspective—in the case of

---

9. The case for the global nature of current problems and the necessity of cooperative action to solve them is developed in Richard A. Falk, *This Endangered Planet* (New York, Random House, 1971), pp. 1–36, and Garret Hardin, *Exploring New Ethics for Survival* (Baltimore, Penguin, 1972), pp. 101–140.

food and population, decades rather than annual budget cycles. Despite the distance between the United States position and that of the majority of nations, viable solutions to many international problems demand cooperative action among states.

The U.N. represents the sole existing global, general-purpose organization and may be useful in dealing with problems of the interdependent era. Although the U.N. has had limited effectiveness in the past because of unenforceable resolutions and limited support, it may become in the future an increasingly desirable institution for encouraging international bargains. The task of the U.N. will include persuading members to be flexible in their positions, so that interests can be coordinated, and producing a consensual basis for effective action. United Nations action will not always necessarily be in United States interest, but the United States does have a stake in making the U.N. increasingly effective as an instrument for generating cooperative efforts to handle global problems.

II. Basis for Reevaluation of U.N. Policy

Any alteration in United States policy toward the U.N. must be based on examination of three areas of United States policy in an interdependent age. The national interests and global role of the United States must be reconsidered in light of shifting forces in international relations. The functioning of the U.N. itself must be evaluated for potential reforms, and finally, the role of multilateral diplomacy in American foreign policy must be reassessed. As the foreign-policy context has shifted from one of confrontation in the cold war to cooperation in an era of détente, these three aspects of American policy must be reviewed.

Any improvement in the American use of the U.N. may require an alteration in the perceived national interests of the United States and other member states, so that a consensus for action can be achieved. The commonality of interests among states may be recognized only with increasing incorporation of global perspectives. While one may argue about the distance various states should be prepared to move in accommodating other states' positions, the present chasm among states on a variety of issues suggests that the United States must be prepared to make some concessions to produce workable decisions on such issues as the new economic order, peacekeeping, or apartheid.

The direction and goals of American foreign policy have already changed in the past ten years under the guidance of Kissinger, Nixon, and Ford. The world policeman role has been formally rejected and the United States has assumed a posture that has been described as "retrenchment without disengagement."[10] The United States remains a superpower with global interests and influence but with a lower profile, in order to avoid expenses and involvement in the affairs of other countries. Coupled with this posture is a realization that coordination with allies through strengthening alliance structures in Europe and the pursuit of détente with the U.S.S.R. and China are essential. In attempting to restrict the United States involvement while maintaining United States influence on the international scene, the Kissinger effort has already produced major shifts in the American world role and has created the potential for further shifts in the perceptions of American interests in the international organizations.

Although cooperative action through the U.N. is certainly not appropriate for all policy problems, the United States must choose between strategies of cooperation or confrontation on various issues. The initial strategy of the United States in response to the increase in OPEC oil prices was one of direct confrontation. The efforts were directed at organizing oil consumers to confront the producers in order to force a rollback of price increases. The effort met with limited success. On the other hand the response to the food crisis was much more along the cooperative line, with the convening of an international food conference, the structuring of new institutions for monitoring food problems, and the establishment of food reserves. The interdependence of many contemporary issues suggests the need for exploiting the cooperative strategy to pursue United States interests. The success of cooperative efforts depends on flexibility in the perception of United States interests, so that some accommodation with the interests of other nations may be possible.

The second area of policy change is reform of the U.N. to ensure that it is an effective instrument, available to assist states in cooperative ventures. The eclipse of the American majority at the U.N. and its replacement by the nations of the Third World has not only affected United States attitude toward the Organization but

10. Robert E. Osgood and others, *Retreat from Empire? The First Nixon Administration* (Baltimore, Johns Hopkins University Press, 1973), pp. 1-27.

also the capacity of the U.N. to act. The era of an automatic majority for the United States position is past, and the United States is no longer able to use the U.N. to legitimize its policies.[11] The new nations of the Third World now control the agenda of the General Assembly, putting the global spotlight on issues of social justice and economic development. Their overwhelming majority ensures that they can pass resolutions stating their positions but does not guaratee leadership for implementing U.N. decisions.

One result of the Third World control of the Assembly agenda has been a shift from a primary concern with the establishment and maintenance of peace to an intense interest in questions of economic well-being and distributive justice. In the 1970's questions of international economy have come to dominate the Organization. The Sixth Special Session of the General Assembly produced the Declaration on the New International Economic Order, and a charter of rights relating to this order was passed at the 29th General Assembly. The prime issues of discussion within the U.N. system continue to be food reserves, organizations of raw material producers, and transnational corporations. The increasing emphasis on economic issues can be expected to continue, requiring further reform of the U.N. machinery.

The necessity of reform in the Organization is emphasized by the increasing incongruity between voting power and military or economic power, illustrated by the rise of the Third World majority and the concentration on economic issues. Although the Third World nations have an overwhelming majority of the votes, the United States remains an extremely influential member of the Organization, since it provides almost one third of the resources of the U.N. The limited effectiveness of U.N. actions at present indicates that efforts to deal with the disparity between voting strength and actual strength must be an important part of any reassessment of the U.N.

The third policy task focuses on decisions about when to use the U.N. or other multilateral channels as instruments of United

---

11. For discussion of use of the U.N. in past U.S. foreign policy, see Robert E. Riggs, *U.S./U.N.: Foreign Policy and International Organization* (New York, Appleton-Century-Crofts, 1971). On the role of the U.N. in legitimizing U.S. policies, see Inis L. Claude, "Collective Legitimization as a Political Function of the United Nations," *International Organization*, XX (Summer 1966), 367–379.

States policy. The policymaker is constantly presented with a number of choices of instruments of policy: bilateral or multilateral channels; ad hoc arrangements or institutional procedures; general or special organizations; and global or regional bodies. These options regarding instruments of policy may not be sharply defined in the routine of bureaucratic politics, but the choice of instruments influences the success of the policy. The argument for increasing use of multilateral options rather than continually insisting on unilateral action is summarized by Lincoln Bloomfield: "The hard-headed, unilateral, close-to-the-chest, keep-all-your-options-open approach of the 'realist' is increasingly out of keeping with the nature of the external problem this nation faces. The truly hard-nosed advice may well be that which recommends interpreting the national interest far more broadly—that is, by taking bold moves to pool authority and giving a new lead to co-operative rather than unilateral directions."[12]

The case for increasing use of multilateral channels is supported by public opinion. Eighty-two percent of the general public and 95 percent of the foreign-policy leadership agreed with the statement: "Problems like food, energy and inflation are so big that no country can solve them alone, and international cooperation is the only way we can make progress in solving these problems."[13] To a similar question, 60 percent of the public and 58 percent of the leadership responded that "we should conduct more and more of our foreign affairs through genuinely international organizations."[14]

The general questions that form the basis for evaluation of United States policy toward the U.N. and are applicable to other international institutions include:

— What shifts in perception of United States interests may be required to permit cooperative action with other nations on global problems?

— What reforms in the U.N. are necessary to make it an effective instrument of world order?

— When and how should the United States use multilateral instruments for implementing its foreign-policy objectives?

---

12. Lincoln P. Bloomfield, *In Search of American Foreign Policy* (New York, Oxford University Press, 1974), p. 165.

13. Rielly, *American Public Opinion*, p. 21.

14. Ibid.

The analysis presented here will center on two specific issues. The first question is: How can the U.N. be reformed so it is an effective instrument in an interdependent world composed of states with great disparities in wealth and power? The second question focuses on the United States: What "strategies of participation" should the United States pursue in the U.N. arena in order to use the U.N. effectively as an instrument of American foreign policy? Although these questions are discussed separately below, it should be emphasized that they are closely related. The United States exercises great influence on the U.N. through its commitment of resources, use of the veto, and intra and extra U.N. policies. If the U.N. is to become more effective, such reform is largely dependent on United States leadership in the effort—as well as some shifts in United States perception of world events, so that American policy toward the U.N. becomes more constructive rather than obstructive.

III. Future Models of the U.N.

The reform of the U.N. could produce a variety of international institutions in the long-term future. United States actions in this era of transition will have a large impact upon the future U.N. In this period of transformation it is useful to spell out the possible future models in order to gain an appreciation of the longer term results of contemporary policies.

1. *Anarchic nationalism.* The first model suggests a return to fundamental emphasis on the nation state, with a general dissolution of the U.N. The reliance on some 150 disparate nation states for international peace and welfare functions would inevitably have elements of anarchy. Although such a model would maximize diversity and self-sufficiency and might even be desirable for some of the major resource-rich states, it seems unlikely by its fragmentation to solve many of the global problems existing today.

2. *Condominium.* A logical conclusion of an extremely successful process of détente could be a unity in the policies of the two superpowers which would enable them to join in controlling the U.N. and using it for their joint benefit. Although the effectiveness of the Organization might achieve new levels, this rule by the superpowers would meet extensive opposition from the other nations of the

world. The Chinese are constantly accusing the superpowers of pursuing this strategy.

3. *Bifurcated world*. What exists today as a gap between the rich and poor could develop into such a split that the U.N. would come to represent only one side. Whether the Organization stood for either the poor majority or the rich minority, the capacity of the U.N. for dealing with global issues would be severely impaired. The Organization would be transformed into a lobbyist group rather than a universal arena.

4. *Multination directorate*. Although Kissinger's former model of a world dominated by the five major economic powers proved inadequate with the sudden rise of the oil-rich nations, the concept of a group of nations with resources and power joining together to dominate the U.N. remains feasible. Whether this is a ten-nation or a fifteen-nation directorate is irrelevant; the prime point is that a small group of influential nations have the capacity for influencing the Organization and ignoring the remainder of the world.

5. *Conference for coordination*. The U.N. could conceivably continue in much the same role it now plays as conference machinery available for assisting in the coordination of national policies. As a catalyst for cooperative behavior, the U.N. would be serving a useful purpose, but it is not at all clear that it would possess enough authority to enforce decisions necessary to meet critical global problems.

6. *Regionalism*. The model of regional groups provides the capability for nations with similar geographic and cultural interests to unite in meeting their problems. A set of strong regional groupings such as the European Economic Community might be an important step toward collective decision-making on the regional level and could be coordinated with U.N. action. Global issues would require interregional cooperation, or some more overarching organization for problems which separate regional groups could not resolve on their own.

7. *Functional centralization*. The functional centralization model relies on a diverse group of agencies or institutions which are matched to international tasks and follow the level appropriate for achievement of the goal. For example, the control of the school system would be handled on a neighborhood level, but responsibility for nuclear weapons may require a world-wide authority. Although

the issue areas may be separated from one another, the approach has the value that power is not totally concentrated in a single body, infringements on individual freedom are less likely, and functions can be performed at the appropriate levels.

8. *World government.* The ultimate concentration of power would be a transformation of the U.N. into a world government, with military forces and a capacity for authoritative decisions. Such a development might come through Charter revisions or global conquest. Although a world government may be necessary for implementing such tasks as world disarmament, a world tax to re-distribute wealth, and humanitarian intervention to support human rights, a powerful central government certainly has the capacity to violate human rights and transgress the freedoms of world citizens.

Assessment of the desirability of the above models rests on judgments about the nature of such problems as war, economic welfare, and social justice, and of the sacrifices one is prepared to make in terms of national autonomy and personal freedom to seek solutions to these problems. Commissions studying the future of the United Nations have suggested moving toward the functional centralization model, which attempts to centralize sufficient au-thority to meet global challenges while still protecting cultural diversity and personal freedoms.[15] The possibility exists, however, that the problems we currently face simply cannot be met by the statist structure now existing, and that some form of world government in the future will be both desirable and acceptable. The discussion of reform at the U.N. must be undertaken with an

---

15. The general case for some strengthening of the U.N. has been made in two evaluations of it: *Report of the President's Commission for the Observance of the Twenty-Fifth Anniversary of the United Nations* (Washington, Govern-ment Printing Office, 1971) and *The United Nations in the 1970s*, A report of a National Policy Panel established by the United Nations Association of the United States of America (New York, UNA/USA, 1971). For explanations of the case for centralization of some functions, while others are decentralized, see the presentations of James N. Rosenau, "Adaptive Polities in an Interdepen-dent World," *Orbis*, XVI (Spring 1972), 153-173; Richard N. Gardner, "The Hard Road to World Order," *Foreign Affairs*, LII (April 1974), 556-576; Miriam Camps, *The Management of Interdependence* (New York, Council on Foreign Relations, 1974), pp. 90-104; and Richard A. Falk, *A Study of Future Worlds* (New York, Free Press, 1975), pp. 224-276.

understanding that such drastic systems changes as anarchy or world government are possible.

IV. Potential Models for U.S. Participation

The options open to the United States in its U.N. participation can be summarized by five general models. These models not only give an indication of overall strategies open to the United States, but also help to point up the implications of various tactics the United States might pursue. The models suggest general patterns of behavior based on alternative attitudes toward the international institution.

1. *Withdrawal.* The first model is withdrawal from the United Nations. The slogan "Get the United States out of the United Nations and the United Nations out of the United States," which had previously been attributed to extremists, is increasingly being presented in respectable forums. Recommendations have been made that the American response to any attempt to remove Israel from the General Assembly should be a refusal to participate in the proceedings of the Assembly. The Congress has previously withheld funds for such U.N. agencies as ILO and UNESCO and could well use this method of partial withdrawal in the future. A complete cessation of participation in the United Nations remains the most drastic option for the United States.

Many have argued that total withdrawal is neither desirable nor feasible. Most decision-makers do not seriously advocate it, and a Gallup poll in November 1975 found only 16 percent of the United States public favored giving up membership in the U.S.[16] To do so would result in the further restriction of whatever influence the United States does have in the U.N. sphere. A prime question in the UNESCO case has been whether it is better for the United States to cease participation, thus abandoning the field to Israel's enemies, or to remain in the Organization and wield its influence to defend American ideals and friends. Despite intense United States involvement and influence in the U.N., the proposal to withdraw remains a useful threat to hold over the members of the U.N., but this option

---

16. "U.N. Performance Rating," p. 29.

should not be exercised at present. If U.N. members insist on consistently pursuing extralegal policies, or if the Organization proves to be totally ineffective, however, the United States might abandon the U.N. as an unsuccessful experiment.

2. *Opposition.* The case for assuming an opposition posture in the U.N. has been made persuasively by Moynihan.[17] Drawing on his experience as Ambassador to India, Moynihan proposes that the United States posture should be one of the "loyal opposition" in dealing with the new majority in the U.N. He argues that "going into opposition requires first of all that the U.S. recognize that there is a distinctive ideology at work in the Third World, and that it has a distinctive history and logic."[18] This ideology, he says, is Fabian socialism, which has been spread throughout the Third World by the British Empire. As the loyal opposition, the United States can stand up proudly to these challenges by extolling the accomplishments of international liberalism, by explaining that the world economy does not run on egalitarian principles and efforts to influence it in that direction may well hinder or destroy the global economic situation, and by judging states' internal policies on civil liberties and welfare by the same standards that are proposed on an international scale. Moynihan further proposes that the United States stop appeasing the Third World and treating Assembly issues as unimportant. The socialist ideological stance of the Third World permits accommodation with the United States position if America presents its views fully and forthrightly. By assuming the opposition posture, the United States is free to argue the merits of the case and to explain the past accomplishments of the liberal political tradition.

In the sense that opposition tactics demand that the United States stop masquerading at the U.N. and take the Organization and the majority's demands more seriously, this option is desirable. As an overall strategy, however, the focus on opposition is unworkable. By placing the emphasis on Assembly voting and ideological factors, Moynihan underestimates the influence the United States can still exercise on U.N. decisions. When it comes to responsibility for U.N. action, the United States is clearly not just a minority

---

17. Daniel P. Moynihan, "The United States in Opposition," *Commentary*, LIX (March 1975), 31–44.

18. Ibid., p. 41.

member in opposition, with limited impact on the actions taken by the majority as suggested by the traditional parliamentary analogy. The opposition analogy conveys an impression that the opposition might become the ruling group—a prospect that seems unlikely in the case of the United States minority at the U.N. In a parliamentary setting the opposition is appealing to external voters for support, while at the U.N. the only prospect for "coming to power" is not through any external voting but rather by shifts in the views of either the United States or the new majority which would permit them to reach accommodation. In the traditional sense the "opposition" is attempting to sell its program to external votes, while at the U.N. the United States has only the options of persuading the ruling majority to change its views or of changing its own policies to overcome the minority position. Furthermore, by discussing the voting actions within the U.N. and the socialist ideology, Moynihan underplays the extent to which demands for more egalitarian distribution of wealth in the system are backed by real shifts of power toward the Third World interests. Finally, the opposition model does little to solve problems that require truly global solutions. Moynihan has struck a responsive chord in American officialdom with his "opposition" argument, and his case for taking the U.N. seriously with responsible criticism is useful policy advice. As an overall strategy for participation, however, it will not serve. The United States must do more than function as a critiquing opponent.

3. *Selective participation.* The model that most nearly represents United States practice under the Nixon and Ford administrations has been selective participation in the Organization. When the U.N. was needed, the United States did not hesitate to use it, as in the case of U.N. troops for disengagement in the Middle East. The United States has always kept its bilateral options open, however, and has reserved the right of refusing to participate in new developments at the U.N. The implication is that other channels worked better than the U.N. and that the really high priority items—like Vietnam, SALT, and national security—always outranked anything of concern at the U.N.[19]

19. For elaboration of the limited importance attached to the United Nations, see Leon Gordenker, "The Declining American Role in the U.N. System," *The World Today* (April 1973), pp. 169–180.

Bloomfield assesses this aspect of United States policy toward the U.N. by emphasizing that "increasingly the United States, while giving lip-service to multilateralism, has itself acted unilaterally, often in disregard of minority opinion. While arguing that the United Nations was unable to handle vital questions, we have given it fewer important things to do. The effect is to create a self-fulfilling prophecy, to produce a United Nations increasingly incapable of dealing with anything very important."[20] A model of future United States participation requires more involvement by the United States to ensure that the U.N. remains an effective instrument of multilateral policy.

4. *Instrumental reform.* The most feasible and desirable model for United States participation in the next decade is attempting to reform the U.N. to make it an effective instrument for handling global problems in an interdependent age. This model recognizes the current ineffectiveness of the U.N., calls for changes in the patterns of decision-making and other actions, and advocates United States leadership in restructuring and revitalizing the Organization. Writers such as Bloomfield, Gardner, and Cleveland have taken the position that the U.N. can and should be improved to better serve the global community and that the United States should play a major role in readjusting its policy to ensure effective use of the Organization.[21] This essay supports the pursuit of some variant of the reform model as the desirable goal of U.S./U.N. policy.

5. *System transformation.* The final option calls for transformation of the U.N. into a world government. Advocates of this posture suggest that the global challenges are so immense that the evolutionary reform of the U.N. will not meet them. Rather, some drastic system change must occur which results in a transformation of the U.N. from a collection of sovereign states into a supranational authority. Clark and Sohn in their proposal for world government urge this perspective, and Falk calls for a major transformation, although he suggests restraints on the degree

---

20. Bloomfield, *In Search of American Foreign Policy*, p. 163.

21. Bloomfield, *In Search of American Foreign Policy*, pp. 159–169; Gardner, "The Hard Road to World Order," p. 569; and Harlan Cleveland, "The U.S. vs. the U.N.?" *New York Times Magazine* (May 4, 1975), pp. 19–23.

of centralized bureaucracy.[22] Supporters of this option note that problems of controlling the nuclear arms race and providing for the economic well-being of the global community require a centralization of authority. The decentralized system of sovereign states may prove incapable of solving common human problems. Naturally, member governments of the U.N. are not now arguing that the Organization should be transformed to assume their authority, and popular support for this model remains limited. The call for drastic system transformation does raise, however, the important proposition that reform may be insufficient and that a major new international structure may become essential.

Those are the five potential options. The choice recommended here for overall American strategy is to shift from the current stance of selective participation in the U.N. to option 4, an effort to improve the structure and use of the Organization. Implicit in all the models is a perception that the future of the Organization is dramatically affected by United States policy. The shift in United States approach is also based on an increasing awareness of the interdependent nature of the current world which enhances the importance of a multilateral forum like the U.N. Given these perceptions, the reformist model seems most desirable for guiding United States policy toward the U.N. in the next decade.

V. Utility of the U.N. for American Foreign Policy

Decisions regarding United States participation in the United Nations are dependent on an evaluation of the costs and benefits derived from the use of international organizations. Multilateral channels of action are not appropriate for all issues but may be particularly useful in specific cases. The characteristics that distinguish multilateral organizations like the U.N. as policy instruments provide the basis for making choices concerning the utility of multilateral diplomacy in American foreign policy.

1. *Catalyst for cooperative action on global problems.* The U.N. can serve as a universal arena in which to mobilize responses to

---

22. Grenville Clark and Louis B. Sohn, *World Peace through World Law*, 3rd ed. (Cambridge, Harvard University Press, 1966), pp. xv–liv, and Falk, *A Study of Future Worlds*, pp. 277–349.

problems that inevitably require action that goes beyond the jurisdiction of any single nation state. Issues such as the arms race,
international terrorism, the uses of outer space, and the regulation
of multinational corporations all require action on a global scale.
Already in response to problems of environmental protection and
food shortages, the U.N. has produced cooperative working arrangements. Its Conference on the Human Environment in 1972
established a Governing Council for the U.N. Environment Programme, an Environment Secretariat, and and Environment Fund.
The function of the Environment Programme has been to produce
information and proposals that would permit states to coordinate
their national policies to protect and enhance the human environment. Likewise, the U.N. Food Conference in Rome in 1974
produced a Governing Council on Food that is charged with forecasting food supplies and needs, organizing buffer arrangements to
limit famine, and encouraging efforts at agricultural development.
In both of these efforts to confront world crises, the style of action
has been one not of shifting authority from the nation state to an
international body but rather of creating an international management mechanism that provides information and assists in coordinating
state policies.[23]

By raising global problems in the U.N. setting, nation states
have an opportunity to generate cooperation on a universal scale
and to utilize a secretariat with previous experience in administering
international programs. Member states retain flexibility in producing
the final arrangements for action, but the U.N. provides a mechanism
for working out a solution. Using this forum allows the injection of
such political views into the discussion as were raised in the environment conference when the developing countries argued that the
program was simply a plan by the developed countries to block their
progress. Yet such claims must be heard and met if any type of
solution to the environmental question is to be reached. In such
global problems as environment, food, oceans, population,
weather, space, and communications, the solutions must incorporate

---

23. The head of the Environment Programme has discussed the elements
of this new style of international action in Maurice F. Strong, "One Year After
Stockholm: An Ecological Approach to Management," *Foreign Affairs*, LI
(July 1973), 690-707.

commitments from states on a world-wide scale, and the multi-lateral channel provides the marketplace in which to begin the bargaining process.

2. *Insulate United States actions.* By acting through a multi-lateral instrument, the United States is insulated from repercussions of actions which if taken unilaterally might be less effective or produce undesirable results. The provision of development aid through multilateral channels is an example of this effect. The aid is more acceptable to the grantee and may even make a greater contribution to the goal of development if it is provided from an international agency with limited strings attached. The donor state does give up influence and control over the state receiving the aid, but the sacrifice may well be worth it in terms of the impact of the assistance and/or the avoidance of responsibility for failure.

The insulation phenomenon also has an internal dimension. By committing resources to action through a multilateral instrument, the bureaucratic politics within the United States government may be restricted. The assumption of an international obligation locks the United States government into a position of support for longer-run goals of growth and justice and sacrifices some short-term political maneuvering and influence.[24] Participants in bureaucratic politics hesitate to support such commitments to international organizations precisely because they remove resources from the domestic allocation process. Yet such goals as population control and development may require long-term projects protected from domestic fluctuations on a yearly basis.

The insulation potential of action through the U.N. may be particularly useful to the United States in a period when it is attempting to disengage from various global commitments. Efforts to restrict population growth or control narcotics traffic may be actions which the United States favors but which would be judged unacceptable by target countries if pressed by the United States. Yet these can be effective if made through U.N. programs. If aid

---

24. The insulation concept is discussed in the context of a developing region in Lloyd I. Rudolph and Susanne Hoeber Rudolph, *The Coordination of Complexity in South Asia* (A report prepared for the Commission on the Organization of the Government for the Conduct of Foreign Policy, 1974), pp. 53–59. (Mimeographed.)

programs ever reached the stage of following a triage policy of simply abandoning certain countries as hopeless, the United States might welcome a U.N. involvement to shield the United States from responsibility for such decisions. Other situations, such as intervention in civil wars like the Nigerian case or efforts to end apartheid in South Africa, may be actions that the United States simply wishes to avoid by "letting the U.N. do it." The capacity of the U.N. to insulate the United States from certain situations and policies may become an increasingly desirable result of multilateral action in the future.

3. *Serve a third-party role.* At certain points a third party perceived as being neutral is essential to permit states to extricate themselves from a confrontation. One of the more dramatic examples of this type of situation was the decision to inject U.N. peace-keeping forces into the Middle East at the height of the 1973 crisis. With the Soviets threatening to intervene unilaterally if the Israelis did not observe the cease-fire and the United States forces on worldwide alert to forestall any Soviet action, the U.N. force was the mechanism for resolving the confrontation. Had the U.N. not existed, some similar unit would have had to be invented to fulfill the need for an impartial force. Most of the U.N. peace-keeping efforts have been precisely this type of international presence, not capable of fighting an enforcement action but functioning as an international observer unit on the scene to forestall a confrontation of the superpowers through their indirect participation in limited wars. Kissinger continued to rely on the U.N. peace-keeping forces in his step-by-step Middle East diplomacy through a skillful uniting of bilateral and multilateral efforts. Similarly, in the confrontation between the superpowers over the missiles in Cuba in 1962, the U.N. was proposed as a third party for inspecting the removal of the missiles.

In advocating this use of the U.N. as an impartial actor, Ambassador Henry Cabot Lodge, who served both at the U.N. and in Saigon, testified in the Senate: "With the advantage of hindsight, one can now say that much trouble would have been avoided if, before the French left Indochina, we had used the United Nations in the early 1950's, somewhat as the U.N. acted in the Congo in 1960—as an international presence to prevent the area from becoming the cause of big power involvement."[25] Once the United States did end its involvement in South Vietnam, the U.N. became the one channel of aid to relieve the suffering in Indochina. The Organization was perceived as impartial enough to operate in all parts of Indochina. In a variety of contexts from peace-keeping and decolonization programs to peaceful settlement of disputes before the International Court of Justice, the United States may find it useful to utilize the U.N. as a third party to prevent interventions by other nations and to avoid more costly forms of involvement by the United States.

4. *Institutionalized behavior.* The U.N. represents a mechanism for encouraging common behavior among the independent states. Much of the effort to negotiate a new regime at the Law of the Sea conferences has been directed precisely toward this function. When the claims and practices of states varied greatly, there was a high cost for this chaos, which led states to attempt to establish a new regime and set of rules to govern their interaction in the ocean space. The U.N. can regularize the relations among states by institutionalizing the procedures for responding to disaster relief, refugee problems, or development questions. By acting through the U.N., the United States may bind other states to shared expectations about appropriate international behavior. The United States may also be able to expand the contributions it makes to international institutions. A dollar of development aid given to the U.N. Development Programme can generate similar amounts from other developed countries or oil-producing nations, thus magnifying the impact in the developing areas. Action through the U.N. provides an opportunity to increase the leverage of the contribution and to encourage the institutionalization of relations in the interest of greater regularity of interaction on the global scale.

Although the use of the U.N. offers no panacea for solution of global problems, the Organization does possess distinctive qualities as an instrument of policy, and they should be utilized. Frequently in the past the bias toward national or bilateral action has been so strong that the multilateral options have not been given sufficient consideration. The capacities of the U.N. to encourage global

25. Lodge testimony in Senate hearings, *The United States and the United Nations*, pp. 7–8.

solutions, insulate United States actions, serve as an impartial actor, and institutionalize relationships may become increasingly important in the interdependent context of the near future.

VI. *Reform of the United Nations*

If the U.N. is to serve as a useful instrument of world order in the future, the United States must support reforms to revive its effectiveness. The United States should support those reforms which contribute to the establishment of a consensus permitting effective action, but oppose those which further divide the rich and poor nations, escalate the level of rhetoric, and diminish the impact of U.N. decisions. The U.N. faces a conflict between universal participation and effectiveness. The voting power and the real power in military and economic terms are no longer coterminous, as they were during the era of United States dominance of the U.N. The decision-making mechanism must be adjusted to realign a working majority for the U.N.

Both the majority and minority must share responsibility for the present ineffectiveness. The United States suggests that the majority abuses its voting strength by passing outrageous resolutions that do not represent the views of the international community. At the same time, the Third World notes that they have no incentive to moderate their views, because the great powers do not expect any action to result from the General Assembly effort. Regardless of fault, the task is clear. All sides must come to an accommodation that will recognize the significance attached to both participation and effectiveness. For the United States this means accepting Third World states into the arenas of decision-making, while insisting on parameters for action which assure implementation of the decisions.

The decision-making process of the U.N. must be altered from straight voting to mechanisms for producing consensus. Through the consensus mode the values of participation and effectiveness are both respected. At present the system in the General Assembly is a single vote for each state. As a result, countries with 10 percent of the world population and 5 percent of the U.N. contributions possess two thirds of the votes. In such a context voting often fails to produce the working coalition necessary for international action.

The idea of weighted voting has frequently been suggested. A system based on the level of contribution has worked in the World Bank and the International Monetary Fund, but in the U.N. itself there is no agreement on criteria for the weighting. Whether population or wealth is chosen as a criterion produces quite different results. Weighted voting therefore does not seem to be a promising mechanism.

A variety of suggested approaches have been based on some type of consensual procedure as a basis for U.N. action. Bloomfield argues for the United States to take a unilateral initiative in producing "coalitions of the willing" simply by accepting as binding the judgments of the General Assembly if passed by a previously determined meaningful majority.[26] Gardner favors a system of conciliation in small committees composed of weighted representation.[27] Cleveland advocates decisions by consensus among those whose action together is necessary to carry out any given international program.[28] The idea of a concurrent majority of developed and developing states has been suggested in United States proposals regarding a seabed regime.

The U.N. has used the consensual approach with increasing reliance on the conference method of tackling new issues. No halt to the deterioration of the environment is possible without participation by both those countries already industrialized and those attempting rapid industrialization. Similarly, food proposals that do not bridge the chasm between those with famine and those with food are meaningless. The success of an ocean regime is dependent on the participation of all coastal states and all those that use the seas. The decision-making mechanism at the conferences on these topics was the straw vote in committee sessions, but the formal action programs were adopted in plenary sessions by consensus. The impact of the conference approach has been to heighten the awareness of member states, spell out guidelines for action, and create on-going councils and programs to encourage and guide the consensus.

The conference approach will undoubtedly remain an important mechanism for dealing with crisis issues and may be extended in

26. Bloomfield, *In Search of American Foreign Policy*, pp. 166–167.
27. Gardner, "Mirror, Mirror," p. 2.
28. Cleveland, "The U.S. vs. the U.N.?" p. 26.

the future to such topics as world disarmament and human rights, but the consensus mechanism must be incorporated into the general business of the other U.N. bodies as well. Whether the approach is one of informal action on the part of states accepting certain votes as binding or a more formal system of weighted voting remains a matter of tactics. The important point is that U.N. reform must incorporate new decision-making processes that ensure both broad participation and a guarantee of effective implementation. Some system of consensual decision-making seems most likely to provide the basis for solution to the world order problems.

A second general area of reform relating to the U.N. is a redefinition of the functions performed by the Organization. In a sense this is more a case of adapting to demands by member states and shaping the Organization to perform these new functions. Whereas a concern with peace predominated in the first three decades of the Organization, the emphasis for the next decade will be on questions of economic well-being. The Organization has defined its limits and potentials for peace-keeping, and the U.N. will continue to be available for those functions. The questions of primary concern now, however, relate to a new international egalitarianism and demands for redistribution as a means of improving human welfare throughout the globe. Whereas past actions focused on aid targets and development decades, the new international economic order emphasizes access to raw materials, trade patterns, monetary policy, regulation of multinational corporations, and nationalization. The United Nations has had an impressive record for action in the economic field but must improve its capacity to handle the questions of economic and social well-being which will dominate the U.N.'s agenda for the next decade.

In reforming the U.N. to serve economic functions, the coordination of the various structures within the U.N. system ranks as a high priority. The diffusion of efforts through a complicated system of agencies and programs, the rivalry among the Specialized Agencies and the U.N. Development Programme, and the inefficiencies of international bureaucrats are legendary. The Jackson Report, which called for increased coordination among development programmes and agencies of the U.N. system, met the usual bureaucratic inertia and entrenched governmental interests.[29] In 1975 the Secretary General appointed a panel of twenty-five experts to propose changes in the structure of the U.N. economic system. The resultant proposals recommended shifts toward unanimity of decision-making in the Economic and Social Council, greater Third World participation in the World Bank and International Monetary Fund, a centralized trade authority to replace the U.N. Conference on Trade and Development, and a Director-General for Development and International Economic Cooperation who would centralize authority over all U.N. efforts in the economic field.[30] Unless some proposal such as this for effective coordination takes effect, the Organization will be unable to meet the functional challenges of the economic order.

Closely related to coordination is reform of the U.N. Secretariat to provide successful leadership. In the past, U.N. executives have been characterized by longevity, political acceptability, and geographical distribution, with little concern for global vision, charismatic leadership, or demonstrated effectiveness in solving global problems. A strong case can be made that the leadership of the Secretariat is the prime ingredient in successful planning and management in an era of interdependence.[31] In peace-keeping the only formula for action is for the Council to set guidelines and leave actual operations with the Secretary-General. Likewise, in a variety of development efforts the initiative of the Secretariat is key. In most U.N. efforts the role of the Secretariat in preparing background work, encouraging conciliation by member states, and implementing decisions are crucial factors in any effective action.

Given the importance of Secretariat members, high priority

29. *A Study of the Capacity of the United Nations Development System* (Geneva, United Nations, 1969).

30. *A New United Nations Structure for Global Economic Co-Operation* (New York, United Nations, 1975).

31. The centrality of effective international leadership is argued in John McLin, *International Institutions for 'Planetary Bargaining,'"* American Universities Field Staff, West Europe Series, X (March 1975); Camps, *The Management of Interdependence*, pp. 96–103; and Cleveland, "The U.S. vs. the U.N.?" pp. 23–28.

should be placed on securing individuals who can successfully take a long-range, global view of problems and mobilize political consensus among states. As the U.N. turns 30, many individuals who joined at the outset are approaching retirement, and one result of this turnover in personnel could be a new breed of international civil servants.

The provision of increased financial resources for the operation of the U.N. is also a necessary reform. The U.N. suffers from chronic financial difficulties because its reliance on assessed and voluntary contributions puts it entirely at the mercy of member states who never provide sufficient resources. Last year the U.N. system, not including the World Bank and the International Monetary Fund, spent $1.5 billion, of which 80 percent went for development. This may seem like a great deal of money until it is realized that this amount is less than one half of one percent of the world military spending for that year.[32] Adequate financing requires either increased contributions by members or establishment of independent revenues. Funds from an international regime for the seabed or a global tax on international trade or movements have been suggested as potential financial resources for the Organization. Some form of increased monetary support from the member states or independent schemes is necessary to permit the U.N. to meet its expanding functions.

VII. Strategies for the United States at the United Nations

The following general strategies of participation in the U.N. system are designed as policy recommendations for the United States. The goals of these strategies are to adjust the Organization to make it an effective instrument and to optimize United States use of multilateral channels for coping with problems of world order.

1. *Global perspective.* The key to many of the processes of international law and organization is a recognition that the long-run interest in stability may outweigh the short-run gains on specific issues. The need for a global perspective arises in discussions of independence vs. interdependence, nationalist vs. internationalist solutions, and short-run vs. long-run time frames. The basis for

---

32. Cleveland, "The U.S. vs. the U.N.?" p. 23.

reform of multilateral instruments of policy must be an increasing recognition by all states that they have interests which coincide and may be served best by immediate sacrifices to gain future advantages. Whether the case is one of foregoing the use of force to enhance a norm of peaceful settlement or an increase in bread prices in the United States today to prevent famine around the world tomorrow, a sense of the global perspective must be incorporated into American policy at the U.N.

2. *High profile posture.* If the United States is to maintain its opportunities for multilateral diplomacy through the U.N., the United States should assume a high profile posture at the international body. Describing the American posture after serving on the United States delegation to the U.N., Senator Charles H. Percy indicated that "in the recent past, U.S. policy in the General Assembly has been to show a relatively low profile and to train our efforts on 'damage limitation'. The feeling, however, has been generated by these tactics that we are giving lip service to the United Nations while our mind and interests are elsewhere."[33] The United States reputation for not taking the Organization seriously is reinforced by the issues taken to the U.N., the personnel sent, and the United States response made to the actions of the Organization. Although the United States left no doubt that it responded negatively to the New International Economic Order, the United States offered neither a full explanation of its position nor a serious alternative. The pursuit of a low profile in the U.N. by the most powerful nation in the world undercuts the efforts at global solutions and restricts the usefulness of the arena.

The high-profile strategy could be easily implemented if the United States chose that mode. A shift in the comments of high-level officials from contempt to support for the Organization would have a major impact if subsequent behavior signaled they were genuine. Concessions on issues, provision of resources, or increased use of the U.N. could all indicate an altered United states posture. A changed attitude toward the U.N. by United States leaders would also have an impact on the views of the American public and the

---

33. U.S. Congress, Senate, *The United Nations*, by Charles H. Percy, Report to the Committee on Foreign Relations, Committee Print (94th Cong., 1st sess., 1975), p. 18.

member states of the U.N. The appointment of highly respected individuals with some public standing as permanent representatives to the Organization could be a concrete indicator of a new importance attached to the Organization. The appointment of Moynihan was a step in this direction, although he did not command the respect and political influence domestically and internationally that Lodge or Stevenson possessed.

The high-profile position would also incorporate both full United States participation in U.N. discussion and proposals for constructive action by the U.N., like Kissinger's call for a food conference. At the same time, United States delegates should be frank and clear in evaluating and criticizing the proposals of other members, as Moynihan argued in his article.[34] Only by treating the proposals of Third World nations seriously can a consensus be built for global cooperation.

3. *Consensus decision-making.* Consensus as a basis for decision-making can be implemented only with the cooperation of the United States, which should be prepared to alter its general position on certain issues to reflect the demands of Third World nations in order to establish workable agreements. The process of bargaining rather than dictating requires that the United States come prepared to make a trade-off between representation and efficiency. The price of effective population control programs may be a greater voice in development projects for Third World countries, or the basis for securing an extension in a Middle East peace-keeping force may be increased attention to the Palestine question. The United States approach to decision-making should involve accommodation with the Third World in order to achieve effective results. Coupled with the reformed decision-making mechanisms would be an effort to prune the agenda of the Organization so that attention can be devoted to important future issues and not to rehashing such past actions as Korea.

4. *Implementation.* The United States should inject concerns about effective implementation into any discussion of U.N. action. As a starting point the American representatives may find it necessary to separate symbolic and substantive actions. If the point of an item is rhetoric and not action, the United States may choose

---

34. Moynihan, "The United States in Opposition," p. 41.

to ignore it; but if the intent is action, the United States should take seriously the prospects for implementation. Questions of what arrangements for administration will be necessary and what resources will be provided are legitimate parts of negotiation on topics from communication to food questions. By insisting that implementation arrangements be part of the concerns of the original negotiations, the United States recognizes the seriousness of the issues and the importance of establishing workable arrangements.

5. *Leadership coalition.* The U.N. has been floundering without leadership since the United States position of dominance ended. While the United States cannot dominate as it did earlier, it should now take the lead in forming a new coalition of actors to give direction to the Organization and to ensure the potential for implementing its programs. The United States remains so powerful that it must provide leadership, but because of changed conditions it must share leadership in coalitions with others—a process that is bound to be frustrating after a period of individual dominance. The United States must serve as the initiator of leadership groupings but must forge them in relation to particular issues. On questions of science, technology, communications, arms control, and disarmament, the United States and the Soviet Union may play predominant roles, and the increasing coincidences of their interests may well permit them to take the initiative jointly for U.N. action. On economic matters the United States, Western Europe, and Japan may form the leadership group, whereas in the area of development a United States effort might produce leaders of the Third World willing to join in new strategies of assistance.

In all efforts at leadership, the international Secretariat remains an important ally in the process of planning for global action. These officials are essential in structuring the incentives to encourage states to pursue their common interests on problems. Therefore, the United States should act first to strengthen the Secretariat and secondly to exploit the Secretariat's potential for leadership within the Organization.

6. *U.N. resources.* If the U.N. is to assume greater responsibilities in an interdependent world, it must be provided with expanded resources to finance existing programs and future efforts adequately. The reaction of the United States as the largest contributor and wealthiest nation in the world is the key to this expansion. The

budget of the entire U.N. system in 1974 was $1.5 billion, as noted. That is approximately the cost of a single Trident submarine, and the United States contribution of $400 million was less than half the cost of the New York City police department. Although the United States was the largest single contributor, the United States contribution ranked 24th in terms of contribution as a percentage of the gross national product.[35] Clearly the world has not overtaxed itself in the support of the U.N., and the United States could well shift a larger share of its resources to the peace efforts of the Organization.

Attempts to increase these resources must be pursued through new avenues, since the traditional mood in Congress runs toward cutting rather than increasing the U.N. budget. The survey of Congressmen in 1975 found that only 5.7 percent favored increasing United States contributions to the U.N., while 37.6 percent wanted the funds decreased.[36] Aside from simply increasing the amount of United States funding, the United States might shift more of its aid from bilateral into multilateral channels. There has been a slight increase in this area, with the percentage of United States aid going through the U.N. rising from 18 in 1969 to 26 in 1972.[37] A further shift would increase the capability of the U.N. to deal with the problems of the new international economic order.

The provision of any new United States funds coming either from shifts from bilateral to multilateral aid or through increases in United States contributions gives the United States the opportunity to exercise leadership through selective commitments to programs, and to emphasize implementation by insisting on standards of efficiency and responsibility for the use of the resources.

Aside from increased contributions that are not strongly endorsed by the Congress and public, the United States might actively support efforts at generating independent sources of income for the U.N. system. The United States proposal on the seabed provided

---

35. Chadwick F. Alger, "The United States in the United Nations," *International Organization*, XXVII (Winter 1973), 14.

36. "The New Congress and the U.N.," p. 2.

37. U.S. Congress, House Subcommittee on International Organizations and Movements, *Implementation of the Lodge and Katzenbach Recommendations on the United Nations* (93rd Cong., 2nd sess., 1974), pp. 10–11.

for revenue to the U.N. systems but also produced opposition from United States businesses as a give-away scheme. Efforts to impose some taxation on international transactions would undoubtedly result in similar protests from multinational corporations. Any proposal to shift resources to the U.N. will have a cost to American interests, and the U.S. government must simply decide at some point that the global activities of the U.N. are valuable enough to ask the American people and businesses to pay the price. A strategy of increasing the resources for the Organization is essential if it is to contribute to the solution of global problems.

VIII. Conclusion

The evidence presented confirms that the United States now faces critical choices with regard to its participation in a world of interdependent states. The United States is confronting not only greater complexity in the international setting, but also increasing challenges from allies, former enemies, and new states. The U.N. represents an important arena in which these challenges are voiced and efforts to solve common problems are undertaken. The United States cannot stem the tides of change heralded at the U.N., but it can adapt its participation in the Organization to take advantage of this multilateral instrument of policy.

Although the U.N. has several plausible alternative futures, the model recommended here as most likely to handle global problems and protect United States interests is one of functional centralization, where certain problems are handled at the global level but national prerogatives are maintained. The general strategy of United States participation at the U.N. which moves the Organization in the direction of this model is one of instrumental reform. The attempt to reform the U.N. into a more effective instrument for cooperative action should include such actions by the United States as emphasis on a global perspective in United States foreign policy, the creation of a high profile at the U.N., development of consensus decision-making processes in the U.N., attention to the implementation of U.N. decisions, forging of leadership coalitions for initiating and influencing the Organization's work, and creation of new resources for the work of the United Nations.

The success of these strategies will determine whether the

United Nations can function effectively in the new international context. Coupled with improvements in the U.N. must be a shift in the perceptions of the American public and decision-makers to recognize that United States interests are vitally connected with the wider interests of mankind and that the U.N. offers a potential instrument for forging long-range solutions to global problems. United States policy toward the U.N. will remain a key element in this effort to shape instruments of world order which will permit the human community to achieve the common goals of peace and justice for all people.

Index